AIRBORNE ARMOUR

Tetrarch, Locust, Hamilcar and the
6th Airborne Armoured Reconnaissance
Regiment 1938–50

Keith Flint

Helion & Company Ltd

Helion & Company Limited
Unit 8 Amherst Business Centre
Budbrooke Road
Warwick
CV34 5WE
England
Tel. 01926 499619
Email: info@helion.co.uk
Website: www.helion.co.uk
X (formerly Twitter): @Helionbooks
Facebook: @HelionBooks
Visit our blog at https://helionbooks.wordpress.com/

Published by Helion & Company 2004. Reprinted in paperback 2010, 2024
Designed and typeset by Helion & Company Ltd
Cover designed by Paul Hewitt, Battlefield Design (www.battlefield-design.co.uk)

Text © Keith Flint 2004, 2010, 2024
Illustrations © as individually credited
Maps © Helion & Company 2004

Every reasonable effort has been made to trace copyright holders and to obtain their permission for the use of copyright material. The author and publisher apologise for any errors or omissions in this work, and would be grateful if notified of any corrections that should be incorporated in future reprints or editions of this book.

ISBN 978-1-804516-40-9

British Library Cataloguing-in-Publication Data.
A catalogue record for this book is available from the British Library.

All rights reserved. No part of this publication may be reproduced, stored in a retrieval system, or transmitted, in any form, or by any means, electronic, mechanical, photocopying, recording or otherwise, without the express written consent of Helion & Company Limited.

For details of other military history titles published by Helion & Company Limited, contact the above address, or visit our website: http://www.helion.co.uk

We always welcome receiving book proposals from prospective authors.

Contents

Preface iv
Acknowledgments vi

Part One – Hardware
1 Tanks 9
2 Gliders 35

Part Two – Operations
3 Special Service 63
4 Flying Tanks 79
5 D-Day 97
6 Normandy 119
7 Arnhem – Ardennes 133
8 Operation Varsity 149
9 Across Germany 165
10 Postwar 187

Part Three – Perspective
11 Other Countries 199
12 Conclusion 215

Bibliography 220

Preface

The title 'Airborne Armour' covers two strands of investigation. First, the project to support British airborne forces with airlanded tanks during World War Two, and second, the story of the armoured reconnaissance regiment which operated those tanks and which also supported 6th Airborne Division during its ground operations.

The starting point for the work was curiosity regarding two events, both relatively minor in the context of World War Two but nevertheless genuinely unique. These events were the landing of British tanks by glider on D-Day, and again during the crossing of the Rhine 10 months later. These were the only two times in the entire war that the assault landing of tanks from the air was attempted by any of the combatants. Accounts of D-Day all mention, of course, the actions of 6th Airborne Division in their role protecting the left flank of the British landings. In most of these accounts there is some brief mention of the landing of tanks from Hamilcar gliders, but how many, in what role, and what happened to them after they landed is usually skimmed over. It is also occasionally mentioned that some tanks may have landed by glider during the largest Allied airborne operation of the war, Operation Varsity, which supported the crossing of the Rhine. Details of this event are usually even more brief (and are also usually inaccurate). At the heart of this book is the attempt to answer as thoroughly as possible basic questions about both these events. For example, how many tanks of what type were landed? To what unit did they belong? What was their intended role, and how effective were they in that role? How long did their operations last?

Delving into these questions quickly raises others concerning the background to the landing of tanks by glider. How did the idea originate? How were the gliders themselves developed? And was the whole thing worthwhile or a waste of valuable resources? Even at the relatively short distance of sixty years, answers to some of the questions about Britain's glider borne tanks are difficult to find, but I have endeavoured to answer as many of them as I could. Books containing real detail on these matters are not common, and I have had to search out what primary material is available at the various relevant archives.

In the course of the research, my curiosity led me to investigate other areas which related to the original subject. In researching the development history of the Tetrarch light tank I found it had been used in some little known operations by little known units, finding its way to Madagascar and Russia. I have looked into the history of the other airlanded tank, the American developed Locust, and tried to see why it replaced the Tetrarch for the Rhine crossing. I also quickly found that the reconnaissance regiment of the 6th Airborne Division, which operated the airborne tanks, did much more than land from gliders. It spearheaded the advance of the division across Europe and was unique in providing a non-armoured division of the British Army with organic tank support: that is, support from within the organisation of the division, rather than attached from outside units. This led me to attempt a history of the 6th Airborne Armoured Reconnaissance Regiment (usually abbreviated as 6th AARR), particularly its combat operations in World War Two. I have also tried to give a brief background on the other units that helped get the tanks and gliders into action: the Glider Pilot Regiment and the RAF squadrons which provided the tugs.

This, then, is the story of the hardware, the men who operated it, and the operational conditions they encountered. Of the hardware, I concentrate on the Tetrarch and Locust light tanks and the Hamilcar glider, which are all three intimately bound up with the story of airborne armour. The Horsa glider (which is covered only briefly) was also used by 6th AARR but it could not carry their armoured vehicles. The men are those of 6th Airborne Armoured Reconnaissance Regiment and its ancestors, and (in much less detail) the glider pilots and tug crews. Paratroopers, of course, also come into the story at times. The operations are primarily those of the North-West European campaign of 1944-45: D-Day, the breakout and pursuit across France, Arnhem, the Ardennes, and the final dash across Germany following the crossing of the Rhine.[1]

Despite all the published works on airborne forces which have appeared since the war, the full story of Britain's 'airborne armour' has remained untold. This book is intended to correct that omission.

A Note on Weights and Measures

Any weight given in tons in this book refers to tons imperial. Weights which have been given in US tons or metric tonnes in sources have been converted to tons imperial. Similarly, all lengths are given in feet and inches. On some occasions the original weight or length in kilograms or metres is given in addition, for the information of the reader. For the record, one ton imperial is 2240 lbs, one US ton is 2000 lbs, and one metric tonne is 1000 kgs which equals 2205 lbs.

---

1 Operation Dragoon, the airborne element of Operation Anvil which was the invasion of the South of France on 15th August 1944, involved no Hamilcar gliders or armoured vehicles, and is ignored in this book.

Acknowledgments

The archives of four institutions provided most of the primary sources for this book: the Public Record Office, the Museum of Army Flying, the Tank Museum, and the Airborne Forces Museum. The staffs were universally helpful, but I would particularly like to thank Derek Armitage (Museum of Army Flying), David Fletcher, Janice Tait and Nancy Langmaid (Tank Museum) and Alan Brown (Airborne Forces Museum). My local libraries (Yate and Bristol Central) were most useful in obtaining published works.

Many individuals generously shared the fruits of their own knowledge and research, or took the time to write with their memories of wartime service. Paul Middleton and Steve Cox (both private researchers) deserve special mention for generously sharing their own hard won knowledge at the time I was commencing my work. It was they who first suggested to me that 6th AARR were the 'forgotten' regiment of the wartime airborne forces. In addition, I would like to thank the following (in alphabetical order): William Atwater, Michael Bowyer, Bob Bragg, David Brook, Denis Edwards, Paul Evans, John Gibbons, John Greaves, David Hall, Mike Hooks, Frank Kerrell, Major J.S. Knight, Dr R.A. Leake, Capt. G.E. Locker (ret'd), Ian Mathieson, Alastair Mellor, Clive Peckham, Kevin Shannon, Major-General Andrew Stewart, Pip Tyler, Mr A.J. Williams, and Peter Young. My thanks also to Duncan Rogers, Managing Director of Helion and Company, for the decision to publish the book and his guidance during its production. I have attempted to obtain all appropriate permissions for works quoted and for photos and illustrations. I welcome approaches from any copyright holders I have missed.

It was a privilege and pleasure to establish contact with ex-members of 6th AARR, and the information I gained was invaluable. John Banbery and Bob Walklett were my main contacts and their willing help was very much appreciated. In addition, thank you to Ron Allen, Geoff Campbell, George Firth, Fred Ford, Edward George, Bill Gladden, Brian Heape, Derek 'Mick' Hood, Rex Laycock, Fred Murray, Colin Peckham, Norman Stocker and Ian Waters. I would particularly like to thank the members of 'B' Squadron for their invitation to attend the 2003 re-union dinner.

Finally, thank you to my wife Jane for covering the home front during my research visits, and for her support and forbearance during my many hours at home shuffling papers and pecking at the word processor.

Keith Flint, March 2004.

Part One
HARDWARE

Chapter 1

Tanks

Two tank types were used operationally in the airborne role by the British Army in World War Two, the British Light Tank Mk.VII Tetrarch and the American M22 Locust. To start our story, we will look into the development history of both vehicles, as well as providing information on some other vehicles which were either considered for the airborne role or relate to the development of the two main types.

The Light Tank Mk VII 'Tetrarch' was neither designed nor produced as a glider-borne tank. Developed originally as a private venture by Vickers-Armstrong with a view for sale either to the British Army or to overseas countries, it became the penultimate design in the series of light tanks which Vickers had produced for the British Army between the wars. The prototype was completed in December 1937 and was a complete departure in design from the previous Light Tanks Mk I-VI. Not only was it the first light tank to mount a 40mm/2pdr gun, equivalent to the main armament of contemporary 'cruiser' (i.e. medium) tanks, but the suspension and steering systems were entirely novel.

The two main reasons for this new departure have been summarised by the tank historian David Fletcher.[1] Firstly, following the take over by Vickers of the Carden-Loyd company in 1928, the Vickers light tanks had all been based on Carden-Loyd designs. Indeed, John Carden had been chief tank designer at Vickers-Armstrong until his death in an air crash in December 1935. This resulted in Vickers having to pay a percentage to both Carden and Loyd for each tank type based on their work. Secondly, the War Office prevented the export of any Vickers tank incorporating design features attributable to Government engineers. The British government's tank orders between the wars were often very limited in number, and a company like Vickers relied on export orders to keep going. Hence, 'in the design for this new tank the company had at least two very good incentives for breaking away from Carden-Loyd features and Government influence'.[2]

Reference has been made to 'cruiser' and 'light' tanks, and it should perhaps be pointed out before going any further that British doctrine at this time declared the need for three broad classes of tank. The light tank was for reconnaissance and had armour basically capable of keeping out shell splinters, blast and small-arms fire. They weighed less than 10 tons and were supposed to be highly mobile, and generally armed only with machine guns. The second class were the cruiser tanks, designed to be the main equipment of the armoured divisions, and with thicker armour (at this time to a maximum of about 30mm) and the 2pdr gun. The third category were the infantry tanks, which theoretically had armour (of perhaps 60-80mm) capable of resisting the enemy's anti-tank guns even at close ranges. This additional weight meant they were generally slower, and they were intended for di-

1 Fletcher, 'The Flying Tank', pp. 21-24.
2 Ibid, p. 21.

Tetrarch prototype. The original Vickers turret is fitted but without main armament (IWM).

rect support of infantry formations, allocated as necessary from independent tank brigades.

The Mk.VII light tank was designed by Leslie Little, Vickers' new chief tank designer, and to emphasise that it was very much a private Vickers design the project was initially designated PR, for Private Research. The most distinctive feature of the new vehicle was its steering system. There were four equal sized wheels on each side, the rear wheel being fitted with teeth to act as the drive sprocket and having an armoured cover fitted to protect the final drive. In response to the driver turning his steering wheel, the road wheels (all eight together) not only turned but also tilted in order to bend or warp the tracks themselves, making the tank turn. The main idea was to reduce the mechanical strain and power wastage involved in the normal system of braking one track in order to swerve the tank round. Vickers had already employed the system, in a less sophisticated form, on its recently developed light armoured carriers which the British Army were to employ so extensively in the coming war. The suspension system was also a new departure. Instead of the sprung Horstman suspension of their previous light tanks, the Mark VII had a suspension system which used struts with pockets of air for springing, and cushions of oil for damping. Each of the wheels was independently sprung which gave an excellent ride.

Despite the complex engineering of the track-bending system, it appears to have worked reasonably well. The best turn radius available using the system seems to have been around 80 to 90 feet; for tighter turns normal track braking could be applied using a lever separate from the driver's steering wheel. The main drawback seems to have been a tendency to throw the inner track during a 'warp turn', as this track became slack during such a manoeuvre. Despite modification, the tank always needed to be driven carefully when turning to prevent this occurring. The steering wheel itself was also very heavy. The engine adopted was the Meadows MAT, a twelve cylinder horizontally opposed engine whose compact design was suited to the small size of the tank. The engine provided 165 b.h.p. at 2,700rpm and gave the tank an excellent road speed of 40mph. Maximum cross-country speed was given as 28mph. However, the engine was a tight fit in its compartment which always made maintenance difficult. The tank weighed 7.5 tons, with armour varying between 4 and 16 mm.

Although a private venture, Vickers had of course always intended to give the War Office first refusal. Following generally successful initial trials of the prototype during May and June 1938, the War Office decided it was definitely interested in the tank, and specification A.17 was written around it. Following further trials, the tank was accepted for limited production in November 1938. The War Office was generally happy with the light tanks it already had, but in a time of rearmament (it should be remembered that September 1938 was the time of the 'Munich crisis') it was unwilling to turn down what promised to be a good tank. In the original A.17 specification, the standard light tank armament of co-axial 15mm and 7.92 mm Besa machine guns was given. However, Vickers had shown that the vehicle could accept a 2pdr and this weapon was selected for the production tanks. Various fairly minor modifications had been made following testing, the most obvious externally being the fitting of a cylindrical fuel tank on the hull rear to increase range. With its 2 pdr gun, in 1938 the Mk VII was equivalent in armour, gun power and mobility to some contemporary cruiser tanks, such as the A.9 (Cruiser Mark I) and A.13 (Cruiser Mark III) which both saw action in France in 1940. The Mk.VII, however, would not enter production until the French campaign was already over.

Its size limited its crew to three, a driver in the hull and a gunner and commander in the turret, which, the Army was realising, could be too few to fight a true battle tank. A member of 6th AARR was later to summarise the problems of commanding and fighting in this type of tank:

> Commanding a [Tetrarch] tank was like looking through a bloody periscope and shaving, riding a bike, reading a map, talking on the wireless and doing ten other things at once! The gunner had an amusing act as well. He had a seat which went up and down; to his right was the big two pounder gun, and to the right of that a machine gun. He had two triggers – left hand for the two pounder, right hand for the machine gun. By moving his shoulder up and down against a pad, and bumping his seat up and down, he could move the gun. His eye was glued onto a periscope, with a brow pad that held his head steady while his left hand turned a handle with two gears that traversed the turret, and with his left foot he cracked walnuts![3]

Official opinion was in agreement. The gunner or the commander had additionally to act as loader for the 2pdr which could obviously cause delays in combat. The AFV School at Lulworth reported on the tank in January 1941 and concluded that as the commander had to both fight and command the tank, control of a troop in close action would be practically impossible.[4] Consideration had been given to adopting the Mk.VII as a 'light cruiser', but its small size eventually led to it being classed as a light tank by the Army, and it became the Light Tank Mark VII, having

3   Arthur, *Men of the Red Beret*, p.176.
4   Tank Museum, Tetrarch file.

not yet been named. The number to be built was the subject of some vacillation. The War Office had indicated as early as July 1938 an intention to order 70 tanks. A three day conference on tank production held in November by the War Office, which resulted in a definite order, specified 120 vehicles. The tanks were to be built by the Metropolitan-Cammell Carriage and Wagon Company Limited in Birmingham. This company was jointly owned by Vickers and Cammel Laird Ltd, and although fundamentally a rolling stock producer Metro-Cammel had undertaken tank production for Vickers on previous occasions. Production was just beginning in July 1940 when the order was cut to 70, but following discussions the order was increased to 100, and then 220, after Metro-Cammell indicated they had already ordered armour plate for about this number of vehicles.

War Office doubts about the tank had been prompted by a rethink regarding the value of light tanks, either for reconnaissance or any other role. Prewar, light tanks had been preferred for the reconnaissance role primarily due to their superior cross country performance in relation to contemporary armoured cars. War experience had emphasised the need for stealth and the ability to make a quick getaway during scouting missions, and for this the small, two man, four wheel drive Daimler scout car had proved ideal, having also a good cross-country performance. Light tanks had also suffered badly in France when the desperate shortage of any armoured vehicles had resulted in their misuse as battle tanks. Their resultant high casualties had emphasised the vulnerability of this class of vehicle. These points are important as they will be revisited when we come to discuss the suitability of deploying the Tetrarch as part of a reconnaissance regiment in the much changed conditions of Normandy in 1944. In the desperate days of 1940, they meant that light tanks were a much lower priority than cruiser or infantry (i.e. heavy) tanks. Production was also slowed and partly curtailed by extensive bombing of the Metro-Cammell works in April 1941, and the last Tetrarchs were built in the first quarter of 1942, with final deliveries taking place in the latter half of the same year. Final production of the tank is given in most published sources as 177 vehicles. However, a lower figure of only 100 tanks is given in some surviving official documents, and the later perceived shortage of Tetrarchs for airborne use would seem to suggest that this lower figure is the more accurate.[5] The name Tetrarch was adopted following a policy decision by the War Office that all tanks should be named, this policy being enacted from the 22nd of September 1941.[6]

As the new tanks were produced (first deliveries were in November 1940) they initially joined 1st Armoured Division, which had just lost all it tanks in the disastrous French campaign, and the 6th Armoured Division which was a new division just being formed. As light tanks, the Mk.VII's main role was intended to be reconnaissance. The desperate shortage of any tanks in 1940 would probably have meant that in the event of Tetrarchs being used for defence against invasion or campaigns overseas, they would have been committed in whatever role tanks happened to be required, regardless of their suitability.

---

5   See, for example, PRO file AVIA46/189, Light Tanks 1935-44. Two official summaries of the Tetrarch's development history are kept at the Tank Museum, and both confirm 100 vehicles produced.
6   A copy of the official notification can be found in PRO file AVIA22/459.

The most likely fate for the Tetrarch at this stage would have been use in training in Britain before replacement by other tanks, perhaps with a brief period of operational use in the Middle East, then retirement when declared obsolete. However, when the 1st Armoured Division was sent to North Africa in 1941, the Mk.VIIs were left behind as their cooling systems were considered unable to cope, although one Tetrarch did go to the Middle East for trials. During 1942, light tanks were dropped from the establishment of British armoured divisions, and in the words of David Fletcher, 'By the end of 1942 the light tank, at least the British light tank as exemplified by the A17 Tetrarch, was regarded as almost useless'.[7] However, the war had a few surprises up its sleeve for this vehicle. Leaving aside for the moment its selection for the airborne role, three particular uses of the tank occurred before the end of 1942. Firstly, the tank had been used in trials for the Duplex Drive equipment eventually developed for amphibious tanks. Secondly it was sent to Russia in small numbers under lend-lease agreements, and thirdly it was used, in its first operational deployment, in a little known campaign in Madagascar. The latter is best left until we explore the history behind 6th AARR, but the first two developments will be described here.

The 'Duplex Drive' Sherman tanks used by both the British, Canadians and Americans on D-Day feature with justifiable prominence in accounts of that operation. They were a real surprise to the Germans and wherever they arrived successfully they provided invaluable armoured support for the first waves of landing infantry. The method used to make the Shermans 'swim' was developed by Nicholas Straussler, a talented Hungarian-born designer who had come to Britain before the war. The tank had its buoyancy increased by having a large waterproof canvas screen erected around it. It was attached above the tracks, and was erected by 36 inflatable tubes running vertically inside the screen, which were supported by steel struts once the screen was up. The screen gave the vehicle sufficient buoyancy to make it float. When in the water, most of the tank was actually below the water line and the tank commander had to stand on the turret roof to see out. Straussler realised the vehicle would need more power to drive it in the water than the turning of the tracks could provide, and he fitted the tanks with a steerable propellor which was run by a power take-off from the tank's engine. A speed of about 4 knots was possible, and these tanks were seaworthy up to Force 5 conditions. The screen could be quickly collapsed on reaching land using a small explosive charge and the tank was at once ready for combat.

The great thing about Straussler's system was that any tank could be made to swim using it: it was not necessary to develop a purpose built amphibious tank and the design was not limited to light tanks which had been the subject of past trials using bulky flotation chambers, which severely reduced mobility on land. Nevertheless, it made sense to test the design on a small, light tank to start with, and the A.17 was the most modern light tank readily available. The first Duplex Drive experiment was therefore conducted using a Light Tank Mk.VII in June 1941, on the Welsh Harp reservoir at Hendon. Only one tank was converted, which came from 1st Armoured Division. Later trials were conducted on the Solent near Portsmouth, and the success of the trials led to the conversion of heavier Valentine tanks, which participated in further trials and training, and then conversion of

---

7   Fletcher, *The Universal Tank*, p. 42.

The one and only duplex drive Tetrarch with canvas skirt raised (Tank Museum).

Shermans for operations. One author has concluded that this episode was the Tetrarch's 'greatest contribution to the development of the tank'.[8]

The operation of Tetrarchs by the Soviet Union is another little known episode in the story of this vehicle. As with so much other information about World War Two in the East, fuller detail regarding these operations has only come to light since the collapse of the Soviet Union and the opening up of various archives.

Twenty Light Tanks Mk.VII were supplied to the Soviet Union in early 1942 under the 'Lend-Lease' scheme, along with a consignment of Matildas and Valentines. It would seem that after the dispatch of the first 20 had been agreed, the Tank Board had decided (in September 1941) that no more Mk.VIIs should leave the country as they were the only suitable airborne tank at that time.[9] Such a small number was obviously only a token contribution, but the Russians deployed light tanks much more widely than the British at this time and thus the vehicles were thought to be of interest. The cooling problems which prevented Mk.VIIs being used in the desert have already been mentioned. It would seem they were also unsuited for really cold conditions, 'largely for the effect it might have on the suspension and tracks', so operation of the Mk.VIIs was limited to the southern part of the Eastern Front.[10] On arrival the vehicles were thoroughly tested. The Soviets admired the controllability, manoeuvrability and speed of the tanks. They also found they could run on low quality fuel which was not useable in Soviet light tanks. Of

---

8   Chamberlain & Ellis, 'Mk VII Tetrarch and Mk VIII Harry Hopkins' in Crow (ed.), *British AFVs 1919-1940* p.55.
9   PRO file AVIA46/292.
10 Fletcher, 'The Flying Tank', p.22

course, the limited armour protection was noted, and some efforts to fit additional armour plate were made, but these had too great an effect on the vehicle's mobility to be acceptable. Nevertheless, the Soviets also noted that even as it stood, the Mk.VII was still comparable to contemporary Russian light tanks such as the T-70, whilst being lighter in weight. Some Mk.VIIs were photographed for propaganda purposes during operations in the Caucasus in 1942, and it seems that some vehicles were involved in combat. Vehicles sent to a tank training school in Sumgait in summer 1942 are believed to have engaged the Germans. As late as September 19th, 1943, records show the 5th Guards Tank Brigade being reinforced by an independent unit, the 132nd Separated Tank Battalion. Of the 15 tanks of this latter unit, 2 were Tetrarchs. One was knocked out in battle on September 30th, the other was destroyed by German heavy artillery on October 2nd.[11]

We can now turn to the events surrounding the selection of the Tetrarch for the airborne role. There were no British airborne forces before World War Two, and it was not until Churchill put his weight behind their creation that such forces were envisaged on any scale. This process is considered in more detail in chapter three, but we can note here that it commenced in June 1940 with a set of directives from the Prime Minister himself.[12] Once the War Office began to look into what form airborne forces should take, they fairly quickly decided that gliders would be a useful part of such a force. The Germans had already demonstrated their use during the Blitzkrieg in France and the Low Countries. Gliders would obviously be useful, amongst other things, for bringing in the heavy equipment that parachute units would lack. Surviving records indicate that by August 1940 at the latest, it had been decided that such heavy equipment should include some sort of airborne tank. A draft paper on this subject from the autumn of 1940 states that 'in the opinion of the War Office, no airborne force will be sufficiently effective against opposition unless it incorporates armoured fighting vehicles and artillery'.[13] Discussions as to what type of tank and how it should be carried took place between departments of the Air Ministry and the War Office. A key source here is a document in the the Public Record Office entitled 'The use of aircraft to carry tanks'.[14] The document indicates that on the 5th of September 1940 the War Office officially asked the Air Ministry to consider the possibility of the air transport of tanks, weighing a maximum of ten tons, by glider or aircraft. A memo from May 1941 confirms that discussions had been going on for the previous ten months, and gives some idea of what form they had taken. One of the earliest ideas had been to adapt a Stirling bomber (at that time the RAF's largest and most powerful aircraft) to carry a light tank. It was estimated a 5.5 ton tank could be carried for 300 to 350 miles, and that even a tank of 9 tons could be got airborne, although only over a short range due to the correspondingly light fuel load that could be managed. If a powered aircraft was to be used, it was agreed that to lift a worthwhile vehicle over a distance, a specially designed aircraft would be the 'only sound solution'.[15] Using a glider had therefore emerged as the preferred solution

11 Latter details from the Russian AFV magazine *Tankomaster*, No.4, 1999.
12 For more detail, see Chapter 3.
13 PRO file AIR32/2
14 PRO file AIR8/569.
15 Ibid.

Propaganda shot of Tetrarchs in Russia. They still have their British 'War Department' numbers (TankoMaster Magazine)

as such an aircraft would be easier to develop and would also be potentially more flexible in its loads.

Of further interest is that the original proposals, in October 1940, were for a glider to carry an 8.5 ton tank. This could only refer to what was to become the Light Tank Mk.VIII, later to be christened the Harry Hopkins, which was intended as the replacement for the Tetrarch. The development of this tank will be discussed below, but for the moment it will be sufficient to indicate that because this tank was in such an early stage of development, plans for an airborne tank reverted to the Tetrarch. This vehicle was the most modern tank available which fell within the size and weight requirements thought to be acceptable. At a conference on 16th January 1941, held at General Aircraft Limited's works in Middlesex, it was decided that the large airborne glider which GAL were to develop (the Hamilcar) would be designed to carry a Mk.VII tank, or two universal carriers, or a stores container. However, the notion of using the Mk.VIII Harry Hopkins continued to resurface throughout 1941 and beyond, as the War Office was well aware, even at this early stage, of the limitations of the Tetrarch. A War Office letter from October 1941 regarding the formation of airborne forces states that, regarding the Mk.VII tank, 'all of these now obsolescent tanks at present available could be used for this purpose, but [...] no more should be constructed in this country specifically for this use. Meanwhile the US authorities have been asked to undertake the development of airborne tanks'.[16] The initiative indicated in the final sentence was to result in the T9 (later M22) Locust, whose development will also be described below.

Coordination between the War Office and Air Ministry on the issue of airborne tanks during this formative period was evidently lacking, and was criticised in an official summary on the development of light tanks between 1935 and 1944, which seems to have been written towards the end of the war. It confirms that, 'with the autumn of 1940 the notion of airborne tanks acquired some promi-

16 PRO file WO32/9778.

Tetrarch stowed ready for combat with airborne forces. The Littlejohn adapter is fitted, and a Bren gun is carried on the turret side above the 2" smoke discharger (IWM).

nence'. However, the War Office and RAF 'made no real effort to evolve common equipment or concentrate on a useful tactical definition. The War Office expected the RAF to carry such light tanks as might be available, and the Air Ministry expected the Army to put up with such planes as could be spared without major alteration'.[17] This controversy apparently continued from September 1940 to spring 1941, whilst Hamilcar development was not carried forward with any urgency. The narrative also confirms that in October 1941 'it was decided the requirement [for airborne light tanks] should be met by US machines'.

A particularly significant aspect of all the initial discussions was the weight of tank proposed. The British were convinced that 10 tons was about the practical limit, taking into account the performance of aircraft likely to be available as tugs. Indeed, in an official letter of May 1941, the Air Ministry clearly stated that a glider carrying the 8.5 ton Mk.VIII tank 'could not be towed off the ground by any existing aircraft', and they included the most powerful British aircraft of the time, the Lancaster, in this conclusion. By January 1941, then, the Tetrarch/Hamilcar combination had been agreed upon as the way of providing tank support to British airborne forces.

Before looking into the tank that emerged from the initiatives in the United States, we should tell the story of the Mk.VIII Harry Hopkins. This tank continued to be suggested for the airborne role well after Hamilcar development was under way, and no description of Britain's airborne tank effort would be complete without charting this vehicle's progress.

17 PRO file AVIA46/189.

The Light Tank Mk.VIII was another Vickers-Armstrong design which was planned to improve on the Mk.VII, in particular in the area of armour protection. It incorporated wheels, chassis components and a number of other parts from the Tetrarch, and was apparently referred to initially as the 'Tank, Light, Mk.VII, revised'.[18] The proposed tank was submitted to the War Office in February 1941, and three pilot models were authorised in April. The tank was wider and heavier than the Tetrarch, (8.5 tons) as a result of a desire to give more room for the crew and increase armour protection. Frontal armour was 32-38mm (hull) and 38mm (turret), side armour 14-17mm (hull) and 17mm (turret). The design was given the specification number A.25. The turret and hull were also given a better ballistic shape by providing more sloped surfaces than the Tetrarch. The steering system was the same, but hydraulic assistance made life easier for the driver. The vehicle was 9" inches longer and (more significantly) 1' 3.5" wider than the Tetrarch. Both the weight and width meant the tank could never be carried in a Hamilcar, but it should be remembered that, like the Tetrarch, the tank was not designed as an airborne tank but the latest in the line of Vickers light tanks for standard army use. The same flat 12 Meadows engine was installed, and road speed was quoted as 30mph, perfectly respectable but slower than the nippy Tetrarch. Main armament remained the 2pdr gun. The name Harry Hopkins was derived from that of President Roosevelt's special advisor.

The tank was obviously officially considered a useful design as at a meeting of the Tank Board in September 1941 it was decided that 1,000 should be ordered, and it was hoped to commence production in June 1942 at a rate of up to 100 a month. By November, the order had been raised to 2,410. As with the Tetrarch, production was to be undertaken by Metro-Cammel. However, from this point difficulties began to be encountered. Prototype tests in 1942 seem to have raised problems, with a report on tank returns issued in December 1942 stating that modifications were required following these tests, particularly to the front suspension. A minute to the Prime Minister from the Ministry of Supply in September of that year had already noted 'delayed deliveries' of the Harry Hopkins due to development problems.[19] It appears these problems dragged on, as a report from the Fighting Vehicle Proving Establishment of July 1943 indicates serious defects were still being encountered, and the trials here were abandoned early.[20] As of 31st August 1943, fourteen months after the time production was supposed to have commenced, only six Harry Hopkins had been supplied, against a revised War Office requirement for 1943 of 100.

Despite these problems, and despite the question marks over the usefulness of light tanks in general which have already been mentioned, documents show that in November 1943 there was still an official requirement for 750 Harry Hopkins.[21] However, in the end it would seem common sense prevailed. A total of around 100 Harry Hopkins was finally completed (the author has seen estimates varying from 92 to 102), and none was ever used operationally. Production was not finished until February 1945, by which time these tanks were presumably being completed to

18 *British AFVs 1919-1940*, p.54.
19 Both these documents are in PRO file PREM3/425 Tank Returns 1940-45.
20 Fletcher, *The Universal Tank*, p.43.
21 PRO file AVIA22/459, AFV Requirements and Supply.

The Harry Hopkins, intended successor to the Tetrarch (IWM).

fulfill contractual obligations rather than any operational requirement. By the time the tank was becoming available, the War Office realised it had no use for it. There was a requirement for a limited number of light tanks within the organisation of British armoured divisions, but this was met by the American M3 and M5 light tanks. David Fletcher quotes a policy report of December 1942 which suggested possible issue of the Harry Hopkins to reconnaissance regiments, or special light tank regiments for service in overseas locations (such as mountainous areas) where light tanks might be particularly suitable.[22] In the end it was proposed, in 1943, to hand over the production to the RAF for airfield defence as a last resort. However, according to Fletcher, the RAF also had an interest in the tanks due to a new project to get the Harry Hopkins into the air.

As we have seen, carriage of an 8.5 ton tank by air had been proposed since the early discussions with GAL in late 1940 which led to the Hamilcar, although in the end the Tetrarch was selected for this glider. A surviving memo of May 1942 indicates that some in the Air Ministry were still considering the Harry Hopkins for the airborne role, carried in a successor to the Hamilcar.[23] However, all parties were already committed to developing the Hamilcar and there was never a serious possibility that this major project would be curtailed or abandoned to produce an even bigger glider. However, a rather different and radical idea was also put forward in 1942 regarding airborne tanks which featured the Harry Hopkins as a potential load. This was the Baynes Carrier Wing, also sometimes known as the Carden-Baynes Tank Glider or the Allen Muntz Bat. The design came from the Baynes and Muntz Co. Ltd., with Mr Muntz seeming to be the main promoter of the concept. The idea was to use a 'flying wing' design, that is a tailless aircraft with swept wings and rudders at the wing tips. Attaching a pair of such wings to a tank raised the pos-

22 Fletcher, *The Universal Tank*, p.42.
23 AVIA 15/2368

sibility of carrying larger vehicles than the Tetrarch by making a winged tank, flown by the driver, rather than developing a large tank *carrying* glider which carried the vehicle completely within it. In the patent specification filed by Baynes and Muntz in November 1941, it was expected that a 7 ton tank could be carried by a structure weighing only 4000 lbs.[24]

The idea produced some serious interest in various official circles, including the Ministry of Aircraft Production and the Ministry of Supply as well as departments within the War Office and Air Ministry.[25] It received the support of Brigadier Richard Gale, then Director of Air at the War Office and later to command 6th Airborne Division, as well as the then commander of Airborne Forces Major-General Browning and the C-in-C Home Forces. A one third scale model was directed to be produced to test the concept in June 1942, and this flew successfully in August 1943. A separate project was the 'glider frame', an idea for a conventional wing and tail unit which could be attached to a tank, once again without the necessity for designing a glider that could carry a large tank within it. A memo of June 1942 survives from the Director AFVs at the War Office to the C-in-C Home Forces stating that such a device to carry the Mk.VIII tank could be in production by July-August 1943.[26]

These projects were about the closest the Harry Hopkins ever got to becoming airborne, but they were abandoned sometime in 1942 or 1943. The tailless concept was still very experimental at this time, and in addition these 'tank-with-wings' designs seem to have relied on using the tracks of the tank as landing gear. At the touch-down speeds likely to be encountered, it was considered highly problematic whether the running gear, suspension and tracks of a tank could stand the strain. The view from the driver's seat of the tank was also likely to be so limited as to preclude safe flying. In addition, these designs were essentially specific to one vehicle, and lacked the flexibility of the Hamilcar which could be adapted as a load carrier for any cargo that could be lashed inside it, provided the weight was within limits. Perhaps the final clincher was the sober War Office view of the Harry Hopkins as a combat tank, given in April 1942: 'a tank such as this will be of little use in Europe in 18 months time'.[27]

To complete the story of the Harry Hopkins, it only remains to tell the story of the Alecto light self-propelled gun. This vehicle is of interest in that it showed that a self-propelled gun on a light tank chassis, carrying a worthwhile support weapon, was a practical idea that could have been adopted if thought necessary. Such sources as there are on this vehicle are reticent about when it was developed, and the best that can be said is that this took place around the last half of 1942 and the first half of 1943. The chassis of the Harry Hopkins was used as the basis for mounting a 95mm howitzer, with the project numbered A25 E2, and originally known as the Harry Hopkins 1CS (i.e. close support).[28] The turret was removed and the gun mounted low in the hull, producing a very low overall profile whilst

24 PRO file AVIA22/1572.
25 AVIA22/1572.
26 AVIA22/1572.
27 AVIA22/1572
28 The best, though still very brief, published account of this vehicle is in *British AFVs 1919-1940*, p.54

The Alecto I self-propelled 95mm howitzer, based on the Harry Hopkins chassis. A protective cover is fitted over the open-topped fighting compartment (Tank Museum).

providing accommodation for a crew of four in an open-topped fighting compartment. The crew consisted of a commander, gunner, loader and driver. Although based on the Harry Hopkins chassis, the armour was completely rethought and reduced to minimum thickness (varying between 4mm and 10mm) presumably to keep weight within limits.[29] The weight of the vehicle was only 8 tons, but with a width identical to the Harry Hopkins there was no hope of carrying the Alecto in a Hamilcar. A traverse of 15° either side of straight ahead was possible for the main armament. The vehicle apparently turned out to be highly mobile (road speed was quoted as 31mph), and the gun packed a very worthwhile punch. The potential roles for the Alecto included replacing the half-track mounted 75mm guns which were used as support weapons in British reconnaissance regiments, and as an air portable weapon. Once again, it is surprising to read in surviving documents that grandiose plans to produce large numbers of Alectos were formulated. In August 1943, the War Office stated a requirement for 1100 'Harry Hopkins 95mm'. By November of that year, the requirement for 1944-45 had risen to the extraordinary total of 2,900, with a note added to the effect that 'effort should be taken to produce as nearly this quantity as possible'.[30] This was a much larger number than could possibly have been justified by the roles already mentioned, but what use all these Alectos were to be put to is not stated.

A pilot model of an Alecto II with a 6pdr anti-tank gun was produced, and an Alecto III with a 25pdr gun and an Alecto IV with a massive 32pdr anti-tank

29 Basic details of the Alecto can be found in PRO file WO194/118, Tank Data; Drawings, Alecto I
30 AVIA22/459

weapon were proposed but never proceeded with. Small numbers of an Alecto Dozer were produced with the gun removed and a dozer blade added. All work on the Alecto ended in 1945 as the war came to an end. After the war a few Alectos were issued to replace the half-track mounted 75mm guns in the 'heavy troops' of recce units, but service was brief.[31]

A modest diversion is called for here to describe two ideas that were put forward to try to squeeze a vehicle with worthwhile hitting power and/or armour into the Hamilcar. They are described by Michael Bowyer in articles which appeared in *Airfix Magazine*, and as I have been unable to find the original source documents describing these ideas, it will be as well to simply quote in full Bowyer's description:

> What was in mind was a two seater amphibious vehicle carrying a 25pdr gun with recoilless ammunition and a .30 calibre Browning gun with 5000 rounds. There was also the Duplex tank consisting of two separate units connected by a cable. The forward vehicle would be heavily armoured and carry an anti-tank gun and crew, whilst the rear unit provided power from 300 yards aft. It was lightly armoured and provided motive power for both vehicles, the forward one being electrically driven via a cable.[32]

The second proposal is ingenious, effectively dividing a tank into two and putting it into two separate Hamilcars. However, once the detail of how such an unlikely combination might actually be handled in action is considered, the idea loses most of its attraction. On the other hand, the self-propelled 25pdr seems a sensible enough idea, and raises the question of why a Tetrarch chassis was never used as the basis for an air-portable SP gun.

Although the Alecto chassis was a little wider and longer than the Tetrarch's, it would seem that a similar development of the latter tank into an SP gun was entirely possible, but never attempted. This would surely have offered a way to provide airborne troops with the mobile and (lightly) armoured support that the airborne tank project was originally supposed to provide. In addition to raising questions of this sort, the Harry Hopkins and Alecto provide examples of the muddled thinking at the War Office about tanks which was one cause of the generally poor standard of AFVs produced in Britain during World War Two, and which in particular resulted in the British Army crossing the Channel in 1944 equipped mainly with the American Sherman tank. To envisage the production of thousands of vehicles which in the end were never needed would appear to demonstrate that some departments of the War Office concerned with AFVs were rather out of touch with operational realities. However, the story of the only other airborne tank, apart from the Tetrarch, to be used operationally shows that such miscalculations were not restricted to the UK. We should turn now to the development of the Locust light tank.

Unlike the Tetrarch, the Locust was developed in the United States specifically as an airborne tank. As has been mentioned above, the catalyst for the tank's design and development came from a British initiative following the decision in the UK to develop a tank carrying glider. This initiative appears to have taken place sometime

---

31 Fletcher, 'The Flying Tank', p.24.
32 Bowyer, 'Hamilcar Tank Transports', *Airfix Magazine*, April 1977, p.450.

during the first quarter of 1941, and was made initially via the British Air Commission in Washington.[33] As we have also already seen, the British had decided that a vehicle of around 9 to 10 tons was the maximum that could be lifted using the available technology, and correspondence from March and April 1941 gives an idea of the type of tank the British hoped to convince the Americans to develop. A telegram which seems to be from the Ministry of Supply to the British Consul-General in New York, and which obviously formed part of the negotiations with the Americans, survives and states:

> Require 37mm gun and .30 Browning in 360° turret. Space for wireless. Crew of 3. Max speed 40mph. Radius of action 200 miles. Armour basis preferably 40 to 50mm front and turret. Sides 30mm. This would bring weight to about nine tons.[34]

A surviving memo from the War Office Directorate of Mechanisation to the Ministry of Aircraft Production (dated March 1941) also mentions a tank of 9 tons: 'a tank of substantially less than 9 tons would not have the necessary fighting qualities for the operations in view'.[35] These statements are interesting inasmuch as that by this time, in the UK, it had been agreed that the glider to be developed by GAL would carry the Mk.VII Tetrarch of only 7.5 tons. This seems to confirm that many of those concerned with developing airborne tanks at this time already knew that the Tetrarch would be inadequate for its supporting role, and also shows that, despite the need to get on with designing a glider based on available equipment, the tank that might eventually go into action was still the subject of discussion.

According to the limited documentation in the surviving British files, American response to the British proposals was lukewarm. They felt they had no spare capacity to devote to the project. The British had no interest in helping the Americans out directly: after all, it was the lack of design and production capability in the UK that had led them to approach the Americans in the first place. The British decided not to pressurise the Americans too much on the project, but it would seem their approaches had the desired effect. The success of the German airborne forces in the Low Countries had impressed the Americans as much as it had the British, and in February 1941 the Ordnance Department held a meeting with representatives of the Armored Force, Army Air Corps and the General Staff on the subject of an airborne tank and the aircraft to carry it. The early date of this meeting would suggest that the Americans were already interested in such a development ahead of the British overtures. That the Americans were thinking along original lines is further suggested by the quite different form of carriage which they envisaged for their airborne tank: they were thinking of using a powered transport rather than a glider. Nevertheless, the present-day Director of the US Army Ordnance Museum, William Atwater, is confident that it was the British requirement that led to development of the Locust.[36] Perhaps the British pressure gave the de-

---

33 Correspondence from this period survives in PRO file AVIA22/1021, Tank Carrying Aircraft in the US.
34 AVIA22/1021
35 AVIA22/1021
36 Mr Atwater very kindly passed on what he knew of the tank's development in a letter to the author in May 2001.

ciding impetus to American intentions, and it may also be the case that knowledge of American ideas led to the British promptings in the first place.

As a result of the February meeting, the Ordnance Department decided to go ahead with design of an airborne tank and design studies were initiated for a vehicle of around 6.7 tons (usually given in sources as 7.5 US tons), a weight considered feasible by the Air Corps. Atwater is again convinced that this weight limit, along with maximum figures for length, width and height, were part of an agreement with the British, apparently made to ensure the new tank would fit inside the Hamilcar. Designs were requested from three companies, General Motors, J.Walter Christie and Marmon-Herrington. At a conference in May 1941, the latter company's design was accepted. Marmon Herrington, rather like Vickers-Armstrong, had a track record of building light tanks for export and for the US Army.

A pilot model, originally designated Light Tank T9 (Airborne), was completed in late 1941. In appearance it had the look of a miniature Sherman, a resemblance that was to be enhanced by subsequent redesigns. As first built, the tank had a 37mm main armament (broadly equivalent to the British 2pdr), with a co-axial .30 caliber machine gun, mounted in a powered turret. The main armament was fitted with a gyro stabilizer to facilitate firing on the move, a fairly novel feature at this date and unusual for such a light gun. In addition there was a pair of .30 caliber machine guns mounted in the bow on the right hand side. Drive was from the front sprocket, with a large rear idler and two bogie assemblies each side, each of two wheels with vertical volute suspension. The engine was a 162hp, six cylinder, air cooled Lycoming. The turret was cast and the hull welded. Armour thickness varied from 12.5mm on the hull front and the vertical hull sides to 9.5mm on the sloping hull sides. Rear armour was 12.5mm, with 9mm armour on the upper surfaces. A number of sources give the frontal armour as 25mm or 1 inch, but it seems that the well sloped front plate of the final version gave the *equivalent* of 25mm of armour, rather than actually being this thick.[37] As with the Tetrarch, it had a crew of three. The pilot model was made of soft steel plate rather than armour plate.

The T9 was not designed to ride to battle in a glider. The carrying aircraft was to be the Douglas C54 Skymaster, a four engined, tricycle undercarriage transport aircraft which was the military version of the DC-4 airliner, which had been developed in the immediate pre-war period. The tank was to be carried under the belly of the C54, and the four lifting brackets used to raise the tank into place are prominent on each side of the hull on photos of those vehicles designed to be used in this way. The turret would have to be removed and carried separately inside the fuselage, and for this purpose it was designed to be easily detachable. Some sources have suggested that having to remove the turret was an unforeseen development resulting from a design error, but this was not the case. In his definitive work on American light tanks, R.P. Hunnicutt clearly states that the Locust was 'originally designed to be suspended without its turret under a C54 transport.'[38] The tank also turned out to be just the correct size and weight to fit complete inside a Hamilcar,

---

37 See Hunnicutt, *Stuart*, p.248.
38 See Hunnicutt, op.cit. p.255. For the idea that having to remove the turret was a mistake, see Hogg, *Armour in Conflict*, pp.152-153 and Icks, 'M22 Locust Light Tank' in Crow (ed.) *American AFVs of World War Two*, p.100.

Locust prototype. Note stepped arrangement of hull front armour and twin bow machine guns (Tank Museum).

compelling evidence that the dimensions and weight had been chosen for this purpose in conjunction with the British when the tank was first proposed.

Modifications to the pilot model were made during testing, such as a supporting steel beam to strengthen the suspension. Weight began to creep up and, in consultation with the British, a maximum weight of 15,800 lbs (7.05 tons) was agreed. Once again, this was just about the weight that constituted the maximum load for the Hamilcar. Two new prototypes incorporating weight reducing changes and other improvements were ordered in January 1942. The first of these two new prototypes, designated T9E1, was completed in November 1942, the second being completed shortly afterwards. The turret was altered in shape and lightened and the power traverse removed, as was the gyro stabilizer for the 37mm gun. The front of the hull was changed from its initial stepped appearance to a sloped configuration which would provide a better ballistic shape. The twin machine guns were deleted from the bow, and the cooling louvres on the engine deck were changed. The steel beam on the bogie assemblies was replaced by a steel rod, and the bogie frames were slotted in another attempt to reduce weight. Tests of the new tank took place at the Aberdeen Proving Ground.

However, contrary to normal practice, orders for the T9 had been placed in April 1942 before development (including the changes noted above) and service tests had taken place. 500 were ordered in April, followed by 400 more shortly afterwards, then a further order for another 1000 was made, making an extraordinary and massive total of 1900. Deliveries were to begin in November 1942, but not surprisingly production difficulties and design changes put this date back and it was April 1943 before production commenced. During 1943 and 1944 extensive testing began, whilst production peaked at 100 per month between August 1943 and January 1944. However, in February 1944 this headlong pace was arrested as results of the test programme came in and operational difficulties were assessed. Production was halted at this point after 830 tanks had been produced. To clarify the reasons for this decision we need to go back to the design concept of the T9 and in particular how it was to be transported.

We have seen that to fit in place under the C54, the turret of the T9 had to be removed and carried separately *inside* the aircraft. A British report on progress with the T9 from January 1943 gave an idea of the time involved in loading and unloading the tank during trials. For loading, the tank was positioned by the side door of the C-54 where the aircraft's own internal hoists could be used to raise the turret off the tank and bring it inside the fuselage. The hull was then driven into position under the belly of the aircraft where a four point hoist lifted the tank up until four sprung locks engaged with the lugs on the side of the tank. Using a group of six untrained men, this whole process took 24 minutes. For unloading, the pilot could release the four locks to drop the hull onto the ground, which only involved a fall of about 14 inches. The tank could then be driven back to the side door to be reunited with its turret. This process took about 10 minutes, though the report noted that this could probably be improved with practice.[39] The unloading and re-assembly time was actually surprisingly quick, but in a combat situation even those few minutes would make the unloading aircraft an excellent target. The heavily loaded C54 itself would require a large airfield to land on. Operational use of the T9 would be restricted by the availability of such airfields, which might not be in the right place and would have to be captured in advance if a landing behind the enemy was contemplated.

By 1944 it was also realised that the tank itself was obsolete. The armour was in some areas shown to be incapable of resisting even the AP ammunition of the .50 calibre machine gun, and the 37mm gun carried by the tank would be ineffective against most of the battle tanks in service with the Axis. The tank was also proving to be mechanically unreliable, and it is also commonly described as being underpowered. The engine was in fact of similar horse power to the Meadows engine in the Tetrarch (a tank of similar weight), so the problem must presumably have derived from the torque characteristics of the engine or problems with an inefficient transmission system. Overall, the Americans realised that they had a faulty operational concept which would result in the delivery of a weapon of dubious value. The production of such large numbers of T9s as occurred must be judged a significant waste of American resources.

It should be noted, however, that by the end of the war, America had developed transport aircraft which could carry the Locust internally without any dismantling (though the aircraft were not specifically designed for this purpose). The British report noted above recorded that loading trials with the Douglas C-97 Globemaster had taken place. This massive four engined transport could take a load of up to 48,150 lbs (21.5 tons), and a Locust could be loaded complete by hoisting through the aircraft's belly hatch. The C-97 had been in development since 1942 but did not fly until December 1945. The Locust could also be carried by the Fairchild C-82 Packet, a twin engined aircraft of twin-boom design which

---

39 Tank Museum files, Locust Tank.

Late model Locust tank with Littlejohn adapter (IWM).

could load vehicles through double clamshell doors at the rear of the fuselage.[40] The C-82 first flew in September 1944. The availability of these aircraft did not improve the operational prospects of the T9: any flights that took place seem to have been trials only.

The T9 was destined never to be used in action by US forces, and no operational units were ever formed with the tank. In September 1944 the tank was classified as 'limited standard' and received the designation M22, but it seems the only use the vehicle was put to in the US was for training. However, the British still had a requirement for the Locust as a more modern alternative to the Tetrarch for use in Hamilcar gliders. Documents at the Public Record Office indicate that the first prototype T9 may have been shipped to England as early as late May 1942, and was used for static trials to demonstrate that the tank would fit in a Hamilcar and to work out the modifications necessary to stow the vehicle securely for flight.[41] It was over a year until a T9E1 (in fact the second of the two T9E1 prototypes) flew in a Hamilcar, on 13th July 1943. The slow production of the Hamilcar meant that potential operations were well in the future, which doubtless reduced the urgency of progress. In addition, the British had to wait for the availability of the modified and lightened T9E1 before flight trials could commence.[42]

40 See Icks, 'M22 Locust Light Tank' in *American AFVs of World War Two*, p.97.
41 PRO file AVIA15/1677.
42 PRO files AVIA15/1677,2368,2369.

Locust and Hamilcar. The wrinkles in the fuselage were common on well used Hamilcars (Tank Museum).

During 1943 the T9 was evaluated by the British, and the results of the trials held at the Experimental Wing of the AFV School at Lulworth have survived. In March that year, brief trials resulted in a favourable conclusion that the tank 'should prove entirely adequate in the airborne role for which it was intended'.[43] However, further trials at the same establishment in November 1943 resulted in the comment, 'this vehicle has shown itself to have a number of weak points both from a mechanical and gunnery point of view ... it is just adequate for its intended role'.[44] We will see in part two that the Locust was first issued to the Airborne Light Tank Squadron in October 1943, but was withdrawn from use before D-Day due to the defects encountered. These defects appear to have caused deliveries of the T9 from the USA to be held up for a while whilst they were corrected, but appropriately modified tanks were being produced by January 1944 and during the course of that year deliveries recommenced.[45]

Eventually, 260 Locusts were allocated to the British under lend-lease. Most ended up being stored in tank parks until scrapped at the end of the war. Some may have been employed by the Royal Artillery as command tanks for self propelled batteries of either field guns or anti-tank guns (or both), but details confirming this use have not been discovered by the author. In the end, only eight ever found their way into action with 6th AARR. The use of Locusts by this unit is covered in Part Two.

43 Tank Museum files, Locust tank.
44 Ibid.
45 Tank Museum files, RAC Policy and Progress Report, Dec. 1944; RAC Liaison Letter No.9, Jan. 1944.

Two other tanks appear in our story, and should be briefly described. These are the Valentine and the Cromwell. The first fought alongside the Tetrarchs in the Madagascar operation and was considered for one (rather outlandish) airborne tank project; the latter was the tank used by 6th AARR in its campaigns in North-West Europe when the regiment was supporting 6th Airborne Division as a conventional recce unit.

The Valentine was another Vickers product and was meant as an infantry tank, that is with a relatively low speed but thick armour to be deployed in independent tank brigades in support of infantry divisions. It was developed in response to a government initiative for a possible new infantry tank which was made in January 1938, around the time the Tetrarch was first being tested by the company. Vickers based the new vehicle on the chassis and suspension of an earlier company design, the A10 Cruiser Mk.II, and as a result the design was quickly finalised and was submitted to the War Office in February 1938. The vehicle was a fairly compact design, with 65mm of frontal armour and a three man crew, the turret mounting a 2pdr gun. Length was 17ft 9ins, width 8ft 7ins and height 7ft 5ins. Weight was around 16 tons. Maximum road speed was 16mph, with an average cross country speed of about half that. The problems of a three man crew have already been discussed, and the tank was initially rejected for this reason. However, after to and fro discussions of possible changes, the desperate need for tanks in the immediate pre-war period convinced the War Office to order the Valentine 'off the drawing board' (that is without building and testing a prototype) in July 1939. The first vehicle was running by May 1940, and proved to be a success, being reliable and judged a good gun platform.

Eventually, 8275 Valentines were produced in eleven marks, making the vehicle one of Britain's most important tanks of World War Two. It saw its main operational service in the Middle East, serving in the North African campaigns up to and including Tunisia. Despite its low speed, it was of necessity used in armoured regiments within armoured divisions as a cruiser tank. After the initial marks, the Marks III and V were fitted with a three man turret, but when the tank was upgunned in 1942 take the 6pdr (the Marks VIII, IX and X) the turret crew had to be reduced again to two men to accommodate the bigger gun. In the final mark, the Mark XI, the 6pdr was replaced by the 75mm gun as fitted to the Sherman and Cromwell in the late war period, still of course with a two man turret plus a driver. In the Marks VIII to XI, weight crept up to about 17 tons. By the end of 1942 the vehicle was considered obsolescent due to its slow speed and three man crew, being replaced by the Sherman and Churchill at the time of the invasion of Sicily and Italy. The 75mm armed Mark XI was not in production until late 1943 and never saw operational service. Production, however, did not cease until April 1944. The main reason Valentine production continued seems to have been that the Russians (who had received a considerable number of Valentines) continued to rate it as a worthwhile tank, preferring to receive Valentines when offered the bigger and faster Cromwell.[46] During its period of British operational service the Valentine was a useful tank, characterised by good reliability, but often considered undergunned, though in this it only shared the same problem as all other contemporary British designed tanks. Having been designed as an infantry tank, its armour protection was quite reasonable even at the end of its career.

46 See Zaloga & Grandsen, p.207.

The Cromwell tank was one of the last designs in the line of British 'cruiser' tanks. It was the most successful of three parallel designs which arose from a specification for a tank intended to replace the Crusader. All three vehicles looked basically the same, the other two being the Cavalier and the Centaur, and the original design work was done by Nuffield Mechanisation and Aero. The basic difference between the three tanks was the engine. The Cavalier and Centaur were in effect interim designs which were powered by a version of the American Liberty engine until the intended final engine, the Rolls-Royce Meteor (a tank version of the famous Merlin engine), became available. The original order for the Cavalier (the first of the three to be made) was placed in January 1941. By January 1942 a prototype of the Cromwell was running, and the first production Cromwells were made in January 1943. There were some problems with the tank to start with, broadly centering around reliability, but by 1944 these had generally been ironed out and the tank was issued to British armoured divisions to equip their armoured reconnaissance regiments, one of which was included in each division. The three armoured regiments which formed the basic tank strength of the armoured divisions were equipped with the American Sherman tank, as a result of the poor performance of the British tank industry which had proved incapable of producing sufficient tanks of the right quality to properly equip British formations. The Cavalier and Centaur were dropped in favour of the Cromwell, most being either converted to Cromwells by fitting the Meteor engine or used for training.

The Cromwell was built in eight versions, the most common versions to see service in 1944-45 being the Mks.IV, V, and VII. The first three marks were designed with the 6pdr gun and did not see operational service. The IV, V, and VII had the 75mm gun. The Mks VI and VIII, produced in fewer numbers, had the 95mm close support howitzer (see below). The Mks VII and VIII were modified to have thicker armour on the hull front (101mm rather than 76mm) and wider tracks, which raised the weight from 27 tons to 28 tons. The armour was unimaginatively arranged, the structure being box-like rather than sloped which would have increased effectiveness. The 600 hp Meteor gave the tank excellent mobility, with a road speed of 40mph for the earlier versions, until the drive ratios were altered in the Mks.VII and VIII to limit road speed to 32mph. Length was 20ft 10ins, width 9ft 6ins, and height 8ft 2ins. The tank was broadly equivalent in combat value to the Sherman, though its good mobility made it a natural choice for the armoured recce regiments. As with the Sherman, it was comparable with the contemporary German MkIVH, although the medium velocity 75mm gun was slightly inferior to the longer 75mm gun fitted to the MkIV. However, the two Allied tanks were significantly inferior to the Panther and Tiger, both in armour protection and main armament. As the vehicle of the armoured recce regiments, the Cromwell was the obvious choice to re-equip 6th AARR when it was not involved in airborne operations, as we shall see in later chapters. The Mk IV or Mk V would have been used in Normandy, upgrading to the Mk VII in the period of action after the Rhine crossing.

Finally, a word on tank armament. The 2pdr gun with which the Tetrarch was armed had been introduced into service with the British Army in 1935, being the tank version of the 2pdr anti-tank gun supplied to the infantry. The weapon was the standard main armament of all British cruiser and infantry tanks at the start of the war. It had a calibre of 40mm and a length fifty times its calibre (usually expressed as L/50), the latter meaning it had a relatively long barrel which would increase the muzzle velocity of its round and hence its armour piercing ability. It fired a round which in fact weighed a little over two pounds, varying slightly with the type of shell. In comparison with weapons of similar calibre produced around the same time by other countries, the 2pdr was superior to most and was a good weapon for its time. The basic armour piercing (AP) round, fired at a muzzle velocity of 2800 feet per second (fps), would penetrate 40mm of armour angled at 30° from the vertical at 1000 yards, according to one source.[47] Other official sources suggest the figure may have been nearer to only 25 to 30mm at this range.[48] The difference in the figures probably relates to the type of armour used in the tests, and/or the angle at which it was set. An improved round called armour piecing capped, ballistic cap (APCBC), introduced in May 1942, increased the figure of 40mm to 49mm. One drawback of the weapon was the light weight of its shell, which meant the high explosive round which it could fire was not very effective. Indeed, for most of time during which the gun was the standard main armament of British tanks, the HE round was not issued at all, severely limiting the ability to take on infantry, soft vehicles and anti-tank guns. Operational experience quickly taught the lesson that it was important for tank guns to have a dual purpose ability, able to fire a powerful armour piercing projectile but also a worthwhile high explosive round for taking on 'soft' targets.

The 2pdr was effective against all German tanks of the 1939-40 period, the standard German medium tanks of the time (the Pz III and Pz IV) having frontal armour of 30mm sloped only 10° back from the vertical. However, the war quickly initiated a competition between anti-tank guns and tank armour in which thicker armour was developed to provide better protection, resulting in a need for more powerful anti-tank guns which in turn meant thicker armour was developed, and so on. This is not the place to describe that process, but it is sufficient to say that by the end of the 1940 campaign in France, the need in the near future for a better tank gun than the 2pdr had already been recognised. By 1944, the 2pdr was completely obsolete as a tank or anti-tank gun, having been supplanted by 6pdr (57mm) and 17pdr (76.2mm) weapons as well as the 75mm guns fitted to the Sherman, Cromwell and Churchill. For example, the frontal armour of the latest version of the Pz IV, the Pz IVH, was now 80mm and the other standard German medium tank, the Panther, also had 80mm of armour on its hull front, but sloped back 55° from the vertical to make it much more effective.

In 1944, only those armoured vehicles whose turrets could not mount a bigger gun than the 2pdr still carried this weapon. Basically, this meant the Daimler armoured car which was widely issued to recce units, and the few Tetrarchs of 6th AARR. (It is worth noting in passing that the Daimler used the same turret design as the Tetrarch, with a few detail differences).

One development had occurred, however, which made the 2pdr a little more effective, and this was the 'Littlejohn Adapter'. This device made use of the 'tapered bore' or 'coned bore' principle, which had been known about since the be-

---

47 Official figures from the booklet *Fire and Movement*, RAC Tank Museum, 1975.
48 Beale, p102.

ginning of the century. The principle was explored by the Germans during the war but the guns they developed saw little service, mainly due to the limited supplies of tungsten carbide which was required for the special ammunition. As the name would suggest, the barrel of a coned bore gun reduces in calibre along its length. When the gun is fired and the bullet or shell moves down the barrel, the explosive force of the charge is exerted on a steadily diminishing area, increasing its effect and increasing muzzle velocity. While the principle is simple, the practicalities of machining the barrels and developing projectiles for such guns are complex. The Littlejohn adapter was Britain's only venture in this field to see operational service, and the idea for this particular version of the coned-bore principle was originally developed in Czechoslovakia in the late 1930s by a Czech arms manufacturer called Dr.F.Janacek. 'Littlejohn' is the anglicisation of his surname. When Czechoslovakia was occupied, Janacek brought his idea to Britain, and after some trouble he managed to convince the appropriate authorities to develop it.[49]

The idea was for a coned bore attachment which could be screwed on to the end of the 2pdr gun, rather than having to develop a completely new coned bore weapon. The attachment was smooth bored, and the special round used had an extremely hard and dense tungsten-carbide core surrounded by a soft metal band or sheath. The round went along the 2pdr barrel in the normal way, but when it entered the adapter the soft metal band was reduced until it formed a thin coating around the core with most of it in a lump behind. The increase in muzzle velocity achieved was striking: the so-called super velocity (sv) round left the barrel at 4200 fps. It weighed only one pound but at 1000 yards it would penetrate 72mm of armour angled at 30°. At 500 yards the figure was 88mm.[50] This gave a performance not much less than the new 6pdr and 75mm guns which were coming into service as the adapter was being produced (from mid-1942). Whilst the adapter had the advantage that it could be fitted to a standard gun, and could be removed in the field to fire the gun normally, it had the disadvantage that when fitted to the 2pdr it could fire only armour piercing rounds. Removing it in the field was not easy, and there were times when even the 2pdr's HE projectile could be useful. Obviously, a normal 6pdr or 75mm gun capable of firing either AP or HE rounds was much more useful in a tank than a 2pdr with Littlejohn. There were proposals to develop Littlejohn adapters for the 6pdr and 17pdr guns, but other special rounds (armour piercing discarding sabot: APDS) were developed for these guns which improved their performance without the complexity of the Littlejohn. A proportion of the Daimler armoured cars which served in North-West Europe in 1944-45 were fitted with Littlejohn, however, and all the Tetrarchs which flew in on D-Day seem also to have been so fitted. The adapters were often called 'squeezers' or 'squeeze attachments' by the crews.

The 3" howitzer which was fitted to the close support version of the Tetrarch (see chapter four) was also a pre-war tank weapon. It had been fitted to close support versions of some of the cruiser tanks which were in service at the beginning of the war in an attempt to supplement the poor HE firepower of the 2pdr gun. Although of similar calibre to the 75mm guns which armed most Allied tanks in 1944-45, it was a much less effective weapon. It fired only HE or smoke rounds, at

49 See Weeks, pp. 38-39.
50 *Fire and Movement.*

the low muzzle velocity of 600fps, and official figures give its maximum range with HE as 2400yds, or 1600yds with smoke.[51] However, in his book *The Great Tank Scandal*, David Fletcher suggests these figures may be optimistic. Of the 3" howitzer he says it 'had such a short range that the high explosive shell could rarely be used effectively, and the main purpose of the weapon was to fire a smoke shell to mask the tanks from enemy fire'.[52] Use of the 3" howitzer was never widespread, small numbers of tanks so armed going to the HQ squadrons of armoured regiments and seeing limited service in France in 1940 and the early campaigns in the Western Desert. The advent of genuinely dual purpose tank guns made them obsolete. Some Daimler armoured cars were fitted with the weapon, but it is not clear if they were ever issued to combat units. The handful of Tetrarchs in 6th AARR were the only tanks using this weapon by 1944, and it appears from the war diary they were used in Normandy to fire HE in order to supplement the fire of 2pdrs fitted with Littlejohn.

The 37mm gun fitted to the Locust was very much the American equivalent of the 2pdr, with very similar capabilities. It was an L/57 weapon, with a muzzle velocity of 2900fps, and a penetration figure at 1000yds, against armour sloped at 30°, of 42mm.[53] In 1944-45 it remained the main armament of the American M3 and M5 light tanks that were a minor part of the equipment of both British and American armoured formations. A Littlejohn adapter was developed for the 37mm, but this modification only seems to have seen service on the Locusts of 6th AARR. Even then, it seems to have been removed from the few Locusts that actually saw combat. The 37mm gun was shortened slightly to take the adapter, and the bore of 37mm was reduced to about 30mm at the muzzle of the adapter. The effect was the same as for the 2pdr, raising muzzle velocity to around 4000fps.

One final gun is mentioned specifically above and needs to be briefly described. The 95mm howitzer was first developed in the UK in 1941 as a potential towed infantry gun.[54] In the end the gun was not wanted in this role, but it was adapted for mounting in tanks in order to perform a role similar to that of the old 3" howitzer but with much greater effectiveness: that is, for use in a limited number of vehicles at squadron or regimental HQ level as a close support weapon, firing a more powerful HE round than the 6pdr or 75mm guns fitted to the normal tanks. In 1944-45 both Cromwell and Churchill tanks saw service with this weapon, the normal issue being two tanks at squadron HQ level. It also saw service with the Centaur tanks (see above) of the Royal Marines Armoured Support Group which landed on D-Day and were in action for a short period afterwards. This unit seems to have passed its twelve vehicles on to a formation called X Armoured Battery, Royal Artillery, who on 9th August commenced handing over to another short-lived formation, No.1 Canadian Centaur Battery, which was operational until 31st August. The latter two units were both used in support of 6th Airborne Division. The 95mm gun proved to be very useful in service, firing a 25 pound shell up to a range of 6000 yards, though short range, direct fire engagements were also com-

---

51 RAC Weapons, Military Training Pamphlet No.35, 1942, held at The Tank Museum, Bovington.
52 Fletcher, *The Great Tank Scandal*, p.7.
53 *Fire and Movement*.
54 See Hogg, *The Guns 1939-45*, p.31.

mon. An effective armour piercing round was also developed for the weapon, being a high explosive anti tank (HEAT) round similar in principle to the rockets and bombs fired from the various 'bazooka' type weapons of the time. This could penetrate 110mm of armour at any range a hit could be obtained (as the round relied on explosive effect rather than kinetic energy).[55] As a support weapon for airborne forces, mounted on an armoured chassis, the gun had much to offer, but as we have seen this line of development (the Alecto) effectively went nowhere.

55 *Fire and Movement.*

Chapter 2

Gliders

We have already seen that one of the earliest conclusions reached when British airborne forces were proposed was that such forces should include a significant number of gliders. Although they needed more space to land than parachutists, their loads arrived in a more concentrated manner and could include the heavy weapons which airborne forces so seriously lacked. Britain had no military gliders in 1940, but with the example of the German use of gliders in the Low Countries before them, the British quickly came to accept that these aircraft would be needed as part of any future airborne force. By the end of 1940, specifications for four types of glider had been issued by the War Office. These were not to be experimental designs, nor were they limited to the size of glider so far used by the Germans. Only the first, the Hotspur, was an eight seater like the German DFS 230 used at Eben Emael in Belgium. As for the other three, specification X25/40 called for a 15 seat glider, which became the Hengist. X26/40 specified a 25 seater which was produced as the Horsa. Finally, X27/40 was for a glider capable of carrying a light tank or other heavy loads into action, which resulted in the Hamilcar. The British military was preparing, from the earliest stage, for an airborne force of considerable size and capability, potentially able to exceed that demonstrated by the Germans up to that date.

The success of the Horsa, which became the operational troop-carrying glider, resulted in the Hengist being dropped and the Hotspur being adopted for training duties. The Horsa and Hamilcar became the two gliders which transported the Army's airlanding troops in the great operations of 1944-45. As this is a history of Britain's gliderborne tanks and 6th AARR, we will concentrate on the Hamilcar, the only British glider capable of carrying armoured vehicles, and give a brief history of the Horsa, which transported elements of 6th AARR in training and operations.

The number of firms capable of designing and producing these ambitious wooden aircraft, and which were not already heavily committed to current projects, was limited. As a result, the contracts for developing them were allocated to particular firms as the government saw fit, rather than being the subject of competitive tendering. Slingsby were the main pre-war producers of gliders in Britain, but they were allocated the smaller Hengist as they were judged too small for the task of developing the larger aircraft. Eventually, Airspeed undertook the Horsa, and General Aircraft Limited (GAL) the Hamilcar.[1]

We have already seen, in discussing the selection of the Tetrarch for airborne use, that initial discussions in the Air Ministry and War Office regarding a glider to carry a light tank had been in progress from autumn 1940. GAL had developed Britain's first military glider, the Hotspur, which had first flown in November

---

1 For glider development, see Wood, *The Glider Soldiers*, pp87-105. More detail is contained in Michael Bowyer, 'Army-air Colours', in *Airfix Magazine*, 1976-1978.

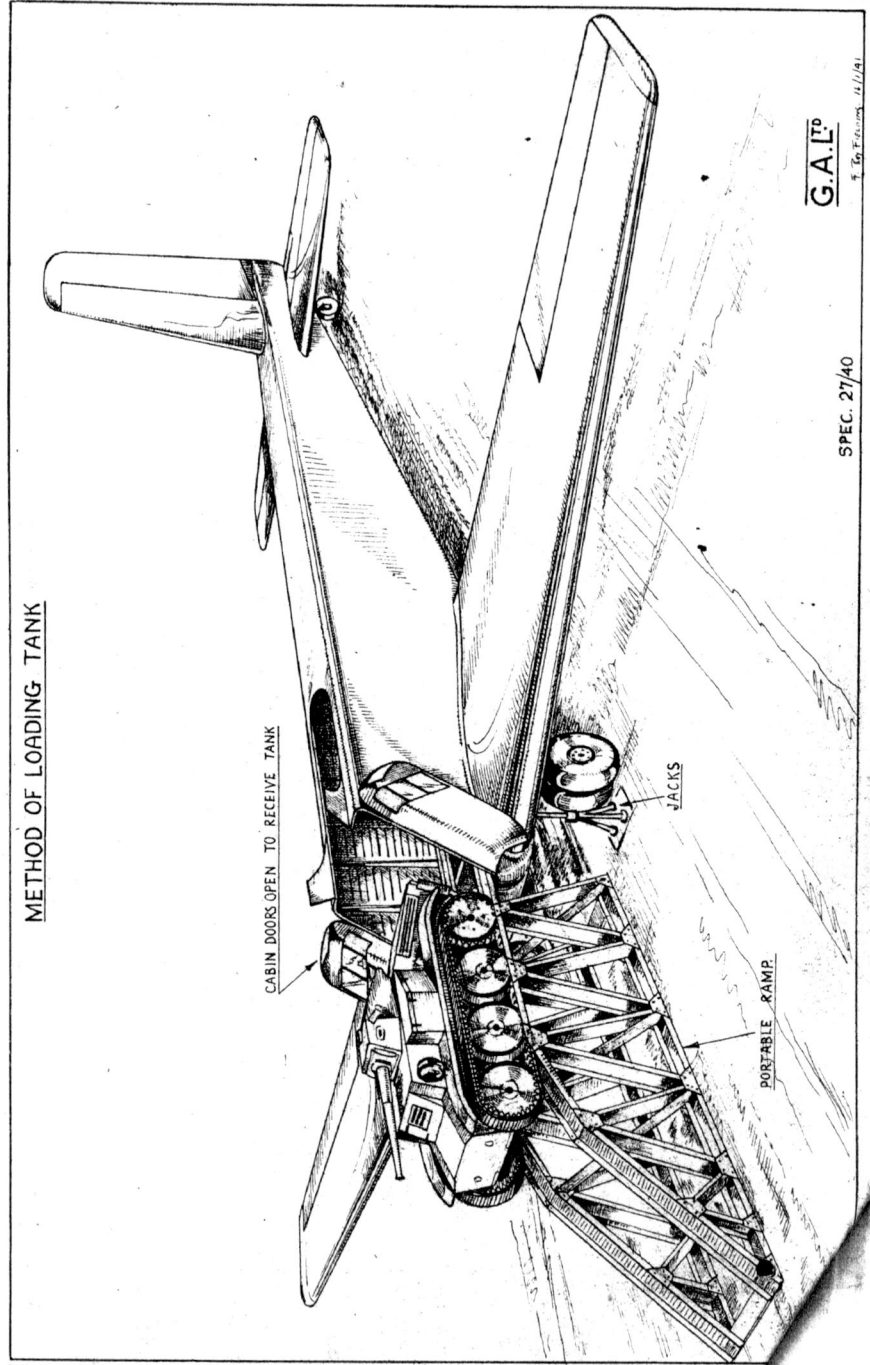

Preliminary Hamilcar proposal, dated 16th January 1941 but marked 'now altered'. The portable ramp looks decidedly impractical (General Aircraft Limited).

GLIDERS 37

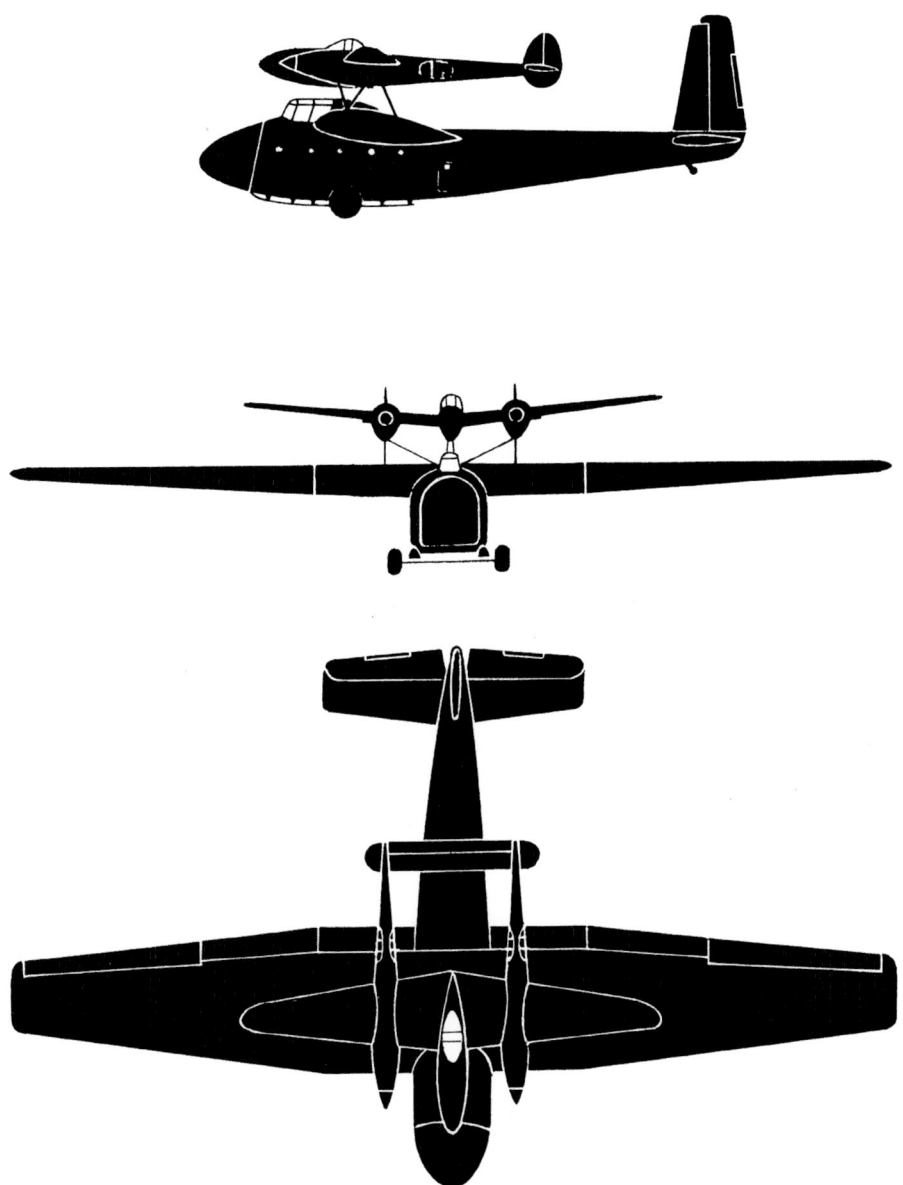

The proposed P-38 Lightning/Hamilcar combination (U.S. National Archives).

1940. Having been selected to develop the Hamilcar, GAL were included in the discussions which refined specification X27/40, a process which seems to have been finalised during a meeting with GAL on 16th January 1941. Previous to this meeting, GAL had been developing designs for a glider designed solely to carry the Mk.VII light tank. This was a low-wing aircraft designed so that the tank driver was also the glider pilot, and flew the glider from his tank driver's seat, involving, of course, internal modifications to the tank. The idea was to save on specifically trained glider pilots and also to bring the tank into action quickly after landing, although the latter objective would have been hindered by an unweildy-looking portable ramp which appears on a GAL drawing of this period. Weight, both of glider pilots and some structure, was also saved. Surviving illustrations show the tank hull enclosed by the fuselage but the turret outside the airframe, apparently ready to engage targets during the approach to landing, though this was a highly unrealistic expectation. However, it was eventually decided that such a design was too inflexible as it only allowed one specific load to be carried. The problem of bringing the tank quickly into action was capable of solution using a more conventional design.

The final form of specification X27/40 was therefore finally arrived at in January 1941. It called for an aircraft capable of carrying the Tetrarch light tank or two universal carriers. It was the dimensions and weight (around eight tons) of these two possible loads which formed the basis for General Aircraft's design. The universal carrier was a small, lightly armoured and open topped personnel carrier, with a load of around four to six men. It usually mounted a Bren light machine gun beside the driver and is often known as the Bren carrier. In specialist versions it was adapted to carry heavy weapons, like the 3" mortar and the Vickers medium machine gun, and tow weapons such as the 6pdr anti-tank gun. The vehicle saw extensive use by the British Army throughout World War Two. In fact, it was the two carrier load, which included 8 crew, which decided the maximum weight to be carried. This was given as 17024 lbs, with the weight of the fully laden Tetrarch including three crew given as 15680 lbs. Wood was specified as the main material to be used in construction. An under-fuselage hatch to allow prone firing of a Bren light machine gun during the approach to landing was a feature of the initial design, which was retained until at least December 1942 but never used in operational Hamilcars.

The original requisition from the Air Ministry to GAL to 'design, manufacture and deliver two tank carrying gliders in accordance with X27/40' survives, dated January 1941, and quotes an agreed cost of £50,000 each. By early February 1941, the basic design had been completed under the direction of GAL's chief designer Mr. F.F. Crocombe, and had been designated the GAL 49 Hamilcar. Wing and cockpit were set above the fuselage to provide an uninterrupted cargo compartment, which was 32 feet 31.5 inches long. Width of this compartment varied between 7 feet 10.5 inches and 8 feet 1 inch, height between 6 feet and 7 feet 7 inches. The nose was hinged and opened to the side for ease of loading and unloading, and included a transparent lower section as well as a glazed tip. The two pilots were seated on top of the fuselage in tandem, and were eventually protected by a bullet-proof windscreen and a plate of armour behind the second pilot. They also received considerable protection from ground fire by having the armoured loads carried beneath them. An intercom was also eventually provided between the pilots and the vehicles or men below. As with all Britain's military gliders, the aircraft was of wooden construction (mainly birch and spruce) with fabric covered plywood forming the skin, and high grade steel reinforcements in critical areas. Use of wood kept use of strategic materials to a minimum, and avoided having to use specialist metal working firms for construction of parts. The aircraft was large by any standards, having a wingspan of 110 feet, a length of 68 feet and a height of 20 feet to

Wooden model of an early Hamilcar concept with low wing and external tank turret. The tank driver would double as pilot (Museum of Army Flying).

the top of the fin. For comparison, the Lancaster heavy bomber had a span of 102 feet and a length of 69 feet 6 inches. The glider weighed 18400lbs empty, and had a military load of 17600 lbs to give an all up weight of 36000 lbs.

It will be noted that the ratio between length and wingspan was practically the same in the Hamilcar as for the Lancaster, in contrast to modern sport gliders which have a particularly large wingspan to enhance gliding performance. This was the result of the way it had been decided to use military gliders on operations. In the first glider operation of the war, Germany's DFS230 gliders had been released from 8000 feet in German airspace to glide into Belgium on their long, elegant wings. This had helped with the element of surprise. Britain's first military glider, the Hotspur, was also designed initially to be capable of long gliding approaches from altitudes as high as 20,000 feet. As early as October 1940, however, the War Office had changed its views on tactics. The new idea was for a low altitude release close to the landing zone, and a steep descent to landing, reducing time in the air and exposure to enemy fire to a minimum.[2] This resulted in the Hotspur Mk.II, with a wingspan reduced from 62 feet to 46 feet. For the same reason, both the Horsa and Hamilcar had wingspans comparable to powered aircraft of the same length, and were also fitted with the massive 'barn door' flaps which show up so prominently in photos of these gliders coming in to land. Deployment of the flaps assisted in a steep and rapid descent, and by adjusting their angle during the ap-

2   *The Glider Soldiers*, p.101.

proach a precise control over descent rate and point of landing could be achieved. They also allowed a slower touchdown speed to be attained, shortening the landing run. In the Hamilcar, the flaps were powered by compressed air, from a bottle only big enough for one deployment. This saved weight, and was also safer because the bottle would become potentially explosive if punctured by enemy fire. The smaller it was, the better.

To minimise the risks inherent in developing such an unprecedented design, a half scale model was flown first (and given the type number GAL 50), which still needed a Whitley tug to get it airborne. This was first flown in September 1941, at the Great West Road aerodrome owned by Fairey Aviation which was later to become Heathrow Airport. Trials were successful and the first full scale aircraft was completed at GAL's Hanworth, Middlesex works in March 1942. GAL's airfield here was too small for the Hamilcar, so for this reason, and probably also for security reasons, the glider was transported to RAF Snaith in Yorkshire which had a 2000 yard tarmac runway. First flight was on 27th March 1942, the tug aircraft being a Handley Page Halifax. A member of the design team, Charles Prower, has left the following account of this time,

> There could hardly have been a more inconvenient arrangement. Snaith airfield was 200 miles from the factory and ten miles from a train service to London. It was a fully operational RAF station housing Wellington bombers and, quite understandably, they did not want to know us. Our men working on the aircraft were accommodated in the sergeant's mess where the difference in pay scale between civilians and servicemen was a continual source of ill-feeling.
>
> I spent eight weeks at Snaith on design liaison in February and March 1942. During that time the ground was continuously covered with snow. [...] When all was ready for a test flight, it all had to be cancelled at the last minute because the squadron's Wellingtons were sent out on a raid.[3]

The only tugs suitable for the Hamilcar were the new four engined bombers being developed for the RAF: the Stirling, Halifax and Lancaster. The performance as tugs of these aircraft differed between the various mark numbers. For example, the Stirling Mk.1 suffered from engine overheating problems whereas the Mk.IV was considered a good potential tug for training purposes, though it lacked range for operational sorties. The choice for operations was between the Halifax and Lancaster. Both could tow the Hamilcar off in a run of 2000 yards. Radius of action for the Halifax (assuming the glider was cast off halfway) was 250 miles, and for the Lancaster 390 miles.[4] The RAF did not want to part with any Lancasters, which they considered to be the best heavy bombers they had, so the choice fell on the Halifax, which was the towing aircraft for the first flight and all the operational sorties.

The Hamilcar pilot's notes indicate that during take off the Hamilcar would get airborne at 80mph, the Halifax lifting off at around 95mph for the Mks.II and V, or 105mph for the Mks.III and VII (see below for details of Halifax versions). Normal towing speed was 120-125mph for the former two marks of Halifax, 135mph for the later marks. It should be noted that it needed the full power of all

---

3 Prower, 'Gliding Into Battle', *Aeroplane Monthly*, August 1993, pp27-28.
4 Table of flight test results contained in PRO file AVIA 15/2368.

four engines to tow off a Hamilcar: an engine failure on take off meant an immediate cast off and some quick reactions from the glider crew. For the Hamilcar, the standard approach speed was 100mph, though for a shorter landing run the approach could be flown at 80-85 mph. Stalling speeds were 64mph with flaps up, or 52mph with flaps deployed.

Testing and development took place at a number of different airfields after Snaith, including the airfield at Newmarket racecourse and Chelveston on the Bedfordshire-Northamptonshire border. The latter airfield offered a sufficiently long run on its grass runways for full load trials using the second prototype, which had been completed in June 1942. As more pre-production machines were built, trials took place at the Airborne Forces Experimental Establishment (AFEE) which had been formed at Beaulieu, and also at Cranwell, as well as at the Royal Aircraft Establishment at Farnborough.. All flight trials appear to have been successful, and there was very little difference between the prototypes and production machines.

The question of undercarriage was a design problem common to both Horsa and Hamilcar. In both cases, a jettisonable undercarriage was considered worth having, as this would reduce weight and drag during towing, whilst landing on skids fitted to the belly of the gliders would shorten the landing run and would probably be more appropriate for landing on rough, unprepared ground. Tests showed that a fully loaded Hamilcar would come to rest in only 200 yards when landed on skids. As it turned out, however, both aircraft went into action with their undercarriages firmly fixed on for landing. This was a result of pilots preferring to land on wheels due to the increased control it gave them on landing, using differential wheel braking and, on the Horsa, a steerable nose wheel. Pilots could steer clear of potential collisions on crowded landing zones, and skilful (or lucky) pilots could turn their gliders clear of the landing area to make way for following aircraft.

The Hamilcar had originally been designed for two alternative types of undercarriage. On operations, the jettisonable undercarriage would be fitted for take off only, being dropped immediately after the glider became airborne. This undercarriage was a simple beam fitted under the fuselage with a wheel on each end, and was consequently lacking in shock absorption. Pilots were cautioned against landings using this undercarriage as the lack of any springing usually caused severe bouncing which was difficult to control. The 'ferrying' or 'training' undercarriage was a more complex affair, with the wheels attached to stub axles at the end of beefy 'V' struts which attached to the lower fuselage sides, supported by oleo-pneumatic struts running down from under the wing root. This is the undercarriage which appears on most photos and drawings of the glider. It was found that, after landing the Hamilcar on skids, it was awkward to drive vehicles straight out of the nose. In contrast, it was discovered that by deflating the oleos of the training undercarriage, the front sill of the cargo compartment was lowered sufficiently for unloading tracked vehicles without ramps, and the balancing effect of the collapsed undercarriage actually held the aircraft at a more convenient angle, making it easier to drive vehicles out. Some published sources refer to the additional practice of letting down the tyres as well as the oleos. This may possibly have been tried experimentally but seems to have formed no part of regular practice as it was quite unnecessary. The discovery regarding the oleos may have occurred quite late in the glider's development: a surviving document indicates its adoption was considered during a visit to Tarrant Rushton by a Group Captain Mole from the Ministry of Aircraft Production which occurred in February 1944.[5] The preference of pilots for landing on the training/ferrying undercarriage was also discussed during this visit. It was found that use of the brakes produced a landing run 'corresponding favourably with that for a skid landing', as *Flight* magazine put it in a detailed article in December 1944. Until mid February 1944, the official line was that the Hamilcar ferrying undercarriage was unsuitable for operational landings with full load, a decision reversed in time for D-Day.

When carrying tanks and other tracked vehicles, the idea was that engines would be started in the air, usually just before casting off from the tug on instructions from the glider pilots. Special exhaust ducts were fitted to the Hamilcar to take the exhaust fumes out of the aircraft. The Locust and Tetrarch tanks were such a tight fit that their crews normally stayed inside the tank during the flight. After landing, the vehicle(s) anchorages would first need to be released. With the Tetrarch and Locust, the driver could pull a lanyard which was within reach of his driving seat to quickly release these anchorages. He would then drive forward, the tank automatically pulling on a line which operated the door release. Universal carriers relied on a member of the crew operating the door line manually. Meanwhile, the oleos would have been lowered. The drill for this was that the pilots would get out of their cockpits and drop to the ground by means of a controlled slide down the side of the fuselage ahead of the wings. Anyone who has stood beside the sole surviving Hamilcar airframe at the Museum of Army Flying will recognise this as a feat which in itself is a testimony to the fitness and nerves of the glider pilots involved. One would go to each undercarriage leg and release the valves, allowing the hydraulic fluid to gush out. Film of the process indicates deflation took about 5-8 seconds. It was supposed to be possible (if all went well) for a Tetrarch to drive out of the nose of a Hamilcar only 15 seconds after landing, though a few seconds more would have been more usual. If after an operational landing the door was jammed, it was of course perfectly possible for a tank to drive straight out through the unopened forward fuselage by main force, and this occurred on both the operations where airborne tanks were used.

For a load like a 17pdr and tractor, unloading was lengthier. The trails of the gun fitted underneath the rear of the tractor to reduce length when stowed, so that a longer process of releasing shackles and hitching up the gun was required. Ramps also needed to be placed for a wheeled vehicle to drive out, although the oleos were still lowered. Film of this process indicates it took about one minute to one minute fifteen seconds in a training situation.[6] In later Hamilcars, it was possible to release the oleo valves using a control in the cockpit, but the modification was too late for any of the operational deployments during World War Two. It appears to have been made around July 1944.

Before the jettisonable undercarriage was dispensed with, considerable effort was expended in making the dropping of the undercarriage a safe operation. It had to be dropped so as to avoid damage both to the glider (in the event of a rebound) and to the undercarriage itself. It also had to be released soon enough after take off to make recovery of the undercarriage easy, whilst not cluttering the runway with

---

5   PRO file AVIA15/2639.
6   Imperial War Museum, SKC 358/02.

used undercarriages during mass operational departures. Problems encountered in early test flights were described by Leslie Dawson in his book *Wings Over Dorset*, for which he was able to interview the test pilot involved, Charles Hughesdon (who had also flown the aircraft on its maiden flight):

> The main assembly proved unpredictable when released at ninety miles an hour, even when fitted with parachutes.
>
> After the first such release, Charles was requested to perform the next a few feet higher as the undercarriage was rather too expensive to be written off so abruptly. Taking off again, the handle was pulled at the required datum and this time the results were even more spectacular. Bouncing up from the runway, the wheels smashed through the floor of the hold with sufficient force to damage a longeron and though the big glider was quickly brought down to land, the capacious interior revealed a considerable amount of silk, reflecting the surprise and even speedier reactions of the unfortunate crowd of boffins.[7]

Charles Prower has also left an account of some of the problems encountered:

> To see a set of wheels jettisoned was pretty hair-raising, for they weighed about half a ton and were travelling at about eighty m.p.h., bounding and bouncing all over the place, quite unpredictably. In fact we lost one of these units in the countryside near North Luffenham for several days. It would have been a considerable problem to collect them up quickly to get the next tug and glider away in an operational take-off, so they were fitted with parachutes and dropped after the glider cleared the runway.[8]

The eventual solution was to stabilise the jettisoned undercarriage by three small parachutes, with release to take place at not less than 400 feet. The undercarriage would fall well clear of the glider, and slowly enough to avoid damage to itself.

The number of Hamilcars thought to be needed was revised many times, as the War Office and the Army were both on completely new ground with the development of airborne forces. At one stage in May 1942 the War Office was asking for 360 Hamilcars for two major operations.[9] This was unrealistic: apart from the slow production rate of this large and novel aircraft, the corresponding number of tugs could simply not be made available. Later, in November 1943, the War Office indicated it would need a total production run of 800, an even more unrealistic target.[10] Eventually, a total of 344 Hamilcars were built, but the maximum number used on any one operation was 48, on Operation Varsity. GAL produced 22 Hamilcars, including the two prototypes and 10 pre-production aircraft for evaluation trials. After the first 22, production of parts was sub-contracted to the 'Hamilcar Production Group', formed by the Birmingham Railway Carriage and Wagon Company (that led the group) along with the Co-operative Wholesale Society and AC Cars. Parts were also constructed by Peerless Built-in Furniture, Slazenger and CWS Pelaw.

---

7   Dawson, p.186.
8   Prower, 'Gliding Tanks', *Aeroplane Monthly*, July 1993, p.31.
9   Bowyer, 'Army-air Colours: Hamilcar tank transports', *Airfix Magazine*, March 1977.
10 Bowyer, 'Hamilcar tank transports', *Airfix Magazine*, April 1977, p.452.

The rate of production was always slower than hoped for, due in part to the great demand on suitable woods that the gliders imposed, and also to problems of finding suitably large airfields with enough available skilled personnel to assemble and store them. It is also apparent that lack of official priority and mismanagement at GAL were additional factors, as we shall see shortly. An initial planning document from the CLE, dated November 1940 (before the design of the Hamilcar had even been finalised), envisaged production commencing in late 1941, with tank squadron training starting at around the same time, and 40-50 produced by the end of 1941. This all assumed that 'maximum priority' was given to design and production.[11] This schedule turned out to be wildly optimistic. The target of 40-50 available gliders was roughly achieved only just in time for D-Day in June 1944. In fact, quite early in the Hamilcar production programme (around the third quarter of 1942), the slow delivery of Hamilcars was causing concern at the Ministry of Aircraft Production, so much so that they appointed an 'Industrial Panel' of three senior industrial executives to investigate possible problems at GAL.

The panel visited GAL in September 1942 and issued their report on the 24th of that month. The members of the panel were Mr R. Barlow (the chairman) from the Metal Box Company, Mr W. Inghram Gunn from Imperial Tobacco, and Mr T.G. Spencer of Standard Telephones and Cables.[12] The reason for their visit was simple enough: of 18 Hamilcars promised between March and August, only one was delivered. The Hamilcar programme seemed to be breaking down and they were there to find out why and offer solutions. Their conclusions were clear. At the root of the problem was the fact that with the Hamilcar programme GAL seem to have bitten off more than they could chew. They had developed and produced the Hotspur, but in becoming the parent firm for the Hamilcar they had taken on more work than they were capable of handling. In the words of the report:

> The organisation of the company was not sufficiently strong to enable it to take in its stride these additional obligations and we are driven to the conclusion that the management, in planning to handle this work, under-estimated what had to be done and were over optimistic as to the ability of their personnel and organisation to carry it through.

It had been apparent through 1942 that serious problems were occurring, in particular with respect to managing the various sub contractors that were working on the aircraft, and these problems had apparently not been addressed. For example, supplies of parts to the Birmingham Railway Carriage and Wagon Company and to the Cooperative Wholesale Society had been interrupted. On 28th July the Ministry of Aircraft Production had stepped in and set up the Hamilcar Production Group (already mentioned above), appointing their own choice of group controller and thus taking away from GAL control of the sub contracting system. The managing director of GAL, Gordon England, did not agree with this decision and appears to have been less than whole hearted in encouraging the appropriate cooperation between GAL and the Group. Other senior managers in GAL are also criticised in this respect, and there also seems to have been an atmosphere of personal

---

11 PRO file AIR32/2, Provision of an Airborne Force
12 All details of this investigation are from PRO file BT28/424, Investigation by Industrial Panel of GAL Ltd

conflicts between senior managers within GAL and between GAL and the Production Group. The panel reported,

> There is a serious want of cooperation between the Group Control and GAL. Both parties complain of the lack of information of action taken and of the lack of necessary records. [...] We are driven to the conclusion that effective cooperation and coordination are seriously lacking and that personal relationships are strained.

At one stage, an official of MAP had accused Mr England of 'obstruction almost amounting to sabotage of the scheme', but the panel found this was going too far. Documentation included in the PRO file indicates that the bad management and backbiting had lowered morale throughout the workforce. In particular, a letter from the Shop Steward's Committee complains of bad management and poor allocation of labour resources.

It is apparent from the report and from correspondence accompanying it that the removal of Mr England was considered as an option, but it was not in the end advocated. The panel did recommend that the Deputy Managing Director, a Captain Schofield, be replaced as he was both unpopular and not up to his job. New people were recommended for various other senior posts, including controller of the Production Group. The retention of Mr England as MD was, as far as the panel was concerned, conditional on his promoting greater cooperation between the company and the Production Group and his whole-hearted implementation of their various recommendations, which also included significant organisational changes.

Gordon England opposed the demotion of Captain Schofield and some of the other changes proposed, but the documentation is not sufficiently extensive to show how this disagreement was resolved and to what extent things improved at GAL. The report does, however, open a fascinating window into the background to the slow production of Hamilcars. It would be surprising if the serious problems indicated were resolved overnight: any improvements were likely to be gradual. It is only fair to GAL to add that the panel identified a 'piecemeal method of ordering' by MAP as one of the other reasons for production problems (aircraft seem to have been ordered in numbers varying from one to six per month during 1942), and took this as evidence that 'no real urgency was attached to this aircraft until March 1942'. This slow start was considered to have lulled the company into a false sense of security over their prospects of successfully managing the project. This problem is also separately mentioned in a minute to the Minister at MAP from one of his advisers, Air Marshall F.J. Linnell, dated October 1942. He states:

> The Airborne force was launched in a most haphazard manner with no properly defined object and with no appreciation of the problems involved. Orders for gliders started in a small way, but then multiplied and again multiplied until very large numbers resulted.[13]

Certainly, it seems unlikely the continuing limitations of Hamilcar availability would have been tolerated if the aircraft had been genuinely considered at Ministry and War Office level to be of the highest priority.

13 PRO file AVIA9/29

The ten pre-production gliders (which followed the two prototypes) were, in the event, all delivered by the end of 1942, four going to various test facilities as already noted above, and six to individual RAF Maintenance Units, as these latter would be the people who would have to assemble the Hamilcars from the produced components. The first production standard aircraft was made by GAL at Feltham commencing at the end of 1942, this aircraft being actually put together at Lasham airfield in March-April 1943. Production of parts and erection of complete aircraft continued through 1943 but it seems that production schedules were constantly slipping. The problem was made worse as the United States Army Air Force (USAAF) had now become interested and required a significant number for use on D-Day, and the aircraft was also being considered for use in the Far East which would require additional production, as well as flight trials to establish whether the glider-tug combination could operate in tropical conditions. Further pressure was created as a result of the steadily expanding variety of loads the glider was expected to carry. We have seen that the American T9 tank was scheduled to eventually replace the Tetrarch, and from at the latest May 1942 work commenced on the appropriate internal modifications, leading to a first flight with the lightened T9E1 prototype in July 1943. Other loads for which the Hamilcar was eventually cleared were:

Two Universal Carriers
Three Rota Trailers (see chapter three)
17pdr anti-tank gun with tractor
Universal Carrier (3" Mortar) and eight motorcycles
Universal Carrier (slave battery carrier) and Jeep
48 Panniers containing equipment and ammunition
D4 tractor with angledozer
Two Daimler armoured scout cars
25pdr field gun with tractor
Self-propelled 40mm Bofors anti-aircraft gun
Bailey pontoon bridge equipment
Scraper with Fordson tractor
Grader
HD10 or HD14 bulldozer (in three Hamilcars)

My research would indicate that only the first seven on this list were ever carried operationally. Other loads were certainly considered or experimented with: for example, a photo survives of an M5 armoured half track loaded in a Hamilcar, as well as film from 1947 of an Oxford Carrier (successor to the Universal Carrier) unloading from a Hamilcar after flight.[14]

One additional modification to some Hamilcars was the fitting of 'Rebecca' navigational receivers. These were part of the 'Rebecca-Eureka' system for marking landing and drop zones with radio navigation devices. 'Eureka' was a man-pack radio beacon used by the pathfinder paratroop companies. When set up, its signals could be detected by the Rebecca receivers which gave the aircraft or glider crew their range and bearing to the transmitter. The Rebecca receiver weighed 100 lbs, and average range at 2000 feet was 8 to 12 miles. According to Michael Bowyer's

14 Photo, Museum of Army Flying archives. Film, Imperial War Museum, COI 117.

research, all the 34 Hamilcars used on D-Day had Rebecca receivers. What proportion of other Hamilcars had the equipment is not known. The equipment was also extensively used by Allied tug and paradrop aircraft, and in some Horsa gliders, and Eureka beacons were often used to mark the outward route for airborne formations within friendly territory.

The Tetrarch and Locust tanks did not require any significant modifications for airborne use, apart from the welding on of some attachment points for lashing the vehicles down for flight. Other vehicles required significant modification for transport in the Hamilcar. The airborne version of the universal carrier was lightened as far as possible, for example by replacing the armoured engine shields with aluminum and removing the back armour plate protecting the rear axle. The side mud shields and step, along with lamps and rear view mirrors, were also removed.[15] The Morris C8 30cwt tractor for the 17pdr had numerous bits of sheet steel bodywork removed to save weight, and the canvas roof and roof supports were taken off to allow the vehicle to fit into the Hamilcar load bay. The variety of loads imposed a considerable design and testing burden. Hamilcar loads were of great weight and very dense. Their loading position had to be calculated with great care so as not upset the glider's balance in the air. Each load required its own set of modifications to the load bay's floor (for example specific channeling for wheeled and tracked vehicles) and its own unique tie down arrangements. The latter were of particular importance as the load could not be allowed to shift in the air, and had to be held securely enough to survive the heavy landings that were bound to occur during operations. It is worth emphasizing that before a particular operation, all the Hamilcars used would need the appropriate internal modifications made to tailor them for their assigned loads.

American interest in the Hamilcar started in June 1942. They wanted Hamilcars to carry bulldozers and other equipment for airfield building, and also apparently for a light tank, which must presumably have been the Locust, although they were also considering the C54 Skymaster to carry this vehicle as mentioned in the previous chapter. In late 1943 the Americans expressed a total requirement for 140 Hamilcars, and in November it was agreed that 50 would be supplied to them for Overlord.[16] Eventually, the slow delivery of Hamilcars so alarmed the Americans that they decided not to take the risk of the gliders not being available and cancelled their requirement in February 1944.[17] Unfortunately, this also meant withdrawal of American personnel who had been helping with the assembly of Hamilcars, which slowed the pace of completion significantly.

Only 27 Hamilcars had been erected by 1st January 1944, although more (perhaps around 20) were stored in parts. Finding personnel to put the Hamilcars together, and finding airfields where they could be erected and stored, continued to be a problem. No.1 Heavy Glider Maintenance Unit at Netheravon (not far from 6th AARR's base on Salisbury Plain) was one of the main locations. No. 33 Maintenance Unit at Lyneham was another major contributor. In addition to service personnel, GAL workers were also involved at most of the sites where Hamilcars were being prepared. Completed gliders were flown to North Luffenham airfield in

---

15 See van Hees, p.239.
16 Bowyer, 'Hamilcar Tank Transports', *Airfix Magazine*, April 1977, pp.450-452.
17 Bowyer, 'Hamilcars In Action', *Airfix Magazine*, May 1977, p.531.

Rutland where the modifications for their specific loads were carried out. From there they were ferried to Tarrant Rushton, which had been selected as the Hamilcar training and operational base in November 1943. It was not possible to fly the Hamilcar unloaded, so such flights always involved carrying Universal Carriers or concrete blocks as ballast. The production and storage problem was further complicated by concerns over deterioration of Hamilcars stored in the open, as available hangar space was at a premium. The problem was being raised as early as October 1942, with the wooden structure and plywood-fabric skinning being particularly susceptible to the British climate. Gliders stored outside needed a continuous programme of checks to ensure they were still serviceable, and a programme of hangar building was specially instituted at bases where the Hamilcars were to be stored.[18] Eventually, however, the required totals were met for the first operations on D-Day, and production continued throughout the war, assembly of Hamilcars not finally ceasing until late 1946.

Despite the problems with production rate, the design and production of the Hamilcar in time for the major allied airborne operations of the war still represented a considerable effort. The aircraft had to fight for priority with all the other types of aircraft being developed and produced during the massive expansion of the RAF. The glider met its specification with very little change from the original design, and was by all accounts possessed of good flying characteristics. Brigadier George Chatterton, commanding officer of the Glider Pilot Regiment, left his impressions of his first flight in the aircraft in his book, *The Wings Of Pegasus*. He had arranged to fly from Netheravon to Tarrant Rushton with one of the Hamilcar test pilots.

> I found the Halifax Mk.V and the Hamilcar at one end of the airfield. The disparity in their size made them look unreal. I climbed up the ladder nervously, and sat myself down in the front cockpit. It was a strange sensation looking out at the huge wing span, at a great height from the ground, and even more strange was seeing the Halifax – looking like a toy – ticking over, far ahead, with the thick tow rope lying on the ground between the two aircraft.
>
> Soon the tug pilot was calling through the headphones, the rope tautened, and we moved across the grass. As the airfield hurtled past it seemed unreal and ridiculous, then the Hamilcar jumped once, twice, and was airborne. She handled remarkably lightly in the air – surprisingly so – and then the Halifax became airborne, and the whole combination was away.
>
> The flight was uneventful. We sailed down to the south coast calmly enough, then, arriving over the airfield at Tarrant Rushton we released from the tug – and she was alone. How smoothly she flew. How the wind swished past the cockpit. How light she seemed to handle. It was remarkable to think that this huge wooden monster had been built completely 'on spec' – a masterly achievement by General Aircraft.
>
> We circled the airfield and turned into the runway. It seemed a steep descent, and as we levelled out the great nose almost obliterated the view of the runway. She sailed, or rather, floated, and then settled smoothly on terra firma. We experienced a great thrill of satisfaction as we climbed out of the cockpit.[19]

18 See PRO file AIR20/5500
19 Chatterton, pp. 124-125.

The aviation writer Bill Gunston also had some memories of flying in the Hamilcar. Having entered the fuselage by the door on the port side,

> The unfortunate pilots climbed straight up rungs on the right wall, opened a two part hatch in the roof and stepped out, carefully latching the the hatch behind them. My trip was in January, and the top of the Hamilcar was covered with thin ice from freezing drizzle. It was no joke to walk up the steep surface of the wing and along the rounded decking of the fuselage; then it was at last possible to unlatch the front or rear canopy, grab hold and breathe a sigh of relief. Two pilots in tandem shared the flying because it was very tiring work, and a single pilot might in any case be killed before the arrival. [...] In the air the Hamilcar rode like a whale, but at least had powerful trimmers on all axes and, as long as it was kept in the high tow position, could be steered along without upsetting the tug crew. After cast off, with indicated speed having been about 125-130mph throughout, one enquired at the limiting dive speed of 187mph to be told that those who wished to avoid trouble did not try it. The landing, I suppose, resembled that of the biggest aircraft of the 1920s, with plenty of clunks and bumps, though the grass seemed to go past very slowly.[20]

Just about all accounts of the Hamilcar confirm that it was relatively easy to fly, if a little tiring. Despite their size and loaded weight, they proved to be capable of being manoeuvred and landed with consistent accuracy in the testing operational conditions of congested and restricted landing zones. Staff Sergeant Gordon Jenks concluded his account of flying a Hamilcar to Arnhem by describing how he decided to stretch his glide into a more distant field after seeing two Hamilcars ahead of him have problems landing in soft ground:

> That decided me against this particular field. I reckoned that if I put the "Bun House" into a dive now she would have enough speed for me to hold her off the deck until we had cleared the fence and get safely into the farthest of the two fields. I pushed the control column forward and we went into a dive. We must have been halfway across the first field when I levelled out a few feet off the ground. The "Bun House" responded beautifully to my every action. What a gem of an aircraft she was! We were still doing ninety miles an hour when I eased her gently over the fence and put her down in the next field as light as a feather.[21]

The glazed nose sections in the Hamilcar meant the tank and other vehicle crews could see forward during flight, though in the tanks when strapped in for take off and landing the drivers had the best view. During the characteristically steep approach, the sight of the ground rushing up to meet you apparently took some getting used to. The long take off roll, during which the tug commonly swung from side to side, and the end of the runway got closer and closer, could also be rather nerve wracking.[22] What might have been going through the driver's mind during an operational approach such as that described above can only be imagined.

---

20 Gunston, 'Hamilcar Tank Carrying Glider', *Aeroplane Monthly*, December 1977, p.639.
21 Quoted in Chatterton, pp.183-184.
22 Conversation with Bob Walklett, 'B' Squadron, September 2002.

There was only one mark of Hamilcar glider, the Hamilcar I, but the potential requirement for this type of aircraft in the Far East led to a powered derivative which was designated Hamilcar X. Although never used operationally, we should briefly describe this version, and one or two other projects, to complete the Hamilcar story.

When fully loaded, the Hamilcar stretched the potential of its Halifax tug to the maximum. Airfields with the longest available runways were needed, and climb was slow. This was the situation when flying in north-west Europe, but when the use of the Hamilcar in the Far East was considered, it quickly became apparent that tropical conditions would render the combination inoperable. The reduced efficiency of piston engines in high temperatures (and the high altitudes of some Far Eastern airfields) meant that the Halifaxes would not manage the tow of a fully laden Hamilcar without a drastically reduced fuel load, which in turn reduced range to an unacceptably short distance. Two main solutions were originally proposed to ease the strain of getting a fully loaded Hamilcar off the ground, whether in Europe or elsewhere. These were rocket assisted take off (RATO) and double towing. The RATO trials were conducted at Farnborough starting in January 1943 and continuing into the spring. Alan Wood provides a succinct yet detailed account of the RATO design in his book *The Glider Soldiers*:

> The Royal Aircraft Establishment at Farnborough designed 25 inch diameter welded steel cylinders each containing twenty four 3-inch rockets which were fired in pairs at 1.2 second intervals giving a mean thrust of 2000lbs for twenty nine seconds. One rocket cylinder was fitted under each wing, well clear of the fuselage, giving a total thrust of 4000lbs. Once airborne the rocket cylinders could be jettisoned and returned to the ground by parachute.
>
> Trials were conducted at RAF Hartford Bridge, [Blackbushe aerodrome, very close to Farnborough], when two rocket cylinders were fitted beneath the wings of Hamilcar DR854. Towed off by a Halifax tug, the glider pilot waited until a speed of 70mph had been reached then fired the rockets until a height of about 100 feet had been achieved. At 300 feet the rocket cylinders were jettisoned. The tests were successful, reducing the take off run from 1700 yards to 1300 yards but the system was not used as more powerful tug aircraft became available.[23]

Exactly what the 'more powerful tug aircraft' were is not mentioned, but the only possibility would be the later mark of Halifax with Hercules engines. Michael Bowyer's normally detailed account is also fairly reticent on why RATO was not adopted. It would seem the performance of the Halifax was deemed acceptable for the European theatre, but that RATO 'was insufficient to overcome take off problems in tropical regions'.[24]

Double towing had originally been tried with the Horsa glider. Experiments with various towing aircraft included a double tow from two Miles Master single engined training aircraft, and with two Whitley tugs, the Whitley being unable to tow a fully loaded Horsa on its own. Similar trials were conducted with the Hamilcar. In England, trials took place at the RAE and at the Airborne Forces Experimental Establishment at Beaulieu. Two Halifax aircraft were used, the idea being that once airborne and at

---

23 *Glider Soldiers*, p.92.
24 Bowyer, 'Hamilcars In Action', p.536.

Hamilcar X prototype. The underwing stripes are yellow and black high-visibility markings (Museum of Army Flying).

cruising altitude, one of the aircraft would cast off. This second aircraft would be stripped of equipment as far as possible and carry only a light fuel load to enhance pulling performance. Even more unusually, a tandem twin tow was studied (but never flown). It was estimated that a Hawker Typhoon fighter bomber towing a Halifax towing a Hamilcar would provide about the same performance as a Halifax twin tow. In the Far East, tests were to be conducted with two Lancaster tows, but as plans to ship two Hamilcars to India were made, it became apparent that tests could not commence until April-March 1944. It was considered that this date would be too late to find out whether double towing was the answer, and so the powered Hamilcar was proceeded with.[25] Generally, twin towing was found to be practical in daylight but was regarded as a high risk operation, requiring considerable piloting skill and with a high probability of a serious accident if something went wrong, whether due to incorrect coordination between the two aircraft or a mechanical failure in one of them. Fortunately, despite some emergency releases, no actual accidents occurred during the twin tow test programme.

The powered Hamilcar, or Hamilcar X, would have as its main potential role the invasion of Japan. Such a version might also offer the possibility of extended range operations in more temperate climates, the possibility of recovery of the Hamilcar under its own power after an operation by flying empty or carrying a light load, and also the potential for operation from less than ideal airfields. The potential for Far East operations began to seriously concern the authorities during 1943, and it was in November of that year that it was decided to go ahead with the powered version.[26] It was apparently initially estimated that production examples

25 See Bowyer, 'Hamilcar Tank Transports', p.452.
26 Once again, I have relied heavily on Michael Bowyer's well researched articles in *Airfix Magazine* for March, April and May 1977 when describing the genesis of the Hamilcar

could not be expected for two years, a very relaxed level of priority for what was to be a fairly basic conversion, and in the event production aircraft were becoming available about 18 to 20 months later, as the the war in the Far East came to an end.

The first prototype was converted from a standard Hamilcar I, and changes were kept to minimum. There was some local strengthening where the two Bristol Mercury 31 engines were attached to the wings, and the top of the undercarriage struts had to be moved further inboard to clear the engine nacelles. Some strengthening of the fuselage was also required to bear the strain of the engine thrust, and also due to the change in the towing points. The bifurcated arrangement used on the Hamilcar I, where towing points in the leading edge of each wing were used, had to be abandoned in favour of a single tow point attached to the nose.

The engines were those originally used on the now obsolete Bristol Blenheim, and developed 965 h.p. The installation was kept as simple as possible. Fixed pitch, two bladed wooden airscrews were used, the cooling gills were replaced by a fixed, flared skirt on the cowlings, and the mixture controls were linked with the throttles so that only a simple pair of throttle levers was required in the cockpit. All extra controls for the powered Hamilcar were duplicated in the two pilot positions, except that starting was only possible from the rear cockpit. The fuel tanks were in the wings, but an additional fuel tank could be carried in the fuselage for ferry flights. The dimensions and load carrying capacity of the freight hold were unaltered. The Hamilcar X was of course heavier than the glider version, but a higher all up weight was accepted by reducing the 'factor of safety' used when stressing the aircraft from five to four, as the designers were confident they had a good strong airframe following experience with the glider version. All up weight was now 47,000lbs, with a full load now representing about 30% of all up weight rather than the 50% of the glider. It was also possible to fly the Hamilcar X unloaded, without the need for ballast. It is interesting to note that at the time the Hamilcar X project was given the go-ahead, a report from RAE Farnborough sketched a design for a Hamilcar that had been aerodynamically 'cleaned up' to reduce drag, and was powered by a pair of Merlin 32 or Hercules XI engines. This produced a 'self propelled transport' that could take off under its own power fully loaded. Why this more capable aircraft was not proceeded with is another minor mystery of the Hamilcar story.[27]

The first flight (using the aircraft's own power) of the Hamilcar X was made in February 1945 from Lasham airfield, following an epic road journey of the prototype from Feltham. Despite removal of the outer wing panels, many trees and street lights had to be cut down en-route and ramps constructed to get the stub wings clear of traffic lights. Trials at Lasham and at AFEE showed that the Hamilcar X performed pretty much as hoped. When allowance was made for tropical conditions, the addition of engines to the glider allowed a fully loaded Halifax to tow off a fully loaded Hamilcar X, with a radius of action of 900 miles. However, a fully loaded Hamilcar X could not maintain height even at full power, a rate of descent of about 150 ft/min being experienced under temperate conditions. Maximum self propelled take off weight proved to be 32,500 lbs, giv-

X. Despite help from the author, I have been unable to locate many of the original documents to which Mr. Bowyer had access.

27 PRO file WO233/44 Long Term Glider Sub-Committee.

ing a maximum useful load without towing assistance of about 3000 lbs in temperate conditions, sufficient to raise the possibility of use of the Hamilcar X for casualty evacuation after its initial operational flight.

Whilst the aircraft did what was expected of it, and remained essentially easy to fly, as a *powered* aircraft it left much to be desired. Test pilot Wing Commander K. Fry has left his memories of flying the Hamilcar X in post war trials:

> The performance of the powered Hamilcar was abysmal. Even when new it took about 900 yards to unstick and 2000 yards to reach 50 feet and climb speed. (Of course, its all up weight was that of a late Wellington, while its power only half a Wellington's). The Hamilcar took 5 minutes to reach 1000 feet, and during trials we went several times to 10,000 feet, which took about 1 1/4 hours. The rate of climb was so low that we had to be careful to use any wave effect productively off the Malvern Hills. The Mercury engines streamed oil throughout, and the tailplane always shone with oil. [...] The drag of the Hamilcar was enormous. We once flew an entire sortie with a chock on an undercarriage leg – where one of the ground crew had absent-mindedly put it (end on).
>
> Take off involved full power and then brakes off. Brakes could not be used to keep straight, nor differential throttle, as take off performance was so bad. [...] The other unusual thing was that cruise speed was slower than climbing speed. Again wave effects made you sink, but the worse thing was the very slow ground speed sometimes obtained. Twice I flew in very strong winds indeed on the south coast and we had ground speeds of only some 40 mph or so.
>
> I remember the unusual start up procedure: you climbed into the front cockpit to put the brakes on, then into the back to start up, then back to the front cockpit to fly it. It was really the greatest fun.[28]

Two Hamilcar gliders were converted for the initial trials, one for GAL's trials and the other for testing at the AFEE. With satisfactory results from these, a further eight Hamilcar Is were converted, then another ten Mk Xs were built from scratch by companies in the Hamilcar production group. Any further orders were cancelled when the war in the Far East came to an end, but testing continued post war to further explore the aircraft's performance.

American interest in the Hamilcar has already been mentioned, and despite the cancellation of their requirement one Hamilcar was shipped to the United States for trials, were it was towed by a Boeing B-17F bomber during testing at Wright Army Air Force Field near Dayton, Ohio in May 1945.[29] Prior to this, however, an unusual suggestion had been forthcoming from the US Army Air Force regarding mating a Lockheed P-38 Lightning twin engined fighter with a Hamilcar in a 'piggy back' arrangement whereby the Lightning was mounted on top of the glider. This idea appears to have been suggested by the discovery of German trials where an Me109 was used as a piggy-back carrier for a DFS230 glider, in a combination known as the Mistelschlepp.[30] The Hamilcar combination would need towing assistance to get it airborne, but once airborne the Lightning would

---

28 From a letter in *Aeroplane Monthly*, January 1978, p.87.
29 Mrazek, *Fighting Gliders Of World War Two*, pp.65-66. Date of tests from PRO file AVIA15/2369.
30 *Fighting Gliders of World War Two*, p.28.

have enough power to keep the combination flying, thus doing away with the problems of towing and relieving the glider pilots of the task of controlling the glider until it was released, as the combination would be controlled en-route by the pilot of the P-38. After releasing the glider, the fighter would be available to provide air support to the landings. Outlandish as this scheme may seem, Charles Prower confirms in his account of Hamilcar development that the idea received serious attention in the UK. 'All the investigations that we did indicated that the scheme had a very good chance of working and that neither aircraft would require major alterations'.[31] However, the idea was eventually dropped.

The realisation that the Tetrarch was simply not adequate for the role of tank support of airborne troops naturally led the War Office and Air Ministry to consider larger gliders to carry more effective tanks, but in general these considerations were tentative and led to no concrete results. In describing the Harry Hopkins tank in chapter one, the recurring suggestion that a larger glider might be developed to carry this tank was mentioned, as well as the idea for a flying wing design to achieve the same purpose. The amount of effort it was taking simply to produce enough Hamilcars in time for D-Day meant that designing and producing a new, larger glider would take a massive additional effort, and there was never sufficient priority attached to the project to make such an effort possible. During 1943, there was some consideration of how a 16 ton load might be got airborne, using twin-tugging or even a B-29 Superfortress.[32] The main potential AFV in this weight class was the American 15 ton M5 Stuart. This, however, was still a light tank mounting only the same 37mm weapon as the Locust, and though it was a little better armoured it would hardly have been worth developing a new glider to carry this vehicle.

One final scheme, perhaps the most remarkable of all, is worth describing here. This was the Rotaplane or Rotatank, an autogyro-type aircraft designed to lift a Valentine tank. It was the idea of Raoul Hafner, an Austrian who had worked on helicopters in his home country before moving to Britain before the war. He became head of the rotorcraft team at the AFEE, where he first developed the Rotachute and then the Rotabuggy. The former was a tiny one-man autogyro, intended as an alternative to the parachute for landing individual men with greater accuracy. It was developed over the period 1940 to 1942, eventually being successfully airtowed behind a Tiger Moth, though the idea was never adopted. The Rotabuggy was a jeep adapted for flight with a two bladed rotor and a stabilising tail unit. This first flew in November 1943, towed behind a car, and later flights were made towed by a Whitley, which after some modifications were quite successful. Again, the idea was not adopted as the Horsa was quite suitable for getting jeeps into action.

The Rotatank itself was never built or flown, but was intended to use a massive 152 foot diameter two blade rotor to lift a Valentine tank. The rotor would be set spinning initially by the tank's engine, and then the Rotatank would be towed off the ground by a tandem tow of a Dakota followed by a Halifax. After take off, the Dakota would cast off and the Halifax would be able to keep the Rotatank airborne on its own. The tank itself would be fitted with a fairing which formed a sort of rear fuselage with tail unit. The pilot was seated in a small cockpit on top of the tank in

---

31 'Gliding Tanks', pp28-29.
32 See Bowyer, 'Hamilcar tank transports', p.450.

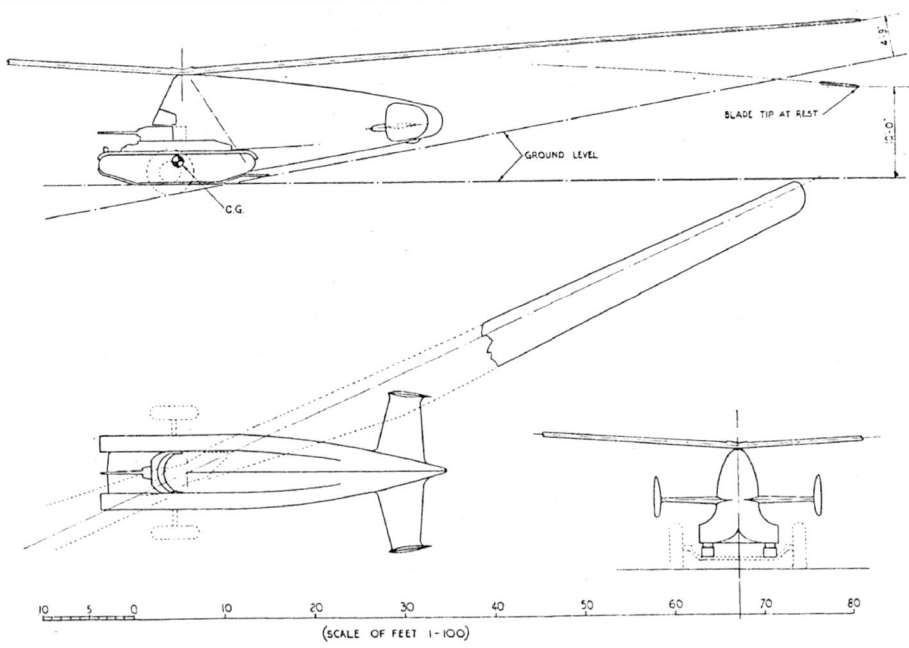

ROTAPLANE FOR VALENTINE TANK

The Rotatank autogyro designed to lift a Valentine tank (via Alistair Mellor).

front of the rotor mast. For take off a pair of large diameter wheels were fitted to a jettisonable undercarriage, and for landing the tank tracks were fitted with a set of wooden rails or skids. Landing speeds were expected to be significantly lower than for an equivalent glider, making accurate landings in small areas easier. Landing was also expected to be quite gentle, as it was planned that low sink rates could be achieved in the final part of the descent. It was calculated that to lift a 35000 lb tank only 5000 lbs of additional airframe weight would be needed. Hafner accepted that the concept was way beyond anything attempted in the rotary wing field up to that time, and that unexpected problems could occur, but in his submission to the Ministry of Aircraft Production (dated December 1942) he was confident that the Rotaplane could be made to work.[33] Although the Ministry's reply remains undiscovered, they obviously thought the concept too risky to be worth proceeding with. The idea did at least have the advantage of being designed around a worthwhile tank.

To carry some of their less heavy equipment, 6th AARR would use the the most numerous British military glider, the Horsa. Before concluding this chapter it would be well to briefly describe this aircraft.

33 My thanks to Alistair Mellor of the present day Airborne Forces Project Team for finding a copy of this submission in the Boscombe Down archives.

The specification for the Horsa had been agreed on 12th October 1940. Eleven months later, on 12th September 1941, the prototype Airspeed AS 51 Horsa was flown, having been transported in sections from the Christchurch factory to the suitably large Great West Road Aerodrome, later to become Heathrow. With a span of 88 feet and a length of 67 feet, the Horsa was as big as a medium bomber, its length and wingspan being closely comparable to both the Wellington and Whitley. It required a medium bomber to tow it, the Whitley being used at first. There was at this stage still considerable uncertainty over the tactical role of gliders. Initial ideas were that the glider would be a paratroop carrier from which troops would jump, with actual landing being a secondary role. It was also thought a significant proportion might be built as towed bombers, a design designated the AS52, to carry an 8000 lb bomb load. These ideas were soon dropped, but were replaced by uncertainty over the number actually needed. Production had commenced in early 1942, and by May of that year 2345 were on order. The Army foresaw the need for 1975 for its first large scale operation with a reserve of 600 for a repeat.[34] The massive diversion of bomber production to provide tugs for such a force was soon seen as out of the question, and Army requirements had to be reduced. Eventually 3655 Horsas in all were produced, but the largest number of Horsas used in one operation were the 392 deployed in Operation Varsity in March 1945.

Only 695 Horsas were built by Airspeed themselves, the remainder being manufactured by a remarkable collection of furniture makers, coach builders and motor companies. These firms had no airfields to fly the gliders from so the gliders were delivered in parts (including 30 major sections) to RAF Maintenance Units for final assembly. The Horsa was an all wood aircraft apart from certain metal fittings, with fabric covered wings and tailplane and a plywood covered fuselage. It had two pilots side by side in a large, well glazed cockpit which gave excellent visibility. It could carry up to 31 troops. The largest equipment loads possible were two jeeps, a combination of a jeep and six pounder anti-tank gun or a jeep and 75mm pack howitzer. Horsas were used extensively to carry jeeps, which became the staple motor transport of airborne forces, but the glider was not designed to carry this vehicle. On the arrival of the first jeep in the UK in November 1941, trials were arranged and it was found by happy chance that the vehicle could just about be squeezed into a Horsa without any major modifications.[35]

Despite its rapid development the aircraft apparently flew well even when fully loaded. To facilitate landing, it was fitted with very large split flaps which lowered to 45 degrees to produce a rapid rate of descent and steep glide angle, and could also be fitted with a tail arrester parachute to reduce the landing run. The latter appears only to have been used operationally by the coup de main force dispatched to the Orne River and Caen Canal bridges on D-Day. There was a large door on the port side ahead of the wing and a smaller door opposite to starboard. On the Mark I, used in Normandy, the unloading of large loads could additionally be accomplished by detaching the tail section of the glider after landing. This was achieved by means of a set of quick release bolts. An earlier idea for a Cordtex belt around the fuselage which would be ignited to blow off the rear fuselage after landing was fit-

---

34 Bowyer, 'Army-air Colours: Enter the Horsa', *Airfix Magazine*, September 1976.
35 Otway, p.40 & p.46.

ted to some gliders but was not used in action. The Mark II was improved by making the whole nose section hinged and able to be swung open for loading and unloading. Whilst often useful, the tendency for damage to the nose during rough landings made the continued ability to remove the tail essential. Additionally, axes, a saw and wirecutters were usually carried to allow troops to force their way out in an emergency. The Mk II also featured a twin nose wheel. The Mark I had an unladen weight of 7500 lbs and a fully loaded weight of 15250 lbs. The Horsa suffered from some difficulties that mirrored those of the Hamilcar, such as obtaining enough of the proper quality wood, the lack of space for storage, and the need for continual modifications as new loads and detail improvements were proposed. One result of these problems was a lower than forecast production rate, but enough Horsas were eventually available to fulfil the operational requirement. Overall, the Horsa was a successful project which fully lived up to its required role.

Having detailed the development of the Hamilcar, it would be appropriate before ending the chapter to give some details of its tug aircraft, the 'airborne' version of the Halifax bomber. Very brief details will also be given of the Stirling and Albemarle tugs that towed 6th AARR's Horsas into combat.

Britain deployed three heavy bombers in World War Two, the Short Stirling, the Handley Page Halifax and the Avro Lancaster. The Halifax was the second to be developed, with a first flight on 25th October 1939, and was much more effective than the Stirling, though usually considered inferior to the Lancaster. The early marks of the aircraft (B.Mks.I, II and V) were powered by Merlin engines, with which it was slightly underpowered, a situation made worse by the steady addition of extra operational equipment. This led to the eventual relegation of the bomber to less hazardous targets from October 1943 until February 1944, as the lower and slower flying Halifaxes had suffered an unacceptable rise in loss rates. The design was revitalised by re-engining with Bristol Hercules radial engines (the B.Mk.III) which restored the performance and led to the aircraft being reinstated on operations on a par with the Lancaster.

Bomber Command was never prepared to give up Lancaster aircraft for tasks other than bombing, as it justifiably regarded these aircraft as its best four engined bombers. Indeed, the whole issue of giving up any type of bomber for other tasks, such as maritime reconnaissance, para dropping or transport was one which caused constant wrangling between Bomber Command and other commands of the RAF, as well as with the Army and Navy. The limited supply of para-dropping and tug aircraft was to be a major reason behind the interrupted development of Britain's airborne forces, a problem which will be explained in more detail later in this book. However, the inadequacy of the Armstrong Whitworth Whitley in the towing role meant that some of the less capable bombers (Stirlings and Halifaxes) would have to be spared if the airborne force was to develop as planned. Compared to the Lancaster, the larger capacity fuselage of the Halifax actually made it more suitable for conversion to roles such as transport.

The first Halifax for airborne use went to the Airborne Forces Establishment at Ringway near Manchester as early as October 1941. This location was at that time the centre for all airborne forces trials, testing and training. The aircraft was first adapted for para dropping by cutting a hatch in the fuselage floor, and then in

December a towing rig was developed. A small number of Halifaxes went on to take part in the early trials of the Horsa and Hamilcar gliders during 1942. It was a converted Halifax Mk.II that towed the prototype Hamilcar into the air. Halifaxes were the towing aircraft for the first British glider operation of the war, Operation Freshman, when two Halifaxes towed two Horsas loaded with Royal Engineers across the North Sea to attack the Norwegian heavy water plant at Vemork, a plant thought to be associated with German efforts to create an atomic bomb. The raid was a high risk one, and was sadly a total failure, but the Halifaxes were not to blame.

The first issue of aircraft to an operational airborne forces squadron to include the towing role was in February 1943 when Halifaxes replaced the Whitleys of 295 Squadron at Netheravon. All wartime airborne Halifaxes were essentially airborne conversions of the equivalent bomber marks. The basic conversion of the early Halifaxes had involved removing the nose and mid-upper turrets (to save weight) and the addition of a parachute dropping hatch and towing attachments. By February 1943 the nose turret of the bomber Halifax had been replaced by a glazed nose fairing mounting a single machine gun as part of a weight saving and streamlining exercise, and the first production airborne version, the A.Mk.V (A for Airborne, of course), generally had the same glazed nose as the B.Mk.V, except some early examples which had a faired over nose turret. The A.Mk.V had Merlin XX engines. The bomb bay was also converted to take supply containers rather than bombs, and a cradle was eventually developed to fit in the bomb bay from which up to two jeeps, or a jeep plus a 6pdr anti tank gun or 75mm howitzer, could be dropped. All 'airborne' Halifaxes were dual purpose para-dropping and towing aircraft, and the squadrons were trained in both roles. It should also be noted that Halifaxes did not only tow the Hamilcar. They were assigned Horsa towing duties on a number of operational missions, most notably towing the six Horsas used in the famous *coup de main* operations against the Orne River and Caen Canal bridges on D-Day. The RAF seem to have sometimes referred to airborne forces Halifaxes using a 'GT' prefix (for glider towing) rather than an 'A' prefix, but the 'A' prefix is the one most commonly used in published sources.

As the RAF wing devoted to airborne operations (No.38 Wing) expanded to a group in 1943, there was a rejigging of squadrons. No. 295 re-equipped with Albemarles (see below) and 38 Wing ended up with two Halifax squadrons by the time of D-Day, 298 and 644. In the months leading up to D-Day, the Merlin XX engines were replaced by Merlin 22s. These were no more powerful, but significantly more reliable, and were progressively fitted with more efficient four bladed propellers, although not all aircraft had the new propellers by 6th June. After D-Day, two more Halifax squadrons were created in 38 Group by converting 296 and 297 Squadrons onto A.Mk.Vs traded in by 298 and 644 Squadrons. From September 1944, the two original squadrons began receiving the Hercules engined A.Mk.III. The new engine produced 1615hp at take off, compared with 1280hp for the Merlin XX, and in conjunction with an increase in span (also standard to the B.Mk.III) from 98' 10" to 104' 2", the performance of the aircraft was significantly improved. The two new Halifax squadrons were not ready for 'Market Garden', but the two original squadrons used a mix of A.Mk.Vs and A.Mk.IIIs for this operation. By the time of Operation Varsity (March 1945), all four squadrons were mostly equipped with A.Mk.IIIs and they provided 120 aircraft for this operation (30 each). Some of this number were still the old A.Mk.Vs, but there were also seven of the new A.Mk.VII, which had slightly more powerful Hercules engines and various detail improvements which again enhanced performance. The A.Mk.VII formed the basis for the A.Mk.IX, the final airborne version, which began to be delivered in October 1945. The performance was unaltered, the main modifications being internal to incorporate the various lessons learned on operations during 1944-45. Post-war, the airborne squadrons were wound down and the last airborne Halifaxes were withdrawn in 1948, to be replaced by a specialised transport aircraft, the Handley Page Hastings. The airborne versions of the Halifax had, however, outlasted the bomber variants which were already being phased out during the last stages of the war in favour of the Lancaster, and had disappeared from Bomber Command in 1947.

Two other aircraft were involved in towing members of 6th AARR into action on D-Day and for Operation Varsity. These were the Short Stirling and the Armstrong-Whitworth Albemarle.

The prototype Stirling first flew on 14th May 1939. The Stirling was the first of Britain's four engined heavy bombers, but the least efficient. It was slower and flew lower than either the Halifax or Lancaster and its loss rates were higher. Consequently, of the three heavy bombers it was the first choice for conversion to para-dropping and towing duties, and this resulted in the introduction of basic towing gear in all production Stirlings from March 1942. The aircraft was found to be capable of towing off a Hamilcar, but there were problems with overheating at the slow speeds that were achieved, and the aircraft was working so hard that range was also less than required. However, the Horsa could be towed satisfactorily and it was for towing this glider, and as a para-drop aircraft, that the airborne Stirlings were used. The Stirling B.Mk.III, the final and best of the bomber versions, was eventually chosen for mass conversion, the prototype of the new airborne version flying in August 1943, and being designated A.Mk.IV (or GT.Mk.IV). As with the Halifax, the conversion involved removing nose and tail turrets (and sometimes, but not always, the rear turret), introducing a floor hatch for parachuting and converting the bomb bay to take supply canisters. Squadron service did not commence until January 1944, but the planned four squadrons were available by D-Day. By the time of Varsity, six squadrons of Stirlings were available, all being of the same A.Mk.IV type.

The Albemarle was developed as a fairly large, twin engined reconnaissance-bomber, and first flew in March 1940. In order to guard against possible wartime shortages of specialist materials the aircraft used wood and steel construction, and was also put together from sub-assemblies which could be made by non-specialist firms. Unfortunately, these features resulted in an aircraft whose speed, operational load and service ceiling were all below specification and the aircraft was not adopted for its intended role. Eventually, in June 1942, the desperate need for aircraft for airborne forces led to the idea of using Albemarles for the para dropping and glider tug roles, to replace the Whitleys then in service and to provide aircraft for expansion. The aircraft proved capable of towing a fully loaded Horsa, although the fuel carried had to be restricted which reduced the available range. The tricycle undercarriage, which was an unusual feature of the design, was found to make take offs with a glider under tow rather easier than for those aircraft with tail wheel undercarriages. By D-Day, four Albemarle squadrons were operational holding 97 aircraft in total, but thereafter the aircraft was steadily retired and by the time of Operation Varsity all squadrons had converted to the Halifax and Stirling. A total of 602 Albemarles were produced, of which 380 were delivered as pure transports, the remainder being allocated to airborne forces in four versions, the A.(or GT) Mks.I,II,V and VI. Differences between the marks were minor.[36]

One general point worth making is that from mid-1942 the Air Ministry ordered all bomber aircraft to be modified during production to make them suitable for rapid conversion to glider tugs. This mainly involved strengthening the rear fuselage area, and the provision of a kit of parts for the fitting of towing apparatus if required. In addition, all Stirlings, Halifaxes and Albemarles were to be produced with the appropriate modifications for paradropping to enable the rapid switching of roles if needed.[37]

By the beginning of 1944, then, the British glider and tug force was essentially complete and training hard for D-Day. The airborne armour project had crystallised into the combination of the Hamilcar glider towed by a Halifax with either the Tetrarch or Locust as its load. The problem was, that as a source of real armoured support for the airborne troops (the reason for which the project had been started) these light tanks would not be up to the job, and all involved – from senior officers in the War Office and Air Ministry to the tank crews themselves – were well aware of this. As we shall see in the next part of this book, the role of these tanks had consequently gradually evolved into one of reconnaissance rather than support, and if support was called for the light tanks would just have to do their best.

The half-hearted attempts at projects to carry the Harry Hopkins or develop other lightweight airborne armoured vehicles were evidence of a recognition that the Hamilcar-Tetrarch combination was inadequate for the job as originally conceived. At the same time, none of these alternative projects offered a sufficient increase in effectiveness over what was already being produced to be worth proceeding with. The British had convinced themselves from the outset that developing a glider to carry a worthwhile battle tank (say, in the twenty ton class) was simply not possible. The Germans had come to other conclusions, and in the final part of this book we will briefly examine the results of their efforts as a comparison to the British experience.

Before that, we should turn to the main part of the book, the story of how the unit that was to operate the airborne tanks came together, and how they were to carve out a fine operational record as part of 6th Airborne Division (one of Britain's two elite airborne divisions), operating both with or without their airborne tanks.

---

36 For more detail on these two aircraft, see Barnes, *Shorts Aircraft Since 1900*, Tapper, *Armstrong-Whitworth Aircraft Since 1913*, and also Bowyer, *Aircraft For The Many: A Detailed Survey of the RAF's Aircraft in June 1944*.
37 *Airborne Forces*, pp.53-54, and see also PRO file AIR39/132, Airborne Forces – History, Organisation, Training and Operations.

Part Two

OPERATIONS

Chapter 3

Special Service

The original ancestor of the 6th Airborne Armoured Reconnaissance Regiment was 'C' Special Service Squadron, Royal Armoured Corps. This was one of three tank squadrons created in mid-1941 for special operations overseas, particularly in an amphibious role, and designated 'A', 'B' and 'C' Special Service Squadrons, RAC. 'A' Squadron was formed on 29th April at Wickham Market from men and vehicles drawn from 48th Royal Tank Regiment, and 'B' on 6th July at Shoreham-by-Sea from elements of 47th Royal Tank Regiment. These two squadrons were each equipped with 8 Infantry Tanks MkIII (the Valentine) and 6 Light Tanks MkVIc, along with three scout cars, three universal carriers and various lorries for administrative support. Troop strength was authorised as 8 officers and 97 other ranks for 'A' Squadron, 7 officers and 96 other ranks for 'B' Squadron. The tanks were organised into an HQ of two Valentines, two troops of 3 Valentines and two troops of 3 MkVIcs.[1]

'C' Squadron's war diary begins on 31st July 1941, and on that date it records that 'orders were received to form and mobilise for service overseas (Tropical Climate) under supervision HQ Southern Command, 'C' Special Service Squadron (Light) RAC'.[2] Similar instructions had formed the basis for the formation of the other two squadrons. Volunteers for 'C' Squadron were called for from the three tank units in 2nd Armoured Brigade, 1st Armoured Division. These were The Queen's Bays, 10th Royal Hussars and 9th Queen's Royal Lancers. The brigade had seen service the previous year in France. C.F. Sheffield (later a Corporal in 6th AARR) remembered the process:

> In 1941 the 10th moved to Ogbourne St George, near Marlborough. While we were there, about July, the regiment congregated in the dining hall and the CO, Lt.Col. Hignett, asked for so many volunteers, combined with others from the Queens Bays and 9th Lancers to form a special unit, for some unknown mission. He promised us plenty of action, blood, and if lucky and we got back, plenty of medals. There was a good response from all ranks.
>
> Capt. Llewellyn Palmer and Capt. Malyon were also in the unit and I felt especially proud when Capt. Palmer came over to me and said, "Sheffield, I'm very pleased you are coming, once again, to continue where we left off in France." He was a fine officer and a gentleman.[3]

Sgt Clegg, then serving with The Queen's Bays, recalled what happened next:

> All the officers and crews assembled in the banqueting room [a country house at Ogbourne was being used as a temporary base] where a Major Asquith,

---

1 All details from war diaries held at PRO, files WO218/155 and WO218/156.
2 From War Diaries of Armoured Airborne Squadrons, Bovington Tank Museum Library.
3 'Madagascar and the Special Service Squadrons', *Royal Hussars Journal*, summer 1990, vol. 20, p.151

who was the senior officer, informed us that we were going to be mixed up, then split up into small squadrons or units, formed as A, B, and C Special Service Squadrons.[4]

There is no evidence that the men from 2nd Armoured Brigade were 'mixed up' in any way between the three squadrons – they were indeed mixed up together but all went to 'C' Squadron. The 'special service' tag meant a unit which would receive special training for an out of the ordinary role. They were amongst those units involved in the developing idea of 'combined operations', which in particular meant cooperation between Navy and Army in amphibious training. They would be involved in pioneering work which would develop some of the techniques eventually used in the invasion of Europe, and it was likely that they would be taking part in novel operations in places far from the UK. As a result, all the men were volunteers. The commanding officer was Major D.V.H. Asquith of The Queen's Bays.

The war diary of 'C' Squadron records that three tank troops were formed, two to be provided by 9th Lancers and one by 10th Hussars, with the Queen's Bays providing the Squadron HQ. The tanks were all Tetrarchs, which also came from units of 2nd Armoured Brigade. Each troop had three tanks, with a further three in Squadron HQ. The squadron initially formed at Ogbourne St. George on Salisbury Plain, but as early as 3rd August parties were setting out for Scotland, where the unit's home would soon be and where training would commence. The same was true for 'A' and 'B' Squadrons who were also sent to Scotland for training very soon after being formed. The initial destination in Scotland for all three squadrons was Inverary, the training area for Britain's Commando forces. One of the early volunteers was Trooper, later Sergeant, Charles Collins, who had these memories of joining 'C' Squadron:

> Our first move away from the 1st Armoured Division, was to put the tanks on flats and proceed to the north of this country. It seemed to take days, two days in fact, it seemed longer. Very uncomfortable. We eventually finished up at a little station called Dalmally, West of Scotland where we got the tanks off the flats and proceeded to drive.
>
> I remember, I was commanding the tank, and I remember coming over the top of a hill and looking down on a Loch, it was Loch Fyne, actually, Inverary. A Loch full of landing craft and I said to my driver 'I can see it all'. He said 'What is it?' I said 'Its landing craft and I think we are Commandos.' And we were Commandos. [...] So we went down to Inverary and we stayed there for some considerable time. Practising landing and taking tanks onto ships, and getting them ashore.[5]

Sgt Clegg also remembered this early period.

We moved to Inverary on Loch Fyne where we teamed up with the 5th Army Commando and 41st Marine Commando. We were given "Special Service" flashes to sew on our sleeves at the shoulder prior to the training starting.[6]

---

4 Ibid.
5 From Charles Collins: 6th Airborne Recce Regiment, in the archives of the Bovington Tank Museum.
6 *Royal Hussars Journal*, p.152

From 8th August, training and exercises in the new area had commenced, in cooperation (according to the war diary) with 1st Guards Brigade and the Marines Brigade. Training centred around embarkation and disembarkation from ships and the use of landing craft, in the Clyde, at Inverary and at locations around the west, north and east coasts of Scotland. Commando-style training in unarmed combat was also received. All three of the special service squadrons were receiving the same training, and their role quickly became clear. They were to be the armoured element in potential amphibious operations overseas, probably involving support for an infantry brigade. They were developing and testing new techniques, and all three squadrons were involved in the some of the first exercises of the war involving landing tanks from the sea. Although all three special service squadrons were based in the same area of Scotland during the time they were formed, they seem to have operated as three distinct commands, although the war diaries indicate that 'A' and 'B' cooperated occasionally during training.

In early September 1941 elements of 'C' Squadron departed for their first operational deployment. Six tanks, along with a scout car and a carrier, were dispatched as part of a force which sailed to Freetown, West Africa (now Sierra Leone). 'A' and 'B' Squadrons departed for the same destination at around the same time, but these two squadrons took all their fighting vehicles with them. At this period of the war there were worries that Spain might enter the war on Germany's side and the force was standing by to capture the Spanish held islands off the West African coast. Cpl Sheffield remembers that some at least of the squadron thought they might be destined for an attack on the Vichy French town of Dakar, which had been the subject of an unsuccessful assault a year earlier. It is entirely possible that both operations were considered. The war diary records embarkation on 2nd September 1941. Lt. Malyon, a troop leader who was given command of the half squadron, recalls a later departure date,

> We took ship in October and sailed in convoy to Freetown, West Africa where we remained in somewhat hot and cramped conditions on board for six months.
>
> Our ship, the 'Ennerdale', was a fleet auxiliary tanker of 6000 tons. Her task was to refuel our naval vessels as they came into port off Atlantic convoys. Its secondary role was to carry our tanks to the beach and so enable the landing craft, in which the tanks were stowed on deck, to take us to the shore. We practised this operation innumerable times but such are the vagaries of wind, tide and human error that it was a red letter day if we ever got to the beach without mishap. [...]
>
> Finally, in March 1942, we were ordered home. During our stay our tanker had grown a fine crop of barnacles on its bottom so that our maximum speed was precisely one knot. Gradually the colder Atlantic seawater brushed them off and after a few anxious days we caught up the convoy and felt much better. It took 28 days to reach the Clyde which, when we arrived, was shrouded in fog. We thought our journey was over but almost immediately we got orders to proceed up Loch Fyne to Inverary. A delightful journey but after six months away not exactly how we had planned to spend our first night ashore.

The rushed move was because the return of the Freetown party had coincided with orders for a new operation. The other half of the squadron had continued training in Scotland while their comrades were away. There had been a move to Hoddon Castle Camp, Ecclefechan, on 19th September 1941, and on 29th December came a move to Melrose, Roxburghshire, where the squadron came under command of the Royal Marine Division. But the day after Lt. Malyon's return on 16th March, orders were received 'to prepare 2 troops of personnel complete with 6 Lt tanks and slave carrier ready to move overseas'.[7] The history of the 9th Hussars records that the embarkation of the troops involved was covered by the announcement of yet another exercise.[8] But this move was for real: the troops were to take part in the invasion of Madagascar.

In March 1942 Madagascar, the third largest island in the world with an area larger than France, was under Vichy French control. With the advance of Japanese naval forces into the Indian Ocean, it represented a tempting target for the Japanese. The main port of Diego Suarez at the northern tip was an excellent modern harbour from where the Japanese Navy might dominate the Indian Ocean and threaten Allied convoys routing around the Cape to the Middle East. Following the rapid Vichy French capitulation to the Japanese in Indo-China, Churchill and the British Chiefs of Staff came to the conclusion that the island must be occupied by British Forces. The combined naval and land forces finally committed were significant. Combined Commander-in-Chief for the operation was Rear-Admiral E.N. Syfret, and as well as his flagship, the battleship Ramilles, he had two aircraft carriers, two cruisers and nine destroyers, plus other smaller vessels.[9] The land forces, under Major-General R.G. Sturges RM, comprised 5 Commando, 29th Independent Brigade Group, and two brigade groups from 5th Infantry Division, 17th and 13th, the latter forming the emergency reserve. 29th Brigade, with four battalions and having been extensively trained in amphibious assaults, formed the core of the force and under command of the brigade was 'B' Special Service Squadron, with 6 of its own Valentine tanks amalgamated with the 6 Tetrarchs drawn from 'C' Squadron. Like some of 'C' Squadron, 'B' had also just returned from the detachment to Freetown, and a hurried turnaround and selection of suitable men and tanks was necessary in both units. The 29th Brigade and the Special Service tanks already knew each other; they had trained together in Scotland. The whole operation was codenamed 'Ironclad'.[10]

On 19th March, three officers (Capt. P.G. LLewellyn Palmer, Lt. B.M.M. Carlisle, Lt. W.R. Astles) and 18 other ranks of 'C' Squadron, along with the Tetrarchs and the 'starting and charging' carrier, entrained at Glasgow and set off to join the operation, being placed under command 29th Independent Infantry Brigade from this date. They joined 3 officers and 21 other ranks from 'B' Squadron. Major J.E.S. Simon of 'B' Squadron was in command, and he organised his vehicles into a Squadron HQ of three Valentines and one Tetrarch, a Valentine troop with three tanks, and two Tetrarch troops, the first with three tanks and the second with two. Operation Ironclad was to be the combat debut of the Tetrarch as well as of 'C' Squadron, although they would officially go into battle as part of 'B' Squadron.

7   A 'slave carrier' would be a Universal or Loyd carrier adapted to carry batteries to aid tank starting.
8   Quoted in *Royal Hussars Journal*, p.155.
9   For details of the naval side of this operation, see Roskill, pp185-192.
10 The best overall account of the operation can be found in Buckley, *Five Ventures*.

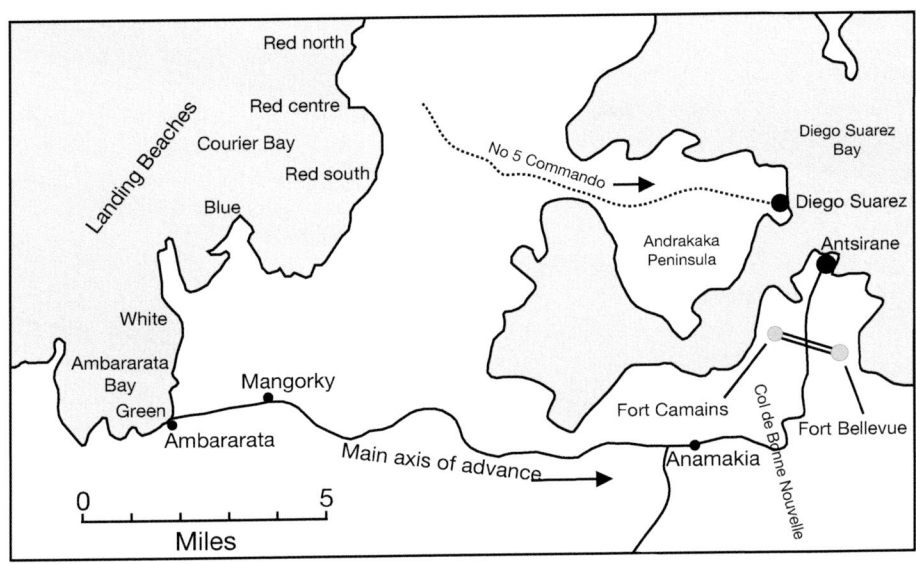

Northern tip of Madagascar, 5th-7th May 1942.

The large force which this small contingent joined was finally assembled off the west coast of the northern tip of Madagascar on 4th May, having proceeded via Freetown and Durban. The naval base of Antsirane and the bay of Diego Suarez within which it was located were on the eastern side of the northern tip of the island. The amphibious assault was to take place onto four beaches on the west side so as to approach the harbour from the 'back door', as the main entrance to the harbour was well covered by shore batteries. This land approach would however involve covering a distance of around 10 to 20 miles to the objectives, although the island was fairly narrow at this point. Rather worryingly, when orders were issued at sea during the voyage from Durban, information regarding the terrain and the location of likely defences (apart from coastal batteries) was very limited, although the squadron was doubtless cheered to be told that the French were thought to have no weapons capable of knocking out a Valentine.[11] The maps issued were found on arrival to be old and out of date. The troops also faced a hostile climate, featuring intense tropical heat, dust and mosquitoes. It is interesting to note that no mechanical problems with the Tetrarchs in these hot conditions seem to have been reported, in contrast to the problems with cooling that apparently prevented deployment in the Western Desert and parts of Russia.

Thirty four transports were needed for the invasion force, and 'B' Squadron travelled in three separate ships with two of each tank type on each ship. These ships also carried the landing craft which would carry the tanks to the landing beaches. Interestingly, the fleet contained Britain's first tank landing ship, a converted tanker called the Bachaquero, but this vessel was used to carry a battery of

11 Bright, p.340.

25pdr field guns and accompanying trucks. Two sets of beaches were selected, in Courrier Bay and the more southerly Ambararata Bay. Landings commenced at 0430 on 5th May. 5 Commando landed in Courrier Bay and headed for the docks at Diego Suarez itself. The infantry brigades and their armoured support began landing in Ambararata Bay with the objective of taking the town and naval base of Antsirane. Air support from the two aircraft carriers was effective in neutralising the small contingent of the Vichy French Air Force on the island. Unexpectedly heavy swells caused some delays, particularly with the heavier guns and tanks, and one of the two southerly beaches, White, was closed at one stage with a Tetrarch stranded on it after being swamped. Landing from three separate ships did nothing to speed up the arrival of the tanks.[12]

As efforts to land the tanks continued, the infantry had moved ahead along the road to Antsirane, and eventually Major Simon decided to take his three available tanks (two Valentines and a Tetrarch) and catch up with them, which he did at the town of Anamakia, about 12 road miles inland. On a ridge just east of the town (known as the Col de Bonne Nouvelle) was the first line of unexpected defences the advance had encountered. Photo-reconnaissance had been ordered, but the area covered had not extended far enough east to reveal the main French defended locations, of which the positions on the Col de Bonne Nouvelle were the first line. The French position on the Col included camouflaged trenches along with earth and concrete pillboxes. Arrangements were in progress for an outflanking move to take the position, but on arrival the tanks were ordered to attack straight away. This they did, and they silenced those French positions which could be identified with machine gun and 2pdr fire. However, the rocky terrain meant the tanks could not leave the road, and the appropriate close infantry back-up was also not available. As a result, when the tanks moved on, the position had not been properly cleared and the French were able to engage the British infantry when they eventually followed up. The ridge here was finally taken by 1500, with the aid of four more Valentines which had moved up from the beaches.

Meanwhile the leading group of tanks had been joined by two further Tetrarchs and this group of two Valentines and three Tetrarchs continued the advance along the road, with the Valentines in front. At about 12.15 a lorry was encountered and shot up, but almost immediately afterwards the French main line of defence was encountered, about 4 miles beyond the Col. Here, where there was a flat and fairly open plain, a strong belt of prepared defences had been created, based on fortifications built just before the First World War. This belt included pillboxes, anti-tank ditches, trenches, machinegun posts and dug-in 75mm field guns which could be very effective in the anti-tank role. At each end of the line was a fort (one named Caimans, the other Bellevue) with well concealed gun emplacements, with the flanks of the forts protected by steep slopes and mangrove swamps. The leading Valentines were engaged with solid shot from 75s located both along the road and in the forts, and were knocked out by multiple hits. The CO's report continues:

12 *Royal Hussars Journal*, p.157. See also Jim Stockman, 'Madagascar 1942', *British Army Review*, no.83, August 1986, p.66. The details of the armoured action are in Major Simon's report, contained in the war diary of 'B' Special Service Squadron, PRO file WO218/156

The Tetrarchs behind, seeing that the leading tanks were under fire, with great gallantry advanced and engaged the enemy. Unfortunately they followed the Sqn Comd down the road instead of deploying off the road to the right, where they would have been hull down at least to the gun down the road. In the event the two leading Tetrarchs were hit, and immediately caught fire.[13]

Sgt Clegg (at this time actually L/Cpl Clegg) was in Captain Palmer's tank which had become detached from the leading five vehicles. This is his memory of the advance and subsequent losses:

> Our Squadron Leader, now Major Jocelin Simon, pushed on ahead followed by Captain Llewellyn Palmer, and myself, followed by Lt. B.M.M. Carlisle, Sgt. Grime and Corporal Watkins. Sgt Major Allen brought up the rear. Capt. Llewellyn Palmer had a Union Jack which we intended to raise over the town hall in Diego Suarez, once we had taken the town. By sheer bad luck the Captain's tank threw a track in very deep soft sand, so Lt. Carlisle took the flag, promising to have it flying by the time we reached the town which was on the northern tip of the island opposite to our landing place. Lt. Carlisle, with Cpl Taffy Watkins, went tearing after Major Simon. If only they had done a recce, or proceeded with caution. The town was protected by dozens of French 75mm howitzers, some in huge concrete blockhouses, others in concealed positions, and bullock drawn. They were manned by Senegalese gunners, under the command of Vichy French officers. As soon as they, the tanks, were in range, the guns opened up and all four tanks were knocked out. Trooper Bond, a driver, managed to scramble out of the driver's flap but fell in front of his tank which was still rolling forward and he died with the track across his body as he begged Major Simon to shoot him. Cpl Watkins was incinerated in his tank whilst his driver died of horrible burns, and was buried at sea from the hospital ship.
>
> Left behind were four combatant and three wounded men. By using their automatics judiciously Major Simon, Lt. Carlisle, Lt. Whitaker and Sgt. Grime (Royal Tank Regiment), who later received the DCM for his part in this stand, were able to keep the patrols off for three and a half hours until their ammunition was exhausted and they were overrun. All the time they were under heavy fire from guns of all calibres. They lay concealed in high grass and were stalked by Senegalese, who revealed their presence by low jabberings as they came to within twenty yards of the party's position. At the end Lt Whitaker was killed in a hand-to-hand fight with a Senegalese, and it was only the intervention of a fine-spirited French officer which saved the rest of them from a similar fate. He intervened and the small party was disarmed and taken prisoner.[14]

The remaining Tetrarch, under the command of Lt. Astles, was ordered back to report the French resistance. (There is a discrepancy here between Clegg's account and the official report. Clegg mentions Sergeant-Major Allen being in the last tank, but Allen commanded a Valentine rather than a Tetrarch). On the way back to Brigade HQ Astles encountered a motorcycle combination and a truckload of French reinforcements which he shot up, killing or wounding most of the occupants. At HQ he was able to link up with the four Valentines and two further Tetrarchs of the squadron. Capt. Palmer, the squadron second-in-command who

---

13 WO218/156
14 *Royal Hussars Journal*, p.158.

had been left behind in the initial attack when his tank threw a track, was told to take this force of seven tanks and once again advance towards the French positions. According to the CO's report, he was ordered to 'locate the precise position of the 75mm guns which had disabled the leading tanks'. In accordance with these orders, Palmer devised a plan to deploy to the right hand side of the road out of sight of the French, then advance through the scrub and sugar cane to hull down positions from which the enemy guns would be engaged. Privately, he told his own crew (he was now in a Valentine) that he would expose his tank over the crest to draw French fire and thus uncover the enemy gun positions. This, at least, is what the official report tells us. Sgt Clegg recalls a rather more gung-ho approach to the problem,

> Captain LLewellyn Palmer, who was now our senior officer, called a brief conference and, being hidden from the enemy by a large plantation of tall pampas grass, it was decided that he would take the lead in one of the heavier Valentine tanks. We would then form up with our lighter Tetrarchs in arrow head formation, charge through the pampas grass at full speed and burst out in an effort to surprise the gunners, and make a frontal attack. It was a rerun of Balaclava[15]

Whatever the plan, there is no disagreement about the results. Sgt Clegg continues,:

> As soon as we were clear of the pampas grass all hell descended on us. How the few of us survived I shall never know. The crack of shells as they flew over the turret and around us sounded as if the artillery was on our hull. We made for the cover of a wood to our right like one man but Sergeant Major Allen's tank, another Valentine, had been hit. He and his crew, though they were wounded, managed to evacuate their tank and reached the cover of the pampas field. It looked as if the rest of us were going to make it to the wood when Captain Llewellyn Palmer and his crew leapt out of their tank and made to run for cover, but he was not to make it. The driver suddenly went down. Whether it was due to his wounds or being hit by machine gun fire we shall never know, but he must have cried out and Captain Llewellyn Palmer turned and ran back to help him reach cover. As he caught hold of the fallen trooper a high explosive shell fell on them. One moment they were there, as if held motionless, and in that terrible flash they were gone. I still maintain to this very day that he deserved at least a DSO for his sacrifice, he was a very gallant gentleman, of whom the 10th Hussars can be justly proud, as I am to have served with him.[16]

Palmer's tank was apparently the first to be hit, again several times, followed by Staff-Sergeant Allen's. The CO's report indicates that Lt. Heywood took over the remaining five tanks, and that once again he advanced to engage the French guns. An exchange of fire ensued, but thankfully there were no further casualties. With the light failing, the squadron withdrew at around 1800hrs.

Attacks by 29th Brigade in the late afternoon had also been unsuccessful. These attacks must have been taking place at around the same time as 'B' Squadron's, but there is no mention in the various accounts of the infantry and tank attacks being coordinated. A further attack by 29th Brigade in the early hours of the

---

15 Quoted in Fletcher, 'The Flying Tank', pp21-24.
16 *Royal Hussars Journal*, p.159.

6th also met with no success. During this time the remains of 'B' Squadron were held in brigade reserve. During the 6th, 17th Brigade moved forward from the landing beaches and put in an attack on the night of the 6th-7th commencing at about 2030. This also encountered heavy resistance, but the earlier attacks from the British had weakened the French position and the defences began to crack. In addition, during the afternoon of the 6th a daring raid on the French rear by fifty Royal Marines had departed from the main naval force. They were shipped directly into the harbour that night by the destroyer HMS *Anthony* and landed at Antsirane. Their unexpected arrival in the town had an effect on the French much greater than their numbers really justified and precipitated the start of a surrender which soon included the French naval and military commanders. Caught between these two British assaults the main defences eventually collapsed and by 0300 on the 7th the British were in control of the harbour and town. The Royal Navy's main force sailed into the harbour that afternoon.

For most of the 6th, the remaining vehicles of 'B' Squadron (two Valentines and three Tetrarchs) had occupied defensive fire positions on some high ground near 29th Brigade HQ. The French were obviously infiltrating men forward, as the tanks were subject to sniper fire throughout the period. At 1500 on the 6th the squadron was ordered out on a patrol to locate and engage some of these troops, but before they could move out a Valentine was immobilised by artillery fire. The patrol subsequently took place, and contact was made with French troops who were eventually mopped up by supporting British infantry. During the final advance into Antsirane, the squadron (one Valentine and three Tetrarchs) remained in reserve, advancing through the French positions once they had been broken through by the infantry. The following morning they were briefed for a possible supporting role in further offensive operations against the Orangea Peninsula east of Antsirane, but with the success of surrender negotiations the operation was cancelled.

It had been a brutal introduction to war for the squadron. Only four of the original 12 tanks were running by 7th May, and from a starting strength of 6 officers and 39 other ranks, 2 officers and 5 other ranks were killed, and 6 men wounded. The party who had been captured, including the CO, were re-united with the squadron after the surrender. Sgt Grime of 'B' Squadron was awarded the D.C.M. for his part in the fighting, and Capt Palmer was recommended for the Victoria Cross, but received instead a posthumous Military Cross. Overall the operation, the first major British amphibious operation of the war, was counted a considerable success. In only three days the objective of capturing the main port had been achieved. Nevertheless, some hard fighting had been necessary by the infantry and tanks. 'B' Squadron had shown a strong fighting spirit, and there had been numerous examples of bravery under fire. However, the accounts of the fighting also show that cooperation between tanks and infantry had been lacking, as was common in the British Army at this time. The evidence given above, and particularly some of Sgt Clegg's comments, would also indicate that a more cautious approach and more careful tactics by the squadron may have brought better results and fewer casualties.

Although this battle was the main one fought for the control of Madagascar, further fighting continued until early November, by which time the island was fully under British control. 'B' Squadron were not heavily involved, the war diary showing a period of maintenance and recovery followed by training and exercises, except for one fruitless patrol carried out by 2 Tetrarchs along with men of the 2nd Battalion, Royal Welch Fusiliers between 21st and 23rd May. The diary records the squadron left Madagascar for Mombasa, Kenya, on 23rd August. Sgt Clegg's account recalls that he and other men from 'B' Squadron were involved in subsequent amphibious actions against the coastal towns of Majunga and Tamatave that took place in September, and it seems 'B' Squadron returned to the island at this time, some men of the unit operating on foot under the command of 5 Commando, though they saw no serious combat and no casualties were suffered. By October the squadron was leaving again and on its way to Durban in South Africa. Re-organised and re-equipped, the unit went to India in early 1943 still under the command of 29th Infantry Brigade, and eventually took part in the Burma campaign as part of 146 Regiment, RAC.[17]

During this time the rest of 'C' Squadron had continued training in Scotland. The unit moved to Blackford, Perthshire on 9th April 1942 where it now came under command of the 36th Independent Infantry Brigade for administrative purposes. Training and exercises are recorded in the war diary up until 16th June, when notification was received that the unit was to disband on midnight 24th June. After only 11 months in existence, the squadron was destined for an entirely new role. In the words of the war diary,

> ...notification was received from War Office that the Airborne Light Tank Sqdn RAC would be formed from the personnel, equipment and vehicles of 'C' S.S. Sqdn RAC to take effect from 0001hrs 24.7.42 [sic-'7' has been typed instead of '6'] & be carried out by HQ South Highland Area. Formation of A.B.L.T. Sqdn RAC to take effect from that date.

The squadron would still be part of 'special forces', but now it would be airborne rather than seaborne. To get the full perspective on this change, we must go back to 1940. Some explanation of the extraordinary airborne army of which the Airborne Light Tank Squadron was to become a part is necessary.

Initiatives by Winston Churchill in that year are usually credited with being the starting point for the creation of British airborne forces. His minute to his chief of staff, dated 22nd June 1940, calling for "a corps of at least 5000 parachute troops" is regarded by British airborne forces as establishing their birthday.[18] In fact, he had made the same call in a minute of June 6th and on June 19th 1940 the Central Landing School had been established at RAF Ringway near Manchester. The officers and men of this school, taken from the RAF and the Army, were tasked to get Britain's airborne forces off the ground, and had to develop training methods and operational procedures pretty much from scratch. Within three weeks of the Central Landing School being established, Lieutenant-Colonel John Rock, the commanding officer, had written a report on organising and training the airborne forces. Other pioneering officers at Ringway were Wing Commander L.A. Strange

---

17 These latter details from B.T. White, 'The Special Service Squadrons', in *Tankette*, the Journal of the Miniature Armoured Fighting Vehicle Association, date unknown.
18 Crookenden, p.37.

and Wing Commander Sir Nigel Norman. Norman and Rock were both killed later in the war.

Rock had been a Major in the Royal Engineers when summoned to the War Office on 24th June 1940 and ordered to take charge of the initial organisation of Britain's airborne forces. Exactly why he was chosen is a mystery, as he had no specialist knowledge of gliders or aircraft. Furthermore, in his diary he records, "it was impossible to get any information as to policy or task".[19] However, he had the example of recent German operations before him, and the British Army was also aware of the work the Russians had been doing in this field. For example, British observers (including General Wavell) had been present when 1200 soldiers plus supporting weapons had been dropped by parachute in a 1936 demonstration in Russia. British beginnings were, by contrast, modest. A demonstration to the Prime Minister on 26th April 1941 could muster only six Whitley aircraft (converted medium bombers) dropping parachutists, a landing by five single seat training sailplanes and a towed flypast by a single Hotspur glider.

With Churchill taking a keen interest, there was some evidence of urgency in this early period. For example, the requirement for the Hotspur had been put to General Aircraft as early as June 1940, and an initial order for 400 had been placed by the Ministry of Aircraft Production in September of that year. Overall, however, early porgress in airborne forces development was slow and patchy. This can hardly be wondered at when the overall situation in Britain at this period is considered. Military resources of all kinds were in short supply, and airborne forces were going to be expensive in aircraft and specialist personnel, as well as being a totally new and unproven departure in military activity. Nevertheless, as we have seen, in 1940 requirements for gliders much more capable than the Hotspur had been issued by the Air Ministry, indicating that official thinking was already looking ahead to major airborne operations.

Despite generally friendly cooperation at unit level between the RAF and the Army, a process which started at Ringway, the novel nature of the forces being created meant an inevitable clash between higher echelons over which service would control which parts of the force. Eventually, it was agreed that the RAF would have charge of the tugs and transport aircraft, which would be formed into regular Air Force squadrons. The RAF would also own the gliders which would be attached to the tug squadrons as required for individual operations. The gliders would be flown, however, by *soldiers* trained as both infantrymen and glider pilots, and formed into a new regiment, the Glider Pilot Regiment.[20] It should also be emphasised that there was a constant and understandable reluctance on the part of the RAF's High Command, in particular the eventual head of Bomber Command, Arthur Harris, to release valuable aircraft and tie up production facilities to provide transport and tug aircraft. This latter was to be one of the main limiting factors in the growth of airborne troops.

Such was the overall picture. The detail of how a tank unit was to be integrated into the developing airborne force can be followed from surviving official files, and from the semi-official record in Otway's Airborne Forces. During the period when

---

19 Ministry of Information, *By Air to Battle*, p. 7.
20 Chapter 4 includes more detail on the formation of the Glider Pilot Regiment and RAF tug units.

staff at the Central Landing School and its various successors worked out training and operational procedures largely from scratch, and the designs that were to become the Hotspur, Horsa and Hamilcar began to mature, discussions between the Air Ministry and War Office commenced in order to clarify the size and role of the initial airborne force that was to be created. These discussions were protracted, with many disagreements over jurisdiction, and it was almost exactly a year until a Joint Memorandum was completed, on 31st May 1941.[21] Initial ideas had envisaged a force where the majority of the troops were airlanded, and the earliest airborne force designed (its organisation officially presented by the War Office in November 1940) was a so-called Aerodrome Capture Group, which contained two infantry battalions, eight 3.7 inch howitzers, eight light anti-aircraft guns and a light tank squadron of 18 tanks, in addition to signal, medical and supply detachments. It is particularly interesting to note, therefore, that the earliest British concept for an airborne force included tanks. During December 1940 and January 1941, this concept was developed into a force of two airlanding brigades, each now with four infantry battalions, and each with the same artillery, AA and support units as before. An anti-tank battery was added, and the 18 tank light tank squadron retained in each brigade. About half the force was to be capable of being airlifted simultaneously, around 1700 men, including the entire light tank squadron. In contrast, the parachute force was at this time a notional 500 men, whose exact organisation was still undecided.[22]

By the time of the Joint Memorandum at the end of May, these two airlanding brigades were confirmed, each of around 5000 men and each able to be flown into action in two lifts. These would be joined by two parachute brigades, each of around 2,500 men. One of each type of brigade was planned to be based in the UK and the other two brigades in the Middle East and/or India. Practice now started to take over from theory. In November 1941 Major-General F.A.M. 'Boy' Browning was appointed General Officer Commanding Airborne Forces. 1st Parachute Brigade had been formed on August 31st 1941, and the 1st Airlanding Brigade in October. On 1st November 1941, Browning was authorised to form a divisional headquarters to control the two brigades, initially as an administrative measure, but Browning envisaged operations on a divisional scale and it was agreed by the end of November that a headquarters capable of controlling divisional operations would be developed. Thus 1st Airborne Division came into being, a year and four months since Churchill's June 1940 memo. It would be some time before the division was operationally ready: even at the time of its first deployment in Sicily in July 1943 there were still deficiencies in training and equipment.

In the UK, 1st Airlanding Brigade did not include a light tank squadron when formed (it will be recalled that the first Hamilcar did not fly until March 1942) but had a reconnaissance company which was to be equipped with jeeps and which would eventually become the 1st Airborne Reconnaissance Squadron.[23] It was not until January 1942, as the Hamilcar neared its first flight and with the 1st Airborne

---

21 *Airborne Forces*, p.27.
22 See *Airborne Forces*, pp25-28, and PRO file WO32/9778, Airborne Forces, Policy and Requirements 1940-43.
23 Chapter 7 includes detail on the formation of this squadron and its parent brigade.

Division two months old, that the organisation of a specific unit within 1st Airborne to operate light tanks was considered in detail.

If the above all appears fairly logical, it should be remembered that in creating an airborne force the UK military was groping in the dark in an entirely novel field. The early stages of this process of creation were marked by uncertainty and disagreements over what the force should consist of, what equipment it might need, or even if it was worth creating large airborne forces at all. The field of airborne tanks was not immune to this confusion and uncertainty. One War Office letter of December 1940 envisaged the ridiculous total of 600 tanks being required for airborne use.[24] Another anonymous and undated note from about the same period sketched two possible organisations; a light tank regiment with an HQ and three companies with a total of 50 tanks, and a light tank brigade of 180 tanks and 40 scout cars.[25] Even as late as August 1942, RAC records indicate that the Director of Air at the War Office (the Air Directorate having been recently formed in order to look after and coordinate matters relating to airborne forces) foresaw a requirement for 132 airborne tanks for the UK airborne division, and 155 for the airborne division in India.[26] It should be noted that D Air (as he was known) was at this time Brigadier R.N. Gale, later to command 6th Airborne Division. It is hard at this distance to understand how such a well informed officer could be so wildly out in judging future needs, but it is a good indication of the extent to which planners were essentially making it up as they went along.

Having mentioned the intention to form airborne forces in India, we should very briefly explain why this attempt forms no real part of our story. Efforts to form an airborne division in India were protracted and a division (44th Indian Airborne Division) was approaching operational readiness in this theatre only by the end of the war. Tropical conditions could play havoc with the wooden structures of Horsa and Hamilcar gliders, and the 'hot and high' conditions reduced the performance of tugs, which as we have seen led to the consideration of double tows and the powered Hamilcar. In the event the vast majority of gliders used in India and the Far East were American CG-4A Hadrians (see chapter 11), which were of steel tube and fabric construction. Providing sufficient resources for the Indian division was a constant struggle and no tank unit was ever formed within it. Jeeps seem to have been the largest vehicle carried by gliders in this theatre.

Returning to the story of the Airborne Light Tank Squadron, a meeting was convened at the War Office on 19th January 1942 to consider the inclusion of a number of support units within the Airborne Division, among which were the light tanks. Amongst a number of senior officers (of which four were Major-Generals), Major-General Browning was naturally prominent. At this and a smaller meeting on 23rd January, the role and organisation of the airborne tanks were clarified, following some preliminary staff work. It was agreed that the light tank unit had to be an integral part of the airborne division to ensure proper training and availability, and that the unit would probably be formed from amongst the three existing Special Service Squadrons. The Mk. VII was the only real choice for equipping the unit as it was the only tank then able to be carried by the Hamilcar.

24 PRO file AVIA22/459, AFV's - Requirements and Supply.
25 PRO file AIR32/2, Provision of an Airborne Force.
26 Tank Museum archive, RAC Half-Yearly Report No.6, December 1942.

Squadron strength was to be 19 tanks. The role of the squadron was described as follows:

> The role of the Light Tank Squadron will normally be the capture of an objective, in anticipation of a quick follow up by part of the Airborne Division, followed by patrolling in front of the main position.
>
> It was agreed that the likelihood of heavy opposition would entail the withdrawal of the squadron.
>
> The squadron is not likely to operate more than 25 miles from the "landing head".[27]

It was noted that, after landing, the Airborne Division would be fairly static due to its limited transport, and that thus the operations of the light tanks would necessarily be quite circumscribed due to their reliance on supply from the parent division. It is also interesting to note that specific mention was made of the limited glider resources available and the need to keep the size of both the Airborne Division and the Light Tank Squadron to an absolute minimum.

What was envisaged here was still very much a *tank* unit, likely to operate in the *coup de main* role, as opposed to a reconnaissance unit. Despite the various caveats, the squadron was to be employed aggressively, and was considered sufficiently important to be given a high priority in scarce resources to ensure it arrived on the battlefield. This was despite the fact that even by early 1942 it was obvious the Mk.VII had severely limited capabilities on the battlefield and had been overtaken in armament and armour by contemporary tanks. This aggressive philosophy for the use of airborne tanks seems to have been carried over into the organisation and planned role of the later Reconnaissance Regiment on D-Day, as we shall see.

By the end of March 1942 the War Establishment of the Light Tank Squadron was confirmed. It would have 19 tanks, just one more than the total envisaged in 1940. These would be organised into a squadron headquarters of four tanks, and five troops each of three tanks. There would be an intercommunication troop of seven motorcycles and one jeep, an administration troop (airborne) with eleven jeeps, nine 'rotatrailers' and one 10cwt trailer, and an administration troop (non-airborne) with three 3ton lorries, two 15cwt trucks and a two seater car. Manpower would total 138 officers and other ranks. One minor point worth mentioning here, as it occurs in other sources relating to our story, is that the files refer to jeeps as 'Blitz Buggies', evidently contemporary British Army slang. The official designation for the jeep was 'car, 4x4, 5cwt'. A more important point is to clarify what 'rota trailers' were, which will require a brief digression.

This piece of equipment was designed in 1942 as a solution to the problem of extending the operational range of tanks, by means of a trailer filled with petrol and ammunition. It has been concisely described by David Fletcher as 'an armoured box, complete with lid, running on two hollow wheels fitted with solid rubber tyres. [...] The front section was used to stow extra ammunition while the rear part contained a small hand-operated pump and hose. The hollow wheels were then filled with fuel which could be pumped into the tank when required.'[28] After apparently extensive testing in the UK, they were sent out to the desert.

27 PRO file WO32/10388
28 Fletcher, *The Great Tank Scandal*, p.117.

Here, the extreme conditions of heat, sand and rocky ground caused the fuel to leak from the wheel hubs, and the unsprung wheels on their solid tyres often caused the trailers to overturn. They were thoroughly unpopular and their use was discontinued. It was, apparently, hoped that they would fare better under European conditions, as a solution to the requirements of an armoured unit operating with an airborne force that would obviously be short of supply vehicles. They did end up being used in Normandy, but continued to be unpopular as they were difficult to manage under tow. This was exacerbated by the practice of towing more than one trailer at a time to make the best use of the limited vehicle resources available. The most unwieldy combination mentioned is two jeeps towing three trailers, which sounds like a recipe for disaster. The Rotatrailers had a habit of jackknifing and overtaking their towing vehicles under braking.

It was around the time that the above organisation was finalised, in spring 1942, that the third brigade for 1st Airborne Division was authorised. This would bring the division in line with the organisation of normal infantry divisions. It was now obvious that aircraft and glider resources for an additional airlanding brigade would not be available in the foreseeable future, so the third brigade was a parachute unit, formed in July 1942 as 2nd Parachute Brigade. The Airborne Light Tank Squadron then became part of divisional troops (i.e. directly under the command of divisional HQ) rather than part of the airlanding brigade. The same had happened to 1st Airlanding Reconnaissance Squadron which had been part of divisional troops since December 1941.

'C' Special Service Squadron must have been the obvious candidate when the actual creation of the new airborne light tank unit was finally authorised. It was an independent tank squadron trained for out of the ordinary operations, and of the three Special Service Squadrons it was the one which operated Tetrarchs, the designated airborne tank. Transfer to the new role on 24th June 1942 saw the squadron remaining at Blackford, Perthshire. The war diary records 10 officers and 84 other ranks on strength at formation, along with 7 Tetrarchs, 4 scout cars and 3 'T.C.Ps' (Tracked Carriers, Personnel). Lieutenants Carlisle and Astles, who had gone to Madagascar, were still listed as 'detached officers', whilst Major Asquith was confirmed to continue in command. Until mid-August, training seems to have continued as far as possible alongside the various reshuffles of equipment and personnel which were required to bring the squadron into line with its revised organisation. July 15th saw a medical inspection of all ranks to see if they were up to the standard used for recruitment into airborne forces. All but two other ranks were declared fit. Also in July there was a proposal to transfer personnel from 'B' Special Service Squadron into the unit to complete the war establishment. A transfer of soldiers did take place, but after 10 days the decision was reversed and the personnel returned to 'B' Squadron. Small drafts of other additional personnel came in from various RAC training regiments. Of the other two Special Service Squadrons, 'A' Squadron disbanded on 15th June 1942, most of the men being posted to various RAC tank units and training regiments, but five officers are recorded as being posted to the Airborne Light Tank Squadron. We have seen that the main fighting elements of 'B' Squadron ended up in India, but some men of this squadron who had remained in the UK did eventually join the Airborne unit.

It was in August that the Airborne Light Tank Squadron eventually moved down to Salisbury Plain to join the rest of the 1st Airborne Division. It seems their first billets, at Tinkers Firs Camp, were fairly isolated, as Trooper Collins remembered later:

> Our spot on the plain consisted of only a few tin huts and we soon realised that we were a long way from anywhere. Liberty trucks were our only means of visiting the outside world. Trowbridge, Warminster, Frome and Devizes were the nearest towns and from the time of our posting to the Airborne Division until leaving for Palestine some years later we must have made hundreds of trips to these places.
>
> To own a cycle and a dog seemed to be the height of luxury in those days out on the plain and it was surprising how many of the men 'acquired' a cycle to visit the nearest villages, and quite a few town dogs were equally surprised to find them selves in the Army being trained to catch rabbits on the lonely Plain.
>
> Soon, however, the unit was moved to a more civilised location, in fact it was a rip-roaring town compared with Lavington Down; Larkhill – to be our home, on and off, for a few years. There we soon settled down in the married quarters (disused as such) and found that we had such luxuries as a cinema and two cafes.[29]

Major Asquith was promoted to Lt. Col. and posted to a new unit, and his second-in-command Captain W.K.C. Pulteney took over the unit as temporary CO. The major did not leave without regrets. Trooper Willcox (ex 10th Hussars), noted that 'when Major Asquith told us he had to leave and take over as Colonel of the Queen's Bays, he failed to finish his speech and walked away with tears in his eyes'.[30]

On 19th August, as the unit was settling in at Tinkers Firs camp, they were visited by the divisional commander, General Browning. September saw training in their new role beginning in earnest, with the men of the squadron being taken gliding, as well as flying in powered aircraft. Two troops of tanks took part in a divisional exercise and some members of the unit commenced parachute training. Ten men from 'B' Special Service Squadron were (once again) posted in towards the end of the month. Also by the end of September 12 new Tetrarchs had arrived on strength. The Airborne Light Tank Squadron was up and running.

---

29 C.L. Collins, 'Flying Tanks', *Pegasus Journal*, 1949.
30 See 'The Airborne Light Tank Squadron – Sixth Airborne Armoured Reconnaissance Regiment', *Royal Hussars Journal*, vol.20, summer 1990.

Chapter 4

Flying Tanks

The Squadron was destined to be in being for the next 18 months, before it was expanded to a regiment in January 1944. This period saw the departure of 1st Airborne Division to the Mediterranean and the creation of 6th Airborne Division, both of these events being gradual processes which took place over several months.

The move of 1st Airborne to the Middle East began when elements of 1st Parachute Brigade took part in Operation Torch, the invasion of French North Africa which began on 8th November 1942. Eventually the whole brigade was committed to the subsequent operations. It was then decided that 1st Airborne Division would be used in the invasion of Sicily, and during the first half of 1943 the whole division assembled in the Middle East, commencing their part of the attack on Sicily on the night 9th-10th July 1943. However, the division had been required to leave some of its units behind to form a trained cadre for the second airborne division to be formed, 6th Airborne. The division was apparently called the 6th because calling it the 2nd would have made it rather too obvious to the Germans exactly how many airborne divisions Britain had![1]

Orders to raise the 6th Airborne Division were issued in April 1943. HQ 6th Airborne Division was established at Syrencot House, Figheldean, Wiltshire, on 7th May 1943. This was the division that would eventually fly tanks into action. Divisional Commander was Major General R.N. Gale. The main units transferred from 1st Airborne were 7th, 8th and 9th Parachute Battalions, 2nd Battalion the Oxfordshire and Buckinghamshire Light Infantry, 1st Battalion the Royal Ulster Rifles and 12th Battalion The Devonshire Regiment. Also eventually transferred was the Airborne Light Tank Squadron. Curiously, the war diary is silent on the date of transfer. However, the war diary does include a reference to an inspection by General Gale on 26th May, and it is clear that from this time onwards the unit trained extensively with elements of 6th Airborne, regardless of the official date of transfer. In fact, the official transfer did not take place until 11th February 1944, as recorded in the diary of 6th Airborne Division, by which time the squadron had expanded to a regiment.[2]

Returning to the autumn of 1942, it was in October that the squadron moved to Larkhill on Salisbury Plain which was to remain their base for the rest of the war in Europe. Here, just over the road from Stonehenge, they were close to the airfields at Netheravon and Boscombe Down, and the big Army base at Bulford. Training over the next year and more saw the unit gradually acquiring the experience and equipment it needed. Fred Murray, later Squadron Sergeant Major in 'B' Squadron of 6th AARR, remembered the early days of the Light Tank Squadron after their arrival on Salisbury Plain:

1 *The Glider Soldiers*, p.26
2 WO171/425, 6th Airborne Division War Diary 1944, 'G' Branch.

From then onwards it was slog, slog and more slog with officers and senior NCOs being involved with loading trials, making out weight lists which changed every day, and it must be said that a lot of the hard work for our future as a regiment was done in those early days.³

As far as getting into the air went, gliding and air experience flying in powered aircraft was a regular feature of training from the start. The latter would have been in transport aircraft, like the Handley Page Harrow mentioned in the war diary during April 1943. Most initial glider experience was in the Hotspur glider. However, it was the availability of the Horsa and Hamilcar gliders that was most vital to the squadron. Although Horsa production was well under way by late 1942, the Light Tank Squadron was probably well down the list of priorities for their allocation. As we shall see later when the formation of the Glider Pilot Regiment and RAF tug units is reviewed, pilots had to be trained, tug units formed, and the airlanding brigades that were to use the Horsa operationally would naturally get priority. The first record of training with the Horsa in the war diary is the 5th of February 1943, when the allocation of a mock-up to practice loading procedures is noted. The first mention of actual Horsa flying is on 20th March 1943.

As a tank unit, our squadron was of course intended mainly for the Hamilcar. From 18th May 1943 there are regular mentions of loading trials with Hamilcar gliders at Netheravon, and it would appear the Squadron possessed a Hamilcar mock-up in a garage at Larkhill. The first mention in the war diary of possible Hamilcar flying is on 9th December 1943, when the HQ troop proceeded to Tarrant Rushton aerodrome for 9 days. War diaries do not contain everything that a unit does, and so these various dates need to be treated with caution. However, this fairly late date for the first training trips in a Hamilcar is not unreasonable. Despite Hamilcar production having started around a year previously, No.1 Heavy Glider Maintenance Unit at Netheravon had only 10 available in November 1943. Of the 53 Hamilcars produced by that time, the majority were in storage, awaiting erection or short of parts. Tarrant Rushton, in Dorset, had only just been selected as the airfield to be used for Hamilcar training and operations, and so it would appear entirely likely that the coming together of tanks and gliders for their first regular training should occur at this time.⁴ Indeed, a number of sources suggest that the first unit training flights in which Hamilcars carried tanks did not take place until January 1944.

The non-availability of Hamilcars would, of course, have been the main reason the squadron had not accompanied 1st Airborne Division to the Middle East. One member of the squadron, Trooper Willcox, has left his memories of early training on the Hamilcar, which took place without the aid of tanks:

> As we were allocated only a small pool of light tanks to suffice the war, we had to call upon the Royal Engineers to bolt a huge wooden box to the floor of the Hamilcar glider. [...]

---

3 Quoted from some memories of his time with 6th AARR that Fred put together for his comrades of 'B' Squadron in 2002.
4 See Michael J. Bowyer, 'Hamilcar Tank Transports', *Airfix Magazine*, April 1977, p.452.

Securing a Tetrarch inside the Hamilcar cargo hold. Ladder to upper fuselage and cockpit on right (Tank Museum).

Our tank crew was given the job of weighing all the contents of the tanks and then filling the box with ballast to the equal weight of a tank, laden ready for action.

At that time we did not have our forward parachute section, so that when we flew with mock tanks we were issued with safety parachutes ready to jump should things go amiss.

For about twenty minutes it was a hectic ride until the pilots really got the feel of the glider. It was their first really heavy load.

Two weeks later we learned that 4th Troop (nucleus 9th Lancers) were to attempt flying a tank but only using securing ropes. We asked them to check our reports of movement of internal ballast. So it was delayed until REME designed a special form of thin steel wire hawsers instead of rope.[5]

By this stage, expansion of the unit in readiness for the change to regimental size was under way. However, before moving on to the story of this expansion there are many important developments that occurred whilst the unit was still a squadron which should be recounted.

Changes in command, organisation and equipment had occurred. Captain Pulteney had been promoted to Major in December 1942, but left the squadron at the end of February 1943. His second-in-command Captain P.Barnett took over temporarily, until on 24th March 1943 Major Godfrey R. de C. Stewart arrived to take over. Godfrey Stewart was to command the unit until the end of the war in

5   From The Airborne Light Tank Squadron – Sixth Airborne Armoured Reconnaissance Regiment.

Europe. Among his first duties was the supervision of his unit during an inspection by the King which was inspected along with the rest of 1st Airborne Division on 2nd April 1942. According to one source, the King remarked on the number of different cap badges on show in the squadron, and recalled inspecting a similar unit in Scotland earlier in the war. This. of course, had been 'C' Special Service Squadron.[6] (Although all ranks were entitled to wear the maroon airborne beret, they used the cap badges of their parent regiment. Stewart was to make subsequent appeals for a cap badge for 6th AARR, but without success).

The squadron had to be built up to its new strength of 5 troops of tanks, which was stronger than the typical tank squadron of the time which usually had 4 troops of 3 tanks each. It would appear that the number of Tetrarchs available for issue was becoming limited, and from the formation of the squadron all available Tetrarchs were earmarked solely for airborne use. At the first meeting of the Airborne Forces Committee (set up by the Air Ministry) on 24th April 1942, it had been noted that Tetrarch production had ceased but 'the 60-70 which would be available would probably be sufficient'. An appendix to the RAC half-yearly report for December 1942 gives an approximate total from the previous August of only 50 Tetrarchs remaining available. That the number of Tetrarchs available was soon causing concern is shown by a report on the state of 1st Airborne Division made by its commander in January 1943. Regarding the Light Tank Squadron, the report states:

> Despite previous assurances that there were 70 of these light tanks available it was now discovered that there were no reserves of them at all in the country, and this meant that in the event of operations any casualties to the LTS were irreplaceable. Also in spite of requests made many months before that the 2pdr gun in each tank should have its performance stepped up by a comparatively simple modification [i.e.Littlejohn], no action has yet been taken.[7]

A War Office memo on shortages of equipment in airborne forces from around February 1943 mentions about 30 Mk.VIIs in reserve, 'some of which have been issued to replace those rendered u/s by the Airborne Division'.[8] The exact number of Tetrarchs available might be in doubt, but the total was low, and with an authorised squadron strength of 19, it can be seen that with unserviceabilities, losses during training and in particular potential losses in action, airborne forces could easily run out of Tetrarchs before the war ended. It has already been mentioned that during late 1942, a requirement was foreseen for 132 airborne tanks for the 1st Airborne Division, and another 155 for an airborne division to be formed in India.[9] Whilst these requirements turned out to be completely overblown, such thoughts added to the pressure to re-equip with a new airborne tank, which as we have seen was to be the Locust.

---

6 Outline History of the 6th Airborne Armoured Reconnaissance Regt., Tank Museum.
7 PRO file AIR39/132, Airborne Forces: History, Organisation, Training and Operations.
8 PRO file WO32/9778, Airborne Forces, Policy and Requirements, 1940-1943.
9 RAC Half Yearly Report No.6, December 1942, Appendix Q4(a). Archives of the Bovington Tank Museum.

The Littlejohn adapters eventually arrived, but the first firing of these converted guns by the squadron did not take place until 24th September 1943. At some stage, perhaps around mid or late 1943, a decision was also taken (probably at the suggestion of the squadron itself) to fit a few Tetrarchs with the 3" howitzer, presumably to give some capability for firing HE and smoke rounds. The 2pdr, once fitted with Littlejohn, could only fire the specialised AP rounds developed for this gun. The howitzer conversions received the designation Tetrarch 1 CS (close support). The conversion was carried out at unit level with help from Vickers.[10]

Not long afterwards a more fundamental change of equipment took place when on 25th October, 17 T.9 Locust tanks arrived. During November the new tanks were issued, although the Tetrarchs with 3" howitzer were retained in the squadron HQ, and at the end of the month the whole squadron took their new vehicles to Warcop ranges in Westmoreland for firing practice. At least some Locusts had Littlejohn adapters fitted to their 37mm guns but it is not known if they were issued with this conversion. As we have seen in Part One, the Locust and Tetrarch were comparable in weight, although the Locust was a little smaller. The slightly more effective frontal armour of the Locust (due to its sloping glacis plate) would make little difference on the battlefields of 1943-44. The Locust was slower than the Tetrarch which was an important consideration in reconnaissance operations, but the Locust had a significantly lower height (5'8" as opposed to 6'11") which could be a distinct advantage in this role.

However, at this stage the Locust was not to last long in service. Once again, the war diary is silent on when the change back to Tetrarchs took place. Ten Tetrarchs are recorded flying in Hamilcars just after the expansion to a regiment, on 25th January 1944, indicating that conversion back to the older tank was beginning. However, Michael Bowyer's work on the Hamilcar to which we have already referred indicates that as late as 1st March 1944 it was still the intention to fit out the gliders for D-Day to take 17 Locusts and 3 Tetrarchs (with 3" howitzer). Only in early April were the gliders finally modified to take all Tetrarch tanks. The war diary records 37mm firing demonstrations still taking place on 21st March 1944. It would seem that by mid-late March 1944 the Locusts had been disposed of. The reason appears to have been the mechanical and gunnery problems which have already been mentioned in Part One. The *Outline History* to which we have been referring indicates that 'gear box trouble' was one of the main problems at this time, though perhaps not the only one.

Finally, for this period as a squadron, we should attempt to analyse how the unit was to be used, as reflected in its training exercises. The squadron's vehicles were commonly used to provide opposition in exercises where airborne infantry was being trained in dealing with tanks, but this was simply a use of convenient resources to aid in divisional training. On the other hand, the tasks in Exercise Solomon, held in February 1943, were those the unit was intended to perform on D-Day: reconnaissance of enemy dispositions and the engagement of potential counter-attacks. The exercise is titled in the war diary a 'Horsa' exercise, and describes the squadron 'taking off' from Netheravon aerodrome, destination Hurn (near Bournemouth). It must be assumed that pending the arrival of Hamilcars the personnel and any light vehicles were carried in Horsas and married up with tanks on

---

10 Tank Museum files, RAC Policy and Progress Report, July 1944.

landing. On this, as in other exercises, the squadron co-operated with elements of 1st Airborne Reconnaissance Squadron, until that unit's departure with 1st Airborne Division in April 1943. This was logical, as since August 1942, when the Light Tank Squadron had moved down to Salisbury Plain, both units had been part of the divisional troops of 1st Airborne Division. This obviously prefigured the later regimental expansion when a new recce squadron was added to the light tank squadron. (The war diary noted that nine jeeps were taken over by the tank squadron from the departing recce squadron in late April).

In examples of other exercises the squadron provided tank support for 2nd Ox and Bucks during a mock attack, and reconnaissance for 3rd Para Brigade and (in a separate exercise) 6th Airlanding Brigade. In August 1943 the unit practised fighting against another recce unit, with opposition provided by the armoured cars and Bren Carriers of the 24th Lancers. Later that month the war diary proudly records the unit's performance in Exercise Frigate, which is worth quoting in full:

> The whole squadron took part in preventing enemy reserve formations reaching the assaulting sea-borne troops. During the course of the battle the Light Tank Squadron annihilated 1 battalion infantry, 1 coy. anti-tank guns, 1 company strongpoint manned by infantry, and 3 armoured cars. The Brigadier congratulated the squadron upon their excellent work.

The squadron was obviously intended, at least in part, to play the aggressive role originally outlined for it in 1941 and still retained on the eve of D-Day.

On 13th December 1943, the war diary records the first arrival of 'officers and other ranks on expansion of unit'. It had been decided to expand the squadron to a regimental sized unit with a combination of light tanks and more conventional reconnaissance vehicles. The official change came on 14th January 1944, when the Airborne Armoured Reconnaissance Regiment RAC was formed. The regiment officially came under command of 6th Airborne Division on 11th February. On March 27th Major Stewart was promoted to Lieutenant-Colonel. It was not until 1st April 1944 that the regiment officially became the 6th Airborne Armoured Reconnaissance Regiment.

On 15th February 1944 General Gale issued a 'Directive for training and employment of The Airborne Armoured Reconnaissance Regiment RAC'. This gives us the organisation of the regiment on first formation and a good general idea of how the unit was intended to be used.[11] A realistic sense of what the Tetrarch was capable of obviously contributed to a continuing move away from the concept of a unit providing tank support, towards a unit whose main role was reconnaissance. Regimental HQ had 2 light tanks, probably armed with the 3" howitzer. The Headquarters Squadron contained the 'parachute harbour party' of 10 men. This party trained with the independent paratroop company who were the division's pathfinders, and they would drop with the leading parachute units to reconnoitre and secure the harbour area to which the regiment would deploy immediately after landing. In this squadron there was also an intercommunications troop with motorcycles, a 'landing head party' (whose role is not explained) and administrative

---

11 The directive can be found in WO171/425, 6th Airborne Division War Diary 1944, 'G' Branch.

troops. The Reconnaissance Squadron had an HQ of jeep, universal carrier and 3 motorcyclists and had four recce troops each with a jeep and a carrier. The Light Tank Reconnaissance Squadron had an HQ of three tanks and five troops each of three tanks. The Support Squadron had an HQ of 2 jeeps and five motorcyclists, a support troop with two 3" mortars each transported in a universal carrier, and an assault troop containing a carrier and twenty motorcyclists. This organisation was to develop in the time up to D-Day.

The directive noted that the Tetrarchs had the greatest off-road mobility of any of the regiment's vehicles. Noting the overall level of weaponry in the regiment, it concluded that 'the armament is certainly not of sufficient weight to have any offensive value except against the most flimsy resistance'. The three roles envisaged for the regiment were reconnaissance, protection and 'seize and hold'. The first of the three was obviously the major role. The protection role might be needed when contact with the enemy had reduced the need for reconnaissance. In this case the regiment might form 'a protective screen in the early stages of defence or when forward troops have to disengage to take up positions elsewhere', or might be used to protect an exposed flank. For the third role the directive noted, 'the employment of the regiment in this role is justifiable. If sent forward unsupported it is essential that it should be reinforced as quickly as possible'.

The new personnel for the expansion continued to come from RAC units, many apparently drawn from the RAC Depot.[12] However, there are many regiments within the RAC and around this time one veteran, a Cpl. Sheffield, recalled twenty two different cap badges in use within 6th AARR.[13] From now until late May, the regiment had to shake down its new organisation and train for the tasks it was allocated for D-Day.

Actual flying in gliders, particularly for the light tank squadron, was a limited part of this training. Most of the everyday flying at Tarrant Rushton was concerned with training for the tug and glider crews, along with a steady level of operational sorties by the Halifax squadrons. These sorties included dropping of supplies and personnel into occupied France and occasional bombing missions, and were designed to keep the squadrons at the required level of efficiency. Glider training flights would include cross country navigation with gliders under tow, as well as 'circuits and bumps' for training in take off and landing. The latter was described by an ex-Hamilcar pilot in a letter to the author, explaining the pattern of training for a Horsa pilot who had been transferred to a Hamilcar unit,

> Training began with dual instruction and when competent solo flying, this usually took about 2 or 3 hours of dual control. It is this training that consisted of circuits and bumps – bump being the landing which was never carried out whilst attached to the Halifax. Firstly the glider was connected to the tug by a length of thick hemp rope. This was bifurcated just over half way along its length and was attached under each wing. The rope contained the intercom wires so that the Halifax pilot and crew could communicate with the glider pilots. The tug would then move slowly to take up the slack and then put all four

---

12 See Norman Eyre, The 6th Airborne Armoured Reconnaissance Regiment (RAC), another of the brief histories held at Bovington. Eyre was an ex-member of 6th AARR.
13 The Airborne Light Tank Squadron – Sixth Airborne Armoured Reconnaissance Regiment

engines at full power and take off. The glider when fully loaded would be airborne first. The circuit is in fact a rectangle and consists of the climb out, then turn to port still climbing and when about 2000' another turn to port onto the downwind leg, and once past the end of the runway a last turn and now the glider pilot can 'cast off' when ready, turn into line with the runway and land.[14]

Most of the glider-related training for the regiment seems to have involved loading and unloading exercises, and general air experience flying as already noted. It was common for members of any airlanding unit to fly as 'live loads' during glider pilot training, and 6th AARR were no exception. Usually, the first contact between members of the regiment and their glider and tug crews was once they were loaded up ready for an operation. Even during major exercises, vehicle landings were commonly 'simulated', with the units positioned by road to their 'landing zones' for commencement of the exercise. Anecdotal evidence (which is limited) and the lack of entries in the war diary would indicate that the tank crews had a very limited number of chances to take their tanks flying in a Hamilcar. Norman Stocker, who ended the war as a sergeant in the regiment, recalled that 'most of us only did one or two training flights'.[15] The primary concern here must have been the risk of accidents which might cost the lives of highly trained troops and specialised equipment, as well as losses to the still scarce Hamilcars. Exercises involving glider landings generally took place onto airfields marked out with landing zones rather than into the open countryside, to keep risks to a minimum and to avoid the time and cost taken to retrieve the aircraft.[16] For some of the men scheduled to fly in Horsas, D-Day would be their first trip in a glider.

Accidents did occur, but in general were no more frequent than at any training/operational base in wartime. During the training of 'C' Squadron of the Glider Pilot Regiment (the squadron which specialised in the Hamilcar), over 2800 lifts were made, an average of 50 per glider crew. This resulted in seven glider pilots being killed, and in three accidents there were additional casualties to passengers.[17] We can give some examples. The 6th AARR war diary records 10 Hamilcars with Tetrarchs flying on 25th January, of which '3 made faulty landings'. The Operations Record Book (ORB) for Tarrant Rushton also records 10 Hamilcars plus tanks flying on 20th January, and this seems to be the date of the most well recorded accident, the story of which has become rather apocryphal due to its spectacular nature and lack of serious injuries incurred. On this day one of the Hamilcars came in too fast, or landed too long (or quite likely both), and overshot the landing area. It ran into a nissen hut, destroying both hut and glider, and the tank itself 'was thrown clear', to quote the ORB. The reader may take his or her choice of the various stories that have grown up around this accident. In one, the nervous driver of the tank has been instructed before the flight not to get out of his vehicle until told. In the accident, the release mechanism operates and the tank flies out of the nose of the Hamilcar at high speed, screeching to a halt some distance away. In the confusion, it is some time before rescuers approach the solitary tank, to hear a plaintive voice from inside asking 'Is it OK to get out now skip?'.[18] Colonel Chatterton claims to have witnessed the accident, which he says occurred

14 Letter to the author from Mr P.A. Young, 16th March 2002.
15 Letter to the author, August 2002.
16 *The Wings of Pegasus*, pp.121-122.
17 *The Wings of Pegasus*, p126.
18 See, for example, Prower, 'Gliding Tanks', p.29

'Is it OK to get out now, skip?' – result of the Hamilcar crash at Tarrant Rushton, January 1944 (Museum of Army Flying).

on the first time 6th AARR took their tanks into the air, and he has his own version of events. The two Hamilcar pilots in their cockpit were sitting atop the heap of rubble that had been the nissen hut, whilst the tank shot through at eighty miles an hour and came to rest fifty yards away. Chatterton rushed over to find the driver chucking out the debris that had found its way into the tank. Asked if he was alright, the reply was, 'Yes, but I'm coovered in bloody moock!'.[19]

Another dramatic accident occurred when a Halifax burst a tyre just after its Hamilcar had lifted off. The glider pilot cast off, and tried to turn downwind to land back on the runway. The glider crashed into the line of Halifaxes waiting their turn to take off, all with engines running, and severed the rear fuselage from one. Once again, the height of the Hamilcar cockpit saved the glider pilots, and the rear gunner of the Halifax had only seconds before gone forward to get a better view of operations, and so also saved his life.[20] Not all accidents ended without casualties, however. The present day visitor to the site of Tarrant Rushton's main gate will find a poignant memorial to the crew of a Halifax which crashed at nearby Tarrant Keynston whilst engaged in Hamilcar towing on the 27th of May 1944. Three of the Royal Canadian Air Force crew were killed.

19 *The Wings of Pegasus*, p.126.
20 'Hamilcars of Tarrant Rushton', p.190.

For the first five months of 1944, the diary shows an intense round of training for 6th AARR at troop and squadron level, including (for example) gunnery practice all the way from pistols to the tank main armament. As has been mentioned, as late as 21st March this still included 37mm gun firing, indicating training on Locusts was still taking place. The organisation of the regiment had evolved somewhat since the beginning of the year, but documents giving the exact organisation on the eve of D-Day do not appear to have survived. The organisation given below has been developed from a number of sources, some of which differ from each other, and as a result may not be definitive.

Regimental HQ consisted of two Tetrarchs armed with the 3" howitzer (the Tetrarch I CS). The regiment itself consisted of a Headquarters Squadron, a Light Tank Squadron ('A' Squadron), and a Reconnaissance Squadron ('B' Squadron). The HQ Squadron contained medical, signals and administrative detachments as well as a REME light aid detachment for vehicle maintenance. The latter were from 7th Air Landing Light Aid Detachment, and numbered about 25 men, including an officer. Also in this squadron were the Rota Trailers for resupply and the Parachute Harbour Party. HQ Squadron also seems to have been the home of two troops of Vickers medium machine guns (MMGs), each carried in a jeep, with each troop containing four weapons. A troop of two 3" mortars transported in universal carriers, plus the 'Assault' or 'Blitz' Troop of about twenty men mounted on motorcycles were also in the HQ Squadron, as the previous 'Support Squadron' seems to have disappeared.

The Light Tank Squadron had a squadron HQ of four Tetrarchs, of which two had the 3" howitzer. There were five troops each with three (possibly four) tanks armed with the 2pdr modified with the Littlejohn adapter. The Reconnaissance Squadron probably had a jeep and universal carrier in its HQ, as well as some motorcycles. The squadron itself had five troops, each of which had a jeep (usually used by the troop leader), a universal carrier and five or six men on motorcycles, with a troop strength of 11 men. Jeeps and trailers were provided for transport and intercommunication, particularly in the HQ Squadron, and there were also a number of additional motorcycles at various levels. Strength returns for the end of May 1944 indicate the total complement of men was 38 officers and 317 other ranks.

The all-cavalry makeup of 'C' Special Service Squadron was now heavily diluted by men from various RAC regiments and training depots. It should be remembered, though, that even if originally conscripted into the Army, all the men had volunteered for service in 6th AARR. The variety of skills and weapons contained within a single regiment was remarkable. There were tanks, medium mortars and medium machine guns as well as all the usual infantry weapons, and skills varied from those required for tank fighting to reconnaissance, from parachuting to fire support, and of course all the 'normal' infantry skills. Training was intense, and spit and polish generally took a back seat. A common theme in conversation with veterans of the unit is that the atmosphere was relaxed but professional. All wore the airborne red beret, but continued to retain their own regimental cap badges. One interesting element among the men of the regiment was the presence of a number (perhaps as much as 10% of the total) of German Jews, who had escaped to Britain before or during the war and were potentially in great danger if they were captured fighting the Germans. They had adopted English names, and one was reputed to be the son of a German General.[21] The welding together of men with such a diversity of regimental backgrounds and soldiering skills into an elite unit was a considerable achievement for the CO, who seems to have been universally respected as a hard, energetic but fair commander. He could also be something of a character, with a large moustache and wearing a pearl handled pistol, and prone to using a hunting horn in battle. Most of the new arrivals had been interviewed by him personally. One remembers to this day the CO's 'pale blue eyes and bristling moustache: he frightened us to death!'.[22]

In two of the anonymous brief histories written on the regiment, and also in Peter Harclerode's book *Go To It!*, it is indicated that the recce troops contained either two scout cars and a carrier, or two carriers and a scout car.[23] However, no scout cars were carried over on D-Day and the organisation given in the previous paragraph is based on statements from ex-members of the regiment who clearly state that scout cars were not part of the regiment at this time.[24] There are mentions in the war diary prior to D-Day of a 'light scout car troop', but no mentions of any scout cars on operations until the Ardennes campaign in December 1944. I have therefore assumed that the 'light scout cars' were jeeps. As we will see later when the loadings for D-Day are summarised, at least 48 motorcycles were flown over by the regiment on 6th June which tends to support the organisation I have given. It does not seem that scout cars joined the regiment until the unit had returned from Normandy and been significantly re-organised. The few scout cars inherited by the Airborne Light Tank Squadron from 'C' Special Service Squadron seem to have been disposed of fairly rapidly, possibly due to perceived problems with loading and unloading. Regarding this early period, Trooper Wilcox noted that 'having had doubts about only 10" ground clearance on a scout car, REME agreed we would be running a risk in very wet weather. So we left our scout car and went all tanks'.[25]

The final chance for the regiment to practice its operational role came in late April, when 6th Airborne Division held Exercise Mush, with the opposition provided by 1st Airborne Division and the Polish Parachute Brigade. The division moved to its exercise area by road. 6th AARR's involvement took place between 19th and 21st April. It started out from a deployment area near Cirencester called Oakley Wood and practised its roles of reconnaissance and delaying actions. On the 20th the war diary records that the regiment 'carried out successful delaying action throughout the day in area Bibury – Quenington – Ampney St.Peter'. On the 21st it would seem the unit had an even better day. According to the diary, 'recce patrols to contact hostile armour were sent out in areas Swindon and north of Cirencester. RHQ moved to area Down Ampney. By 1700 patrols had penetrated deeply in rear of enemy's positions, and disorganised a Div. HQ area'.

21 See John Banbery, IWM interview. These men are also mentioned in a letter from Ted George, an NCO in the regiment, held at the Tank Museum, 6th AARR file.
22 Brian Heape, conversation with author, June 2003.
23 *Go To It!*, p. 21.
24 Norman Stocker and Ted George
25 The Airborne Light Tank Squadron – 6th Airborne Armoured Reconnaissance Regiment.

Following Exercise Mush, the familiar round of normal training for 6th AARR continued during May, in the Larkhill area. Although the men did not know it, there would be no more exercises before D-Day.

It is time now to pause in order to see how 6th AARR fitted in with the organisation and the forthcoming tasks of 6th Airborne Division. Therefore the order of battle of 6th Airborne Division will now be summarised.[26]

The basic fighting force of a British airborne division was formed by its two parachute brigades and single airlanding brigade. The parachute brigades were formed of battalions from the Parachute Regiment. Broadly speaking, this meant newly raised formations of soldiers who had volunteered for parachute service. The earliest parachute battalions had been formed from volunteers culled from throughout the British Army, but the new battalions required for 6th Airborne were formed from selected line infantry battalions whose personnel were invited to volunteer for parachute service. Typically, around half the unit would volunteer and the battalion would be brought up to strength by volunteers from other units. The airlanding brigade was formed from normal infantry battalions who had been converted to the airborne role. The only soldiers allowed to drop out of this conversion would be those who failed during training for their new role. These battalions retained their previous identities. They would arrive on the battlefield not by parachute but by glider. The airlanding battalions were roughly as strong as a normal infantry battalion, but the parachute battalions were weaker, having only three rather than four companies which gave them a 'jumping strength' of about 550. Parachute battalions also had no anti-tank guns.

6th Airborne Division contained the 3rd and 5th Parachute Brigades and 6th Airlanding Brigade. 3rd Parachute Brigade consisted of 8th, 9th and 1st Canadian Parachute Battalions. 5th Parachute Brigade contained the 7th, 12th and 13th Parachute Battalions. 6th Airlanding Brigade contained 2nd Battalion The Oxfordshire and Buckinghamshire Light infantry (the 'Ox and Bucks'), 1st Battalion The Royal Ulster Rifles ('1st RUR') and 12th Battalion The Devonshire Regiment ('12th Devons').

The division's artillery regiment was the 53rd (Worcestershire Yeomanry) Airlanding Regiment, Royal Artillery, which had been converted from an anti-tank unit to join the new division. They were equipped with the 75mm pack howitzer, usually carried complete in Horsa gliders. Anti tank support was provided by the 3rd and 4th Airlanding Anti-Tank Batteries, Royal Artillery, mostly equipped with the 6pdr anti-tank gun but beginning to receive some of the powerful new 17pdr guns.. These batteries were normally attached one to each parachute brigade, whilst the airlanding brigade relied on the anti-tank guns contained within its infantry battalions. Anti-aircraft support came from the 2nd Airlanding Light Anti-Aircraft Battery, Royal Artillery, using 40mm Bofors guns. With the demise of the Luftwaffe during the late war period, this latter unit was converted to an anti-tank battery within the division in January 1945. Pathfinder duties were carried out by 22nd Independent Parachute Company.

---

26 The main source here is Peter Harclerode, *"Go To It!": The Illustrated History of the 6th Airborne Division* (London: Bloomsbury, 1990). See also Alan Wood, *Glider Soldiers*, pp.8-86.

A Hamilcar loaded with a Morris 30cwt truck and 17pdr is inspected by King George (centre) prior to D-Day. General Gale is on the right (IWM).

Also attached to the division were the usual, and vital, units of the Royal Signals, Royal Engineers, Royal Army Service Corps, Royal Army Medical Corps, Royal Army Ordnance Corps, Royal Electrical and Mechanical Engineers, Intelligence Corps and the Military Police. Many of the men in these units were parachute trained, most of the remainder were glider trained and, due to the nature of the division, all could expect to be in the front line when the division saw action.

And finally, the division contained the unique 6th Airborne Armoured Reconnaissance Regiment. As part of 'Divisional Troops', the regiment was an independent formation which was not part of any of the three brigades of the division. As it was glider-borne it was often associated with the Airlanding Brigade, or else it would come directly under command of General Gale as part of Divisional Headquarters. 6th Airborne Division was unique amongst all allied (not just British) airborne divisions in deploying operationally an armoured reconnaissance regiment. It was the home of those tanks destined to be the first and only such vehicles ever deployed by air directly into action by any country in World War Two.

Before moving on to the plan and final preparations for D-Day, we should once again digress slightly in order to put 6th AARR's operations in fuller perspective. In order to do this a brief outline of the formation of the Glider Pilot Regiment and the RAF tug units is necessary. 6th AARR would rely on the men and machines of these units to get them across the Channel and into action.

The first glider pilot unit was the Glider Training Squadron, which was formed in September 1940 during the early days of the Central Landing Establishment at Ringway. There was a mix of RAF and Army personnel in the squadron, all qualified pilots, and they relied at first on civilian one and two seat gliders as basic procedures were developed. The squadron was essentially a development unit; bringing into being a large force of operational glider pilots would be something rather different. The creation of totally new types of airborne unit required some hard negotiating between the Air Ministry and the War Office over who should provide the personnel, training, organisation and equipment of the new formations. The possible sources of manpower for the new glider pilots, along with procedures for their selection and training, was a particularly thorny problem. To cut a long story short, during August and September 1941 the Air Ministry and War Office finally agreed that glider pilots would be Army volunteers, trained by the RAF, and selected by combined Air Force/Army interview panels. They would conform to the mental and physical standards of RAF aircrews.[27] Following selection, glider pilots would attend a standard 12 week course at an RAF Elementary Flying Training School flying light aircraft (usually Tiger Moths), before moving to a Glider Training School to fly Hotspurs. They would then move on to an Operational Training Unit to learn to fly Horsas, with some Horsa pilots being subsequently selected for the Hamilcar. At the end of all this they would receive the Army Flying Badge, also worn by the Army's other group of pilots who flew with the Air Observation Post Squadrons of the Royal Artillery.

True to the traditions of the British Army, it was decided by the War Office that these new pilots deserved a parent regiment in order to realise fully their esprit

---

27 For the details regarding formation of the Glider Pilot Regiment, the main official source is Otway, *Airborne Forces*.

de corps. As a result it was decided to form the Army Air Corps, and within it the Glider Pilot Regiment, on 21st December 1941. Lt Col. John Rock, who we have already met, was given command of the 1st Battalion, Glider Pilot Regiment. A second Battalion was formed in August 1942. Lt.Col. Rock was tragically killed in an accident in October 1942. His original second-in command, Major G.J.S. Chatterton, assumed command of 1st Battalion, and eventually went on to command the entire Glider Pilot Regiment. Chatterton remained in command for the rest of the war. It was Chatterton who became identified with the concept of the 'Total Soldier', a pilot who could fight as an infantryman and handle any of the heavy weapons his glider could carry, as well as operating radios and driving trucks and jeeps. The introduction of two Company Sergeant Majors from the Brigade of Guards emphasised Chatterton's commitment to a high standard of military discipline. The skills and responsibilities of the other ranks of the regiment were such that all were eventually given the rank of sergeant (2nd pilot) or Staff Sergeant (1st pilot). The gliders used in combat were all designed for a crew of two, and the second pilot received reduced training in order to reduce the training load. His task was to fly the glider on tow or land it in an emergency. Normal take-offs and landings were the responsibility of the 1st Pilot. New badges were introduced to reflect the two levels of skill.

During October 1942 high level disagreements, involving the Chief of the Imperial General Staff, the Chief of the Air Staff, the Commander in Chief Bomber Command and Churchill himself resulted in a slow down in the growth of airborne forces which particularly affected the Glider Pilot Regiment. Airborne forces were expensive in resources, and the supply of sufficient tug aircraft and crews in particular was a direct drain on resources for Bomber Command. The disagreements were resolved broadly in favour of Bomber Command, and training of glider pilots slowed down dramatically due to lack of aircraft. This situation lasted until the spring of 1943 when, during April and May, it was considered necessary to provide increased resources to Airborne Forces if they were to achieve the level of availability for operations which had been planned for them. Training picked up again, but sadly the hiatus in training must be counted as one of the factors leading to the heavy losses suffered in the first large-scale glider operation during the invasion of Sicily. Total GPR casualties here were 13 officers and 88 other ranks.[28]

From this time expansion proceeded steadily. The Operational Training Units became known as Heavy Glider Conversion Units, and by September 1943 nearly 900 glider pilots had reached heavy glider standard. In November an important re-organisation took place designed to improve cooperation and understanding between glider pilots and their tug squadrons. There had been a plan that the two battalions of the GPR would be attached one each to the two existing airborne divisions, but Chatterton and the new CO of 38 Group, Air Vice Marshal Hollinghurst, had a different plan which eventually prevailed. The two battalions became No.1 and No.2 Wings, and the wings were made up of squadrons which in turn were made up of flights. The number of squadrons in a wing, and the number of flights in a squadron, was not strictly laid down. There was, however, an intended arrangement of a flight of twenty glider crews (of two men each) to an RAF squadron with twenty aircraft. No.1 Wing was attached to 38 Group, RAF (for

28 *Airborne Forces*, p.23.

which see below), and eventually No.2 Wing was attached to 46 Group when it formed. Glider pilots lived and worked at the same base as the RAF squadron to which they were attached, and this harmonisation in organisation and location produced better understanding of each other's problems. Brigadier Chatterton (as he had now become) was stationed at HQ 38 Group.

By 31st May 1944, 774 first pilots and 718 second pilots were available. The forthcoming large scale operations in North-West Europe were to prove what an outstanding unit had been created in the Glider Pilot Regiment, both in piloting skills and fighting qualities.

The story of the provision of tugs to tow the British glider force is one of a constant struggle with other parts of the RAF, and in particular with Bomber Command, for aircraft resources. Until the arrival of American Dakotas, the only aircraft with the performance for glider towing were bombers, which were so desperately needed as Britain's main way of hitting back at the Germans in Europe. The bombers that were eventually provided were characterised by being either obsolescent (like the Whitley and Stirling) or otherwise unsuitable for the bomber role (like the Albemarle). The Halifaxes used mainly to tow the Hamilcars of 6th AARR were the only completely first line bombers spared to the airborne forces. The C47 Dakota was of course purely a transport aircraft.

By the end of 1940 only six Armstrong Whitworth Whitleys were at the Central Landing Establishment, to participate in both para-dropping and glider towing trials and training. Also present were a number of light aircraft (mainly Tiger Moths and Avro 504Ns) to tow the light civilian gliders. The first Hotspur glider arrived in April 1941, and it was found that the out of date Hector army co-operation aircraft (a single engined biplane) could perform towing duties for this training glider. The RAF began to prepare itself to provide what resources it could for airborne forces, and the first two squadrons made available early in 1942 were 296 (Glider Exercise) Squadron (Whitleys, Hectors, Hotspurs and Horsas) and 297 (Parachute Exercise) Squadron (Whitleys). A significant step was taken on 15th January 1942 when Headquarters No.38 Wing was created to take charge of the two squadrons, commanded by Group Captain Sir Nigel Norman. The wing was formed as part of the already existing Army Cooperation Command.

This small force was already inadequate for the demands of the expanding airborne units, and pressure from Winston Churchill, who maintained a continuing interest in the airborne forces, was necessary to keep RAF development in this area in pace with that of the Army. Even obsolete bombers were required to train bomber crews at Operational Training Units. In addition the issue of whether a dedicated force of aircraft could be created for airborne operations or whether bomber squadrons might take this role on as a secondary task was still undecided. Nevertheless, 38 Wing gradually grew during 1942, with the 295 and 298 Squadrons forming by the end of the year. The latter included 10 Halifaxes. However, setbacks soon occurred. One was the discovery around August and September that the Whitley could not tow a fully loaded Horsa. Even worse were the high level disagreements about RAF resources for airborne operations which have already been described above in relation to the Glider Pilot Regiment. Air Chief Marshal Harris refused either to allow Bomber Command squadrons to be trained and used for airborne tasks, or to allow the creation of a dedicated transport force. This resulted in the halting of all additional aircraft and personnel resources to RAF airborne forces units until the situation had been resolved.

As has been described, it was the following spring that things began to pick up again. The decision to continue to increase the airborne force (in particular with the creation of 6th Airborne Division) was confirmed, although Air Ministry feathers were smoothed by some recalculations which reduced the requirements for aircraft, gliders and crews for the two airborne divisions. In addition, the Armstrong Whitworth Albemarle had been selected to replace the Whitley (see chapter two). There were also hopes that deliveries of Dakotas from America, also capable of towing Horsas on operations, would further ease the aircraft shortage. 296 Squadron, re-equipped with Albemarles, was sent to the Middle East with 1st Airborne Division in May for the Sicily operation, along with a flight of 295 Squadron equipped with Halifaxes. This further stretched the resources of the wing which was at this time under-equipped and under-resourced for all the tasks it had to undertake. On 15th May, the wing was instructed to cease its leaflet dropping operations over France in order to concentrate on airborne tasks, an order resented as it removed the only opportunity for crews to gain experience on 'live' operations.

However, expansion and re-equipment began to take off during the rest of the year. During October and November the wing was authorised to expand into a group, to be commanded by Air Vice-Marshal L.N. Hollinghurst. The strength was authorised as four Albemarle squadrons, four Stirling squadrons, and one squadron of Halifaxes.. Each squadron would have 16 operational aircraft plus four reserves, giving a total of 180 aircraft. An additional squadron of Halifaxes was later added to this total and aircraft strengths per squadron were increased as plans for Operation Overlord matured. By March 1944 the group was based at five airfields: Brize Norton, Harwell, Keevil, Fairford and Tarrant Rushton, with group HQ at Netheravon. Tarrant Rushton was the base for the two squadrons in which we have a particular interest, 298 and 644 Squadrons, each with 18 Halifaxes plus two in reserve ('18+2' as it was usually written). 298 had formed at RAF Thruxton on 24th August 1942 on Whitleys, but had disbanded on 19th October that year as a result of the development hiatus noted above. It reformed on Halifaxes at Tarrant Rushton on 4th November 1943 from 'A' Flight of 295 Squadron. On D-Day it provided three aircraft to tow gliders for Operation Deadstick, the *coup de main* assault on the Orne and Caen Canal bridges. Fifteen Horsas and two Hamilcars were towed in for Operation Tonga (see chapter five), and one Horsa and fifteen Hamilcars for Operation Mallard. 644 Squadron formed at Tarrant Rushton on 23rd February 1944, from a cadre supplied by 298 Squadron. Its operations on D-Day mirrored those of its brother squadron: three Horsas for Deadstick, eighteen Horsas and two Hamilcars for Tonga, and one Horsa and fifteen Hamilcars for Mallard.

To provide the amount of aircraft needed for Overlord, a second British transport group was officially formed on 17th January 1944. It consisted (by March) of five squadrons of Dakotas, each with the large number of thirty aircraft. The group was technically part of Transport Command, and was to undertake normal transport duties when not required for airborne operations. However, under the latter conditions it would come under the control of HQ 38 Group. It was policy that the squadrons of both groups should be capable of both para-dropping and glider towing, although in the lead up to an operation squadrons would concentrate on training for the speciality appropriate to their assigned role. It was also policy that British transport resources should be capable of supporting American airborne formations and vice-versa, but of course they tended to be assigned to units of their own nationality in practice.

With the demise of Army Cooperation Command in June 1943 (the ground attack resources becoming Tactical Air Forces under Fighter Command), 38 Group came under HQ, Allied Expeditionary Air Force. The group was obviously kept busy during the first part of 1944 supporting the various exercises taking place as well as conducting its own training. In the final big exercise before D-Day, (exercise Mush) around 700 British and American aircraft took part. Nevertheless, the group also resumed live operations by dropping special agents and supplies into enemy territory on the continent. These flights were often routed over the areas of Normandy the squadrons were due to visit on D-Day. We have already noted that the gliders were officially owned by the RAF, and the gliders required were steadily allocated to the two transport groups as D-Day approached. Alan Wood notes that by 6th June, 38 Group had 264 aircraft (Albemarles, Stirlings and Halifaxes), 150 Horsas and 70 Hamilcars ready for operations, whilst 46 Group had 150 Dakotas and 200 Horsas.[29]

On 24th May 1944, 'A' Squadron 6th AARR and the universal carriers from 'B' and HQ Squadrons moved by road for their transit camp at Tarrant Rushton aerodrome. On the 25th, the rest of the Regiment left for its transit camp at Brize Norton aerodrome. RHQ was set up at Tarrant Rushton on 29th May. It was from these two airfields that the regiment was to fly to Normandy, and it was here that the men of the regiment were briefed on their tasks for D-Day, the invasion of Europe.

29 *The Glider Soldiers*, pp.112-113.

Chapter 5

D-Day

In describing and attempting to analyse the actions of 6th AARR on D-Day and during the Normandy campaign, the only aspect of the vast D-Day plan that need concern us is the role of the 6th Airborne Division.

The D-Day operation would be 6th Airborne Division's first battle. The purpose of the division on D-Day was to protect the left flank of the Allied landings by seizing specific objectives at the eastern end of the landing area on the night of 5th-6th June, and, during D-Day itself, consolidating its hold on the ground it had taken. This role was officially described as follows:

> 6th Airborne Division with 1st Special Service Brigade (less one commando) under command, will protect the left flank of 1st Corps by denying to the enemy the use of the area between rivers Orne and Dives north of the road Troarn – Sannerville – Colomnelles. 6th Airborne will also attack and delay enemy reserves and reinforcements attempting to move towards Caen from the east and south-east. [1]

Some of the specific tasks accomplished within this overall role have since become near legendary, such as the capture of the Orne bridge by a brilliant glider coup de main, and the attack, in the face of considerable odds, against the Merville gun battery which threatened the invasion beaches. These occurred during the early hours of 6th June. However, 6th AARR's part in the divisional plan would not commence until the evening of D-Day.

Major-General Gale's plan to fulfil his operational task had been shaped by the knowledge that sufficient resources did not exist to land the whole of 6th Airborne in one lift. Only two brigades could be carried in the first wave, and the third would have to be carried in by a second lift later in the day. Originally, Gale had intended to use his Airlanding Brigade as one of the two initial landing brigades, in order to exploit the concentration of forces which glider landings should provide. However, on 17th April 1944 aerial photographs first revealed the existence of anti-glider poles which were being erected by the Germans on potential landing sites. This persuaded him that 3rd and 5th Parachute Brigades should lead the assault, and that the Airlanding Brigade should wait until the paratroopers had been able to secure and clear the landing zones. Whilst this change affected many of the glider and tug units, it did not affect 6th AARR, who had always been intended for the evening lift.

It was not intended that 6th AARR would operate alone. General Gale's plan for 6th Airborne Division included the formation of what he originally called the Armoured Recce Group, which subsequently became 'Parkerforce' after its commander, Colonel R.G. 'Reggie' Parker. As a Lt.Col., Parker had originally led the

---

1 PRO file WO106/4315, Operation Neptune; deployment of 6th Airborne Division.

12th Parachute Battalion, but by the time of D-Day he was deputy commander of 6th Airlanding Brigade. Parkerforce was to consist of the following units:

6th AARR
'A' Company, 12th Battalion, The Devonshire Regiment ('12th Devons')
211th Light Battery, RA (8 x 75mm pack howitzers)
Troop, 3rd Anti-Tank Battery, RA (4 x 6pdr anti-tank guns)
Detachment, RE
Detachment, RAMC

According to Gale's instructions to Colonel Parker on the use of the force, the infantry were to be to carried in jeeps to create a fully mobile group. 'Instruction No.1' to 6th Airborne Division, a set of orders for the forthcoming operation dated 17th May, says that 'if practicable, 20 jeeps will be made available by 0300 hrs D+1 for transport. These jeeps will be retained during attachment of Coy 12 Devon to Armrd Recce Group'.[2] Gale's instructions to Colonel Parker are worth quoting in full. The surviving document in the Public Record Office is undated but was evidently written before the force was named after its commander.

Instructions issued to Commander Armoured Recce Group

It is my intention to constitute a Force which will be known as Armd Recce Group. You will command this force.

The task of the Armd Recce Group will be to form a small firm base outside the 6 Airborne Div area from which it will

(a) carry out deep recce

(b) impede and delay any enemy movement from the east and SE on CAEN.

[force composition as above]

This force must be prepared to operate without support from the Division. It will not be withdrawn at night.

You will bear in mind that your task cannot be carried out if your force is liquidated. Whilst you must be prepared to fight to achieve your object, you will avoid static battle in circumstances which in your opinion will result in the annihilation of your force.

The force will land by glider in the late afternoon of D-Day. In order that you should be in the picture when your force arrives you will accompany me on the night of D-1/D day.

(sgd) RN Gale, Major General.[3]

Another surviving document adds:

By 0300 hrs D+1 they were to be prepared to carry out a deep reconnaissance towards CAEN in an entirely independent role. They were to send back information and attempt to delay any enemy reserves approaching from the SE and South.[4]

---

2 Copy held at Museum of Army Flying, File 29/E/01A.
3 PRO file CAB106/970, Appendix G
4 PRO file WO106/4315

It was further noted that the use of the force in its intended role would take place only 'if the tactical situation would permit'.[5] The force was to concentrate initially in a harbour area to the north east of Le Mariquet. Expanding slightly on these orders in his book With The 6th Airborne Division In Normandy, Gale makes it clear that Col. Parker was to 'form a firm base in one of the villages of the Escoville type south of the bridgehead near the Troarn-Caen road from where he would sally out'.[6] That these were ambitious instructions is indicated by reference to the parallel orders of 'A' Coy of the Devons. These give the location for the firm base as Cagny, a village which was not eventually wrested from the Germans until 19th July, during the massive 'Goodwood' offensive. The Devon's orders also clarify that the basic idea was for the infantry and artillery to form a firm base from which 6th AARR would 'sally out' on its recce tasks.[7] There is evidence that Colonel Parker had problems coordinating his force prior to departure due to lack of an headquarters staff (including no adjutant or quartermaster) and also the widely separated locations at which his units were based in the run up to D-Day. According to the war diary of 12th Devons, 'it was difficult to find out anything'.[8] These problems are confirmed by Napier Crookenden in his book, Drop Zone Normandy.[9]

As this was the only time any nation in the entire war landed a significant number of tanks from the air (the numbers involved in the Rhine crossing were much reduced) it is worth trying to assess Gale's plan. We can see that Gale intended to use 6th AARR in an important role helping to achieve one of his main objectives, detecting and preventing the arrival of German reserves. Caveats regarding taking excessive casualties and a favourable tactical situation obviously recognised the limited fighting powers of this light force, but nevertheless Gale had decided to use his airborne armour as part of a mobile battlegroup, and to set it an aggressive and independent role. There seems to be a strong link here to the role envisaged for the original Airborne Light Tank Squadron when it was first formed.

At first sight the idea of inserting such a light mobile force deep into enemy territory under the intense combat conditions of Normandy appears rather harebrained. It seems most unlikely the force would be able to leave the airborne perimeter and penetrate enemy lines, and even if it did its limited fighting capabilities would make it extremely unlikely that any base for operations could be secured for a significant period of time. The force would surely be either destroyed or forced to retreat before achieving anything. Countering these arguments is made difficult by the lack of any definite information on the thinking behind the plan for Parkerforce. However, Parkerforce can be made to seem a bit more logical if put into the perspective of similar recce plans for other units, and if some reasonable assumptions about Gale's attitude to the deployment of the force are made.

Briefing his generals for D-Day on 7th April 1944, Montgomery chose at one stage to emphasise three main points. The second of these was 'the need for boldness and enterprise in pushing forward mobile forces; even a few armoured cars 20

---

5   Ibid.
6   Gale, p.91.
7   PRO file WO223/27, 12th Devons, Diary of events 6th June-26th August 1944'.
8   PRO file WO171/1279, 12th Devons, War Diary, 1944
9   *Drop Zone Normandy*, p.228.

miles inside the German lines would create confusion and delay'.[10] There was no knowing what conditions might apply in the period immediately following the landings, and advantage was to be taken to exploit potential gaps in the enemy's front. An example of plans made with this in mind was the mission of 'C' Squadron, the Inns of Court Regiment, who landed with the first wave on Juno beach. This recce squadron was to penetrate any gaps they could find in the German defences and seize and demolish as many as they could of 13 bridges, some as much as 30 miles from the beaches. They were then to hide up and radio back what information they could until relieved by advancing British forces. Some elements managed to penetrate as far as 5 miles south of Caen, but the mission was too difficult under the prevailing conditions and the survivors were withdrawn on D+4.[11] This mission provides an interesting comparison to the Parkerforce plan, and would appear to show that it was not an isolated idea, but part of an overall concept for bold reconnaissance efforts in the period immediately following the landings. If we also take into account the caveat that Parkerforce would deploy only if the situation permitted, then Gale's plan takes on a reasonable perspective. We cannot know just how likely he thought deployment of the force would be, but as we shall see he had the sense to realise that deployment in the conditions that actually prevailed was inadvisable. He cancelled the operation before the constituent units even had the time to assemble. The factors behind his decision will be examined later in the chapter once we have described the events of the initial landings.

It is worth summarising the opposition that 6th Airborne Division and 6th AARR were expecting to meet. 6th Airborne's dropping and landing zones were on the eastern flank of the German 716th Division, which was a 'static' defence division manning the section of the Atlantic Wall which contained all three of the British/Canadian beaches. The 716th was classed (correctly) by Allied intelligence as a 'low category' division, with no motorised transport and very little counter attack capability. It contained mostly men who were under 18, over 35 or else for some reason unfit for a front line infantry division. In addition, two of the division's battalions were 'Ost' battalions of 'volunteer' Russians, with a very low fighting value indeed. Compared to a first class infantry division, intelligence rated the potential of the 716th as 40% in defence and just 15% in attack. Just east of 6th Airborne's landing area (the boundary was the River Dives) was the sector of 711th Division, which was rated very similarly to the 716th. The boundary between the two divisions was also the boundary between two different armies, 7th Army to the west and 15th Army to the east, which would help cause command problems for the Germans. Interestingly, both German divisions were thought to have a 'squadron' of obsolete French tanks (perhaps 10 vehicles each) which were used in the counter partisan role. Those of the 711th Division had been reported by the resistance as Renault R35s.[12]

Much more worrying than these two divisions was the presence of 21st Panzer Division, and the potential presence of 12th SS Panzer Division. These were the main counter attack forces likely to be encountered. 21st Panzer Division was de-

---

10 Hamilton, p.233.
11 Knowles, 'With Armoured Cars to France!' in *The Journal (magazine of the Society of Twentieth Century Wargamers)* no.34, p.2.
12 These details appear in PRO file CAB 106/970.

ployed inland of 716th Division but some of the more northern units were billeted within 6th Airborne's area; for example the 2nd Battalion, 125th Panzer Grenadier Regiment were in Ranville. The division as a whole had been reformed in France following the surrender of the original 21st Panzer in Tunisia in 1943. It was a powerful tank unit which contained, by D-Day, around 16,000 men and perhaps 90 of the latest version of the Mk IV tank, the MkIVH. However, equipment shortages had been such that the second battalion of the division's panzer regiment still contained two companies (each 18 strong) of old French Somua S35 tanks which had been captured in 1940 and had been used for training, as well a company of older models of the MkIV (B or C) with short barrelled 75mm guns and thinner armour. The other company of the battalion had even less effective Hotchkiss tanks, also antiques captured from the French.[13]

The division also contained, in its Assault Gun Battalion 200, more unusual armoured vehicles in the form of converted Hotchkiss H35, H38 and H39 tanks and Lorraine Schlepper armoured tractors. The chassis from these vehicles had been converted into self-propelled artillery (with 10.5cm howitzers) and panzerjagers (with 7.5cm PAK40 anti-tank guns). It is not clear exactly how the conversions were distributed between the assault gun battalion and the divisional artillery regiment but Robert Kershaw states that the two units together fielded 44 Hotchkiss conversions and 45 Loraines.[14] Along with the vehicles mentioned above as allocated to the local static divisions, it would seem that the Tetrarchs of 6th AARR might have the opportunity to encounter armoured vehicles of a similar vintage to themselves, which they might conceivably challenge on almost equal terms. As it turned out, it seems that a few of the old French tanks were encountered by some of the parachute units on D-Day (notably at the west end of the Orne bridges at Benouville by 7th Parachute Battalion) and, as we shall see, it is possible that at least one of the converted SP guns was engaged by a Tetrarch. However, whilst the prospect of Tetrarchs taking on, say, Somua S35s in open battle may seem an engaging one for present day tank buffs, such a prospect never materialised.

21st Panzer was billeted over quite a wide area, with some elements as far south as Falaise, and so would take a little time to collect together for a concerted counter stroke. However, to make such a counter stroke was its allocated role and the time would be measured only in hours. The unit was a direct and powerful threat which would be on 6th Airborne's doorstep almost as soon as they landed. Further away was the second counter attack unit in which General Gale was interested, the 12th SS Panzer Division 'Hitler Jugend'. This unit was billeted over a wide area of Normandy, with some units as far east as the Seine, and others as far west as Vimoutiers. They had been moved south away from the coast and their original assembly area around Lisieux just before D-Day. The division was formed from members of the Hitler Youth and the Normandy campaign would be its first action, in which it would gain a reputation as a very hard-fighting unit. 12th SS was a full strength panzer division and the second closest tank division to the British and Canadian landings. The British estimated at the time that it could be in position

---

13 See intelligence summary for 19-20th June 1944 in PRO file WO171/425, 6th Airborne Division War Diary, 1944.
14 Kershaw, p.28.

south east of Caen as soon as 12 hours after the initial landings if the Germans reacted quickly. The threat it represented explains the need to locate it as early as possible when it moved to counter attack, which was part of the role of 6th AARR. As Napier Crookenden has said, Gale had to face the fact that the Hitler Jugend 'might well have the task of smashing through the 6th Airborne Division into the left flank of the Second British Army'.[15] Besides the anti-tank guns of his division, Gale's main defence against a heavy armoured counter-attack would be air support and the supporting guns of the Royal Navy and 1st Corps, which if needed would be plentiful. In the end, the Germans decided to make their main tank thrust to the west and north of Caen so that 6th Airborne did not have the misfortune to encounter this thrust. The Hitler Jugend would not be one of their opponents in Normandy, and they would encounter only parts of 21st Panzer.

As the above shows, and as General Gale made clear in the book he wrote after the war, he was perfectly aware that 'the counter attack supported by tanks we must expect from the beginning. From this it became obvious that my original fly-in must include as high a proportion of anti-tank guns as I dared include'.[16] With this in mind, it is particularly interesting that he gave over the lion's share of his heavy load-carrying gliders to transporting Tetrarchs rather than 17 pdr anti-tank guns and their tractors.

The first members of 6th AARR to see action would be the men of the Parachute Harbour Party. These men were among the first parachutists of the division to land, being carried in the same wave as 22nd Independent Pathfinder Company whose job it was to mark the landing and dropping zones. 6th AARR's parachutists were to find, reconnoitre and secure the harbour area for their regiment, which would be the unit's first rendezvous after landing. It would appear that from the sixteen men of this party, two groups of five had been selected for the D-Day operation. Lt. Belcher and four others flew in a Stirling of 620 Squadron from Fairford which took off around 2340 on 5th June. They shared the aircraft with pathfinders from 7th Parachute Battalion. Details of their flight emerged after the war in an article in *Pegasus* magazine, written by an officer on an accompanying aircraft.[17] It would seem that, distracted by flak and low cloud, their Stirling (like a number of others that night) mistook the Dives estuary for that of the Orne and so ended up well to the east of their intended landfall. The aircraft was hit by flak and crashed, killing all the six crew and nineteen parachutists inside. The other stick was under the command of Sgt. Dillaway. We lack the precise detail provided for their comrades, but they must be presumed to have travelled from Fairford in another Stirling. Sgt. Dillaway's group landed shortly after midnight on 6th June and successfully completed their task, meeting the main force of 6th AARR at the harbour location on the evening of D-Day.[18]

The main airlift and landing of the two parachute brigades and their various supporting elements in the early hours of D-Day was called Operation Tonga. The follow-up assault by 6th Airlanding Brigade on the evening of D-Day was desig-

15 *Drop Zone Normandy*, p.164.
16 *With The 6th Airborne*, p.41.
17 Shiner, 'The Grangues Memorial', in *Pegasus Journal*, December 1997
18 See *Go To It!*, p.76, and Eyre, The 6th Airborne Armoured Reconnaissance Regiment (RAC).

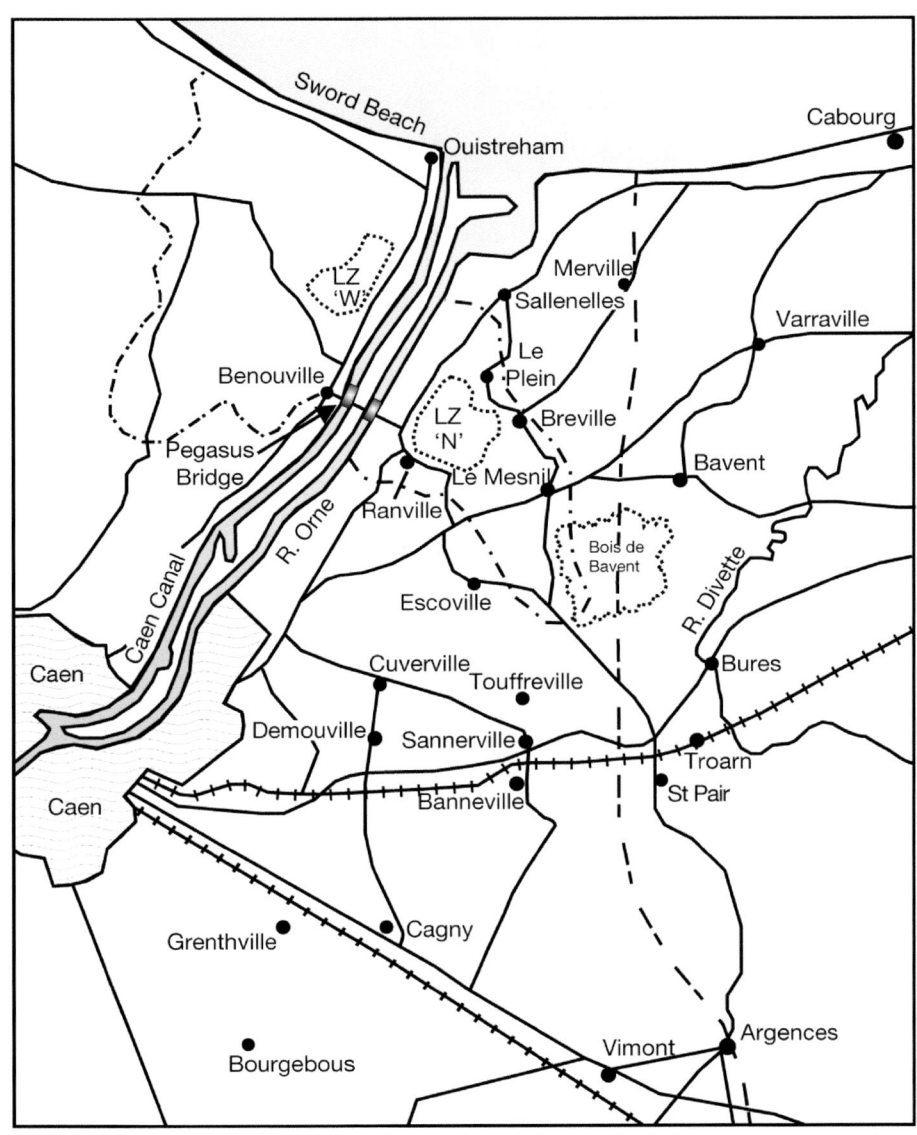

D-Day and Normandy, 6th June to 17th August.

nated Operation Mallard. Tonga included the use of a number of gliders, including some Hamilcars, and in order to give a complete account of the operational use of this latter aircraft its part in Tonga should be described before we move on to Mallard and the landing of 6th AARR.

Ninety eight gliders were used in Operation Tonga. A total of seventeen Horsas were used in the assaults on the Orne and Dives bridges and the attack on the Merville Battery, the first of these taking off before midnight and landing in the first hour of D-Day. A further twenty three Horsas were scheduled to land very early on D-Day (between 0045 and 0103) bringing in HQ troops and heavy weapons for the two parachute brigades. Seventy five gliders, including four Hamilcars, landed a few hours later (between 0300 and 0430) to bring in further HQ, heavy weapon, medical and engineer units to support the parachute landings. This was the first operational deployment of Hamilcars, and they were used not to bring in armoured vehicles but four 17pdr anti-tank guns and their Morris 30cwt prime movers, belonging to the 17pdr troop of 3rd Airlanding Anti-tank Battery. Besides the two pilots, in each glider there was a crew of eight for the gun and its vehicle. The Hamilcars would come in on landing zone 'N', an area just to the east of the Orne and Dives bridges, using strips cleared by the paratroopers. These gliders came from Tarrant Rushton, which as we have seen was the base for all Hamilcar operations. Two were towed by crews of 644 squadron and two by 298 Squadron, using their Halifax V tugs.[19] They took off around 0210 and were due to land around 0330. Release height was planned as 1500 feet. However, only two of the Hamilcars made successful landings and delivered their cargoes. These were the two towed by 644 Squadron, and they landed pretty much on time. Sergeant R. 'Jock' Taylor was second pilot in Hamilcar 'Tom's Gen Tub", named after its first pilot, Lieutenant Tommy Taylorson. After encountering flak in the coastal area (like all the gliders that night) they found their landing zone, and saw it was obstructed by anti-glider poles. However, the poles turned out to be about ten feet in height and passed under the Hamilcar's wing, with its seventeen foot ground clearance. They landed safely. Sergeant Taylor's account of the unloading is instructive:

> After we rolled to a stop we got out, opened the nose door and released the the valves on the landing legs, allowing the Hamilcar to settle on the skids. When the load was released the tractor pulled the gun and ammunition down the the ramps. We looked around to see if any of the other Hamilcars were near, but found only one. This glider had suffered severe damage to the undercarriage, making it impossible for the gun crew to get their equipment through the nose door. Therefore, instead of us going with our own gun, Lieutenant Taylorson and I assisted Staff Sergeant England and Sergeant Hill to cut through their fuselage at the tail end. This proved a considerable task, but with the help of other men, we managed to tow the load through the tail section as daylight was breaking.[20]

Note that it was not possible to let down the undercarriage from within the cockpit, and that the pilots had to open the nose door themselves and then deploy ramps to allow out a wheeled combination.

The first Hamilcar casualty en-route had been due to a broken tow rope over Bognor Regis, and by a combination of luck and judgment the glider landed at the Royal Naval airfield at Ford. The other Hamilcar towed by 298 Squadron had the unusual experience of a parachute hitting the starboard wing of the glider whilst it was still 8 miles off the coast, though no damage was caused. The tow rope then

19 See *The Glider Soldiers*, pp.232-280, for an overall account of Tonga and Mallard.
20 Quoted in Shannon & Wright, *One Night In June*, p121.

Tarrant Rushton with gliders and tugs ready for Operation Mallard, 6th June 1944. The aircraft are lined up on the threshold of runway 01, the longest of the runways at 6000' (IWM).

parted two minutes after they had crossed the coast, but too far from the landing zone for the Hamilcar to reach it. It came down in an orchard near St. Vaast-en-Auge, where at dawn it was attacked by the Germans. Four of the crew were killed and the rest seem to have scattered, at least one eventually being captured.[21]

The crews of the two Hamilcars on landing zone N were not the only men having to desperately hack at fuselages during the night. Damage incurred during landing often made the extraction of loads a problem, from both Hamilcars and Horsas. On the subject of Horsas, it is interesting to note that three of these gliders carried tracked, although unarmoured, vehicles in the shape of three Royal Engineers bulldozers which were to be used to help clear the landing zones for Mallard. These Clark Crawler Tractors had been obtained from the Americans only a month or two before the invasion, and were small enough to fit in a Horsa without dismantling. One of the Horsas went down in the channel. Of the other two, one definitely delivered its load safely, but there is disagreement over the fate of the other whose glider appears to have had a rough landing.[22]

Operation Mallard was to be the largest of the glider landings on D-Day. 256 tug and glider combinations got airborne from seven airfields in England between 1840 and 1935 hours on the evening of D-Day. For this account we will concentrate on the actions of the gliders and troops involved with 6th AARR, which in-

21 *One Night In June*, pp.120-123.
22 See *One Night In June*, pp.103-106, and Lowman, 'The 6th Airborne Divisional Engineers on D-Day 1944' *The Royal Engineers Journal*, June 1982, pp84-85.

cludes all of the thirty Hamilcars dispatched for Mallard. The objective for this operation was primarily that of reinforcement, although as we have seen 6th AARR had a specific task of their own. The gliders involved in Mallard would have the advantage of landing in daylight at the end of the long June day, although twilight would be beginning. They would also have the advantage of much better prepared landing zones. In the confusion of the early hours of D-Day, many lights and navigation beacons intended to mark landing zones had been put in the wrong place or not laid at all, a problem compounded by the short time allowed to complete some of these marking tasks. With several hours of daylight to sort things out, as well as to clear obstructions, the Mallard armada would find it easier to land safely.

Sufficient gliders had been allocated to carry just about all of 6th AARR, if we assume the tank troops had three rather than four tanks each. Exact loadings of the assigned gliders are not now easy to establish but the Hamilcars from Tarrant Rushton were to carry 'A' Squadron, Regimental HQ and the tracked vehicles of 'B' Squadron. Thirty Hamilcars flew in to Normandy for Operation Mallard, but it is worth noting that there are some sources which disagree. A surviving copy of the operation order for 6th Airborne indicates that four 17pdr guns and tractors were allocated to fly from Tarrant Rushton, with the strong implication that four of the 30 Hamilcars would be needed to lift them.[23] These guns are indicated as being destined to support the Ox and Bucks and 1st RUR. A figure of 26 Hamilcars allocated to 6th AARR is also mentioned in some other original documents.[24] Michael Bowyer's magazine article already mentioned gives the loads for only 28 gliders.[25] The confusion seems to be conclusively cleared up by reference to the Glider Raid Reports of 298 and 644 Squadrons.[26] These give the loads of the gliders towed into action on 6th June and they confirm 30 Hamilcars, all the loads generally agreeing with Bowyer's list except for two extra Hamilcars with tanks. It would seem, in fact, that the four 17pdrs were originally to fly in with 6th AARR (though not as part of Parkerforce) making a total of 34 Hamilcars initially allocated to Mallard. In the end it seems General Gale decided it would be better to have these guns available earlier, and they were flown in as part of Tonga. (Confusingly, it was the 6pdrs of 4th Battery and the 17pdrs of 3rd Battery that went by air). Loads, therefore, were as follows.

Twenty Hamilcars carried Tetrarchs, though how many of these had 2pdr guns, and how many had the 3" close support howitzer is not specified. Bowyer gives fifteen 2pdr tanks and three 'CS' tanks, so it would seem there were from three to five vehicles with the howitzer. Although the exact organisation of the tanks is not given for this period, it would be reasonable to assume five troops of three tanks each, with three in squadron HQ, leaving two more in regimental HQ. The only troops on board these gliders were the three crew members. Four further gliders carried three Rota trailers each, with no troops. Three more had two universal carriers each, one carrying 8 men as well and the others two men. The final three

---

23 See the 'Air Movement' appendix dated 20th May 1944 to 'Operational No.1, 6th Airborne Division'. Copy held at Museum of Army Flying, File 29/E/01A. This has been used as the basic source for allocation of gliders to units of 'Parkerforce'.
24 For example, PRO file CAB106/970.
25 See Bowyer, 'Hamilcars in Action', *Airfix Magazine*, May 1977, p.534
26 I am indebted to Mr David Hall (ex-GPR) for drawing my attention to this source.

Hamilcars had mixed loads. Two had a 3" mortar carrier and 8 motorcycles, along with 13 men, whilst the third carried a slave battery carrier and a jeep, along with 6 men. Of the thirty Hamilcars, fifteen would be towed by Halifax Vs of 298 Squadron, and fifteen by similar aircraft from 644 Squadron. Many of the crews had already taken part in Tonga, towing the Hamilcars and also Horsa gliders. The glider pilots for the Hamilcars came from 'C' Squadron, No.2 Wing, Glider Pilot Regiment. The Hamilcars were allocated to landing zone 'N', as the Tonga Hamilcars had been.

In addition, the regiment was allocated a number of Horsas which took off from Brize Norton, and these were assigned to carry 'B' Squadron minus its tracked vehicles, and the Headquarters Squadron. These gliders were also allocated to LZ 'N'. Besides personnel, the loads consisted of jeeps, trailers and motorcycles for the headquarters and supply elements, the recce troops, and for the two MMG troops.[27] The exact number of gliders is uncertain. It would seem possible that nineteen or possibly twenty were allocated, but the Glider Raid Reports of the two squadrons only identify seventeen for certain, fourteen towed by Albemarles of 296 Squadron and three by Albemarles of 297 squadron. These records give a total lift of seventeen jeeps, forty eight motorcycles and 145 men, plus a number of trailers and supply panniers. There may well have been an additional two or three glider loads over and above this confirmed list. Glider pilots were from 'B' Squadron, No.1 Wing, Glider Pilot Regiment.

We should also mention the arrangements for the other units of Parkerforce. 'A' Company of the Devons (CO Major J Rogers) were allocated eight Horsas from Fairford.[28] Four would each carry a jeep, two trailers and six men of company HQ, and the other four would each have 28 men on board. These gliders were destined for LZ 'W', west of the Orne. The rest of this battalion would cross by sea on 7th June due to lack of aircraft. Twenty seven Horsas also from Fairford would carry 211th Airlanding Light Battery. These airlanding artillery units were always expensive in the number of gliders needed to carry them, due to the requirements for towing vehicles, ammunition supplies and the vehicles and trailers to move those supplies. These gliders from Fairford would be towed by Stirling IVs of 190 and 620 Squadrons, with glider pilots from 'C' and 'G' Squadrons of the Glider Pilot Regiment, and would also land on LZ 'W'. The twenty jeeps which would lift 'A' Company may have come in Horsas from Fairford, or from those Horsas allocated to 716th Company, RASC, which departed from Brize Norton. The troop of 6pdr anti-tank guns from 3rd Airlanding Anti-Tank Battery went by sea (along with the other 6pdr troops of this unit) and landed at Lion-sur-Mer at 1300 on D-Day, in time to reach their assembly area within the airborne perimeter in the early hours of the 7th. Colonel Parker flew in as part of Operation Tonga. He had de-

---

27 Details from PRO files AIR 27/1647, Air27/2574 (glider raid reports for 296 and 297 Squadrons) and Appendix B of Instruction No1 to 6th Airborne Division Museum of Army Flying box 442.

28 Most sources give Brize as the departure airfield. However, the Glider Raid Reports of 296 and 297 Squadrons have no loads corresponding to 'A' Coy. At Fairford, the GRRs indicate 620 Squadron as the most likely tug unit for the Coy. Operational Instruction No.1 for 6th Airborne Division (dated 17th May 1944) gives Fairford as the departure aerodrome for 12th Devons.

parted from Harwell at 0128 on 6th June in a Horsa towed by an Albemarle of either 295 or 570 Squadron, along with an officer from 6th AARR. They shared the glider with 6th Airlanding Brigade's advance party. This party was flying in company with HQ, 6th Airborne Division, as Gale had promised in his orders to the Armoured Recce Group.

Something of the atmosphere prevailing during the last hours before departure can be found in the following memories of a member of the regiment, Cpl. Sheffield:

> At last came the big day, when we moved to a camp just outside Tarrant Rushton airfield. We were now confined to camp and learnt of all the plans of where we were landing, which was Ranville in Normandy.
>
> On the evening of June 5th (2300 hrs) the Ox & Bucks took off over the top of us, to take the bridges over the River Orne. It was a beautiful June evening. Our officers were playing football by their tent, and the word went round the ORs lets pile in, we did and the CO came out to see what was going on. He fetched a hunting horn which he used to carry, gave a few calls and shouted at us, "get in lads, give them some stick". I believe it settled us down for the next day.[29]

Corporal A. Darlington was also departing from Tarrant Rushton. His memories give (amongst other things) some insight as to how the 'inner man' was to be catered for during the initial phase of operations:

> Before D-Day we were all penned in near Tarrant Rushton. The gliders were herring boned in formation along the runway which we believed to be the longest in Britain at that time. Our loading was completed, whilst our tow planes, souped up Halifaxes, came later.
>
> Two Tetrarchs were in the hangars both having something wrong with them. An officer asked me whether I could get one good one out of the pair. Cpl Elsey and myself, along with a couple of RAF fitters, decided that changing the good engine to the good rest of the tank would make one good one fit for action. We worked through the night and loaded it into its empty glider, and we reported all was well to the highly pleased officer who gave us permission for a late Reveille. D-Day had been postponed because of heavy gales.
>
> We were of course being briefed with aerial photographs and special lenses on stands that gave us a 3D image of our landing zones. There were, of course, posts erected in some areas to prevent such an airborne landing.
>
> We arrived at the airfield in the morning and were given a meal by the Airforce WAAFs. We even had sugar in bowls and the best meal we'd had in years. WAAFs even refilled our water bottles for us, and gave us what turned out to be a useless object called soap! This we termed the "Last Supper" and for many of us it was. We had been issued with a 48 hour emergency ration, which looked more like a child's compendium of games when opened. Creamy coloured dominoes turned out to be porridge with milk and sugar if reconstituted, the dice were tea, milk and sugar cubes. Chocolate was so hard it could only be knawed with the front teeth, and there were boiled sweets and a couple of 'pink pills' to keep us awake if necessary. Two pieces of tin plate could be slotted together to become a cooker with solidified methylated spirits, and another use-

---

29 From The Airborne Light Tank Squadron – Sixth Airborne Armoured Reconnaissance Regiment.

Fine shot of Halifax/Hamilcar combination in the air near Tarrant Rushton. Identification stripes were only applied immediately prior to operations, so the aircraft are probably bound for Normandy (Museum of Army Flying).

less component was 6 pieces of brown bumph! This 48 hour emergency pack, however, lasted me 10 days, and there was no opportunity to cook them, nor had we any room in the overladen jeep for anything else but our equipment, weapons and ammo, so our food was nibbled with sips of water from our bottles.

We were then taken to our respective gliders which were still in herring bone formation, but this time with the Halifaxes attached with tow ropes and intercom lines connected. We met our pilots for the first time. Two Sergeants called Jones were brothers. One trusts pilots as these are roughly in the same boat as you are, and will pick the easiest landing, as they also became foot soldiers when they rejoined their units.

Our glider was at the back end of the runway, apparently the handiest for several last minute "just in case" packages and we were about to find out that we were slightly overloaded. Door closed. Brakes on. Anchors firm. Strapped in. We're off! A gentle tug, then bump – bump from the wheels. Bump – bump – bump which speeded up as we raced down the runway. Bu – bu – bump – then silence as we became slightly airborne, then bu – bu – bump again. "What the hell have you got in there?" "Take off or cast off!" Then silence – we were airborne. Whether we were flying below the tug or above it we will never really know, as the sound of the wind through the glider carried on.[30]

30 Quoted from a letter held at the Tank Museum library

Staff Sergeant Heaton of the Glider Pilot Regiment was piloting one of the four Hamilcars loaded with rota trailers, which of course were full of petrol and ammunition:

> The pilots of these gliders were issued with parachutes, unlike all the other glider pilots who did not enjoy this privilege, as they usually carried troops; the theory of this was presumably that as the troops did not have parachutes it would have been bad for morale if the pilots were seen to have them! I must say that we did wonder at the time what earthly use the parachutes would have been if we had been hit, in view of the nature of the loads we were carrying.
>
> My memory is of an uneventful trip, and I was greatly impressed by the swarms of Mustang fighters escorting us across the channel and by the sight of the Royal Navy firing broadsides into the German defences on the coast of Normandy.[31]

The take-offs from Brize Norton commenced at 1850 and finished at 1945. At Tarrant Rushton, the tugs and gliders departed between 1925 and 1950. Once the formations had joined up, flight time to the landing zones was about 1 hour 30 minutes. Flying in the gliders was notoriously bumpy, and airsickness was common, though by no means universal. Figures based on reports from the tug squadrons and Glider Pilot Regiment indicate the landings on LZs 'N' and 'W' took place broadly between 2050 and 2120: in 30 minutes 246 gliders had touched down on the two sites, 10 gliders having been lost en-route through various causes. The report on 6th AARR's operations on D-Day says the regiment landed between 2100 and 2130.[32]

Of the ten gliders lost en-route, one or possibly two Horsas belonged to 6th AARR. One definitely broke its tow over England but landed safely near Winchester. This was the glider carrying the second-in-command, Major Welstead, as well as a jeep and 5 motorcycles. Another 6th AARR combination is given as 'missing' in 297 Squadron records but the 6th AARR war diary mentions only the Winchester Horsa as lost. One report indicated a Hamilcar may also have been lost en-route. F.J.Parslow was a navigator in one of 296 Squadron's Albermarles, and he was watching what he believed to be a Hamilcar combination in front of him as he was crossing the channel:

> Suddenly the tank broke through the front of the glider, plummeting to the sea, followed by the glider, which had been cast off from the towing aircraft.[33]

The report of a tank in the channel is also recorded in a message summary of 7th June.[34] However, the war diary, after mentioning the Horsa incident, clearly states 'No further episodes in flight'. We must therefore conclude that the sighting over the channel was some sort of mistake. 12th Devons lost one of their 'A' Company Horsas over the channel. The reports of 6 men tragically drowned would indicate it was one of the jeep carrying gliders. It is just possible that this was the glider seen by Parslow.[35]

---

31 Quoted in Warner, p.50.
32 Report contained in PRO file WO171/425, 6th Airborne Division, War Diary, 1944.
33 The D-Day Landings, p.30.
34 PRO file WO106/4315
35 See for example *Drop Zone Normandy*, p.230.

The 246 surviving combinations arrived over the Normandy coast in two streams, one destined for each landing zone. They were in tight formation to make the drop as concentrated in time as possible. The Horsas had been instructed to fly at ten second intervals, the Hamilcars 'to fly in line astern as close as possible'.[36] The sight was by all accounts awe inspiring, greatly worrying those Germans who saw it and conversely raising the morale of Allied troops. Western elements of 21st Panzer Division had recently reached the coast at Lion-sur-mer, and Robert Kershaw has recorded their dismay in his book on D-Day. 'Unteroffizier Werner Kortenhaus of Panzer Regiment 22 declared 'no one who saw it will ever forget it". They were taken completely by surprise. 'Suddenly, the hollow roaring of countless aeroplanes, and then we saw them, hundreds of them, towing great gliders, filling the sky'.[37] Kershaw concludes, 'The 21st Panzer Division was convinced the airlanding operation was specially mounted to cut them off in the rear' and cites the arrival of the glider force as a major factor in deciding the German division to withdraw its coastal elements inland. David Fletcher concludes that, in combination with the other glider troops, 'the tiny Tetrarchs had an effect on Rommel's crack panzer division out of all proportion to their size or numbers'.[38] Claiming this course of events as 6th AARR's first victory over the Germans is, however, rather stretching a point!

The gliders were cast off at between 1000 and 2000 feet, following which the tugs turned right back to England whilst the gliders turned left, also around to the north, to make their approach to the landing zones. A 'Eureka' beacon was located on LZ 'N', though not on 'W'. However, weather conditions were reported as good, with little cloud in the area and 10-15 miles visibility, so the landing zones were quickly identified visually. Wind on the ground was 10-15 knots from the north-west. The landing zones had been reported ready for use by 1900 that evening and so were marked out as expected. The LZs were marked by a 'T' formed of white panels, each 15 feet by 3 feet, which were used to produce a letter with a 90 foot stem and 75 foot cross piece, the stem aligned parallel to the landing direction. Each LZ was also marked with its identifying letter made from similar panels. White smoke markers would be lit at the 'T's to draw attention to them and indicate wind direction. On zone 'N', four parallel landing strips were indicated, numbered I to IV in roman numerals. Strip number IV was supposed to be for the sole use of Hamilcars, and was to be 1000 yards long by 90 yards wide. There were two parallel strips on zone 'W', numbered five and six, with a west to east landing direction. In the event, the good weather conditions meant that the majority of pilots did not remember using the markings. Most simply followed their comrades in, and the invasion stripes were reported to be an excellent aid to identifying friendly gliders which had already landed.[39]

Despite the careful marking, and the many briefings and exercises, the reader will not be surprised to learn that the landings were not quite as orderly as the planners intended. There were a lot of gliders in the air and each pilot sought his own

36 PRO File WO205/898
37 Kershaw, p.180.
38 'The Flying Tank', p.24.
39 See, for example, Glider Pilot Organisation, Training and Operations, by Chatterton, Museum of Army Flying, file no. 463

approach path and landing direction, even if they were all within the same general trend. And if the landing zones were ready for the gliders, so also, to a certain extent, were the Germans. After his 'uneventful' flight, Staff Sergeant Heaton found 'our landing, however, was much more tricky':

> There was a certain amount of small arms fire, including tracers, coming up at us, and the field in which we landed near Ranville had got telegraph poles erected in it to hinder the landings. We came in rather fast with our wings hitting the odd telegraph pole, which proved to be no obstruction, but just as I thought we were going too fast and would end up in an orchard at the end of the field, a Tetrarch which had just driven out of the Hamilcar landing before we did, proceeded at right angles across our landing path. The tank commander, who was standing in his little turret, took one look, mouthed imprecations and leaped from the tank a second or two before we hit it at a speed of 90 to 100 mph. My first pilot, Charles Channell, and I jumped from our cockpit, forgetting in the heat of the moment:
>
> (a) that my flying helmet with its intercom was still plugged into its socket, thus wrenching my neck; and
>
> (b) that the Hamilcar cockpit was situated on the top of the glider, some 15 feet above the ground.
>
> After looking around we found the tank upside down underneath our load, with grenades and cannon shells dropping like ripe plums from their containers into the field, and a strong smell of petrol. It was somewhat discouraging to see one or two gliders nearby burning fiercely as they had been mortared by the Germans. Staff Sergeant Channell and I managed to get the unfortunate tank driver and gunner out of the tank; I am glad to say they were still alive but not very pleased and somewhat shaken. We then adjourned to the nearby orchard, which otherwise we would have landed in the middle of, and proceeded to dig a hole where we spent a rather disturbed night with a number of other glider pilots who had landed more uneventfully.[40]

Corporal Darlington has left an equally vivid description of the landing zones. He was evidently in the Hamilcar loaded with a jeep and slave battery carrier:

> "Approaching LZ. Ready for cast off. Cast off" Then a gentle tug backwards, the opposite from take off. The nose dipped and turned and the wind whistled through the fuselage. It was as if we had come to the top of a scenic railway at night.
>
> The landing was a roaring, twisting, bumping skidding from high speed to a dead stop, and we were all momentarily knocked out. The side door opened and the pilot looked in and shouted "Sorry for the rough landing, boys" which wakened me up. I unstrapped, dashed out of the door to let the struts down for exit, only to find that the undercarriage no longer existed and parts of the wings were missing. The front was clear and the engines were running. "All clear for exit, sir!" "The damned anchors are jammed!" Out of the jeep again, I took the escape hatchet from the wall, after two or three good swipes, the carrier shot forward. The door opened and off they went. As they left the glider, the glider settled down backwards and our jeep anchor ropes were jammed also. The hatchet came into action once more but the front edge of the exit had risen

---

40 *The D-Day Landings*, p.51.

Hamilcars landing on LZ 'N', evening of June 6th (IWM)

some 2 ft; on hindsight, I realise the tail wheel was also torn off. The jeeps front wheels could not reach the ground as we see-sawed on the edge with the chassis. I got out again, grasping the bumper so that the back wheels could drive the jeep slowly forward and then the front wheels take over. Then we were off, following the carrier. I often wonder how I completed this feat of strength.

On the way, it was obvious from the parachutes scattered around that we were not alone. As we reached the edge of a wood and a small track, we turned and saw the rest of the gliders of our units coming in all manoeuvring for the empty spaces.

I witnessed two Hamilcars heading for the same space, and obviously they had seen each other. As they tried to bank away from each other, one glider's wing tip turned the other over and it crashed sideways into the wood and the Tetrarch shot out of the front on impact. We made a mad dash over and the tank was upright although it had somersaulted out of the glider. The crew of which the driver was Tpr Kewney and two others were unstrapped and dragged out. Their foreheads were bulged and purple and they were unconscious. They were strapped on the back of a passing tank's engine compartment with camouflage nets and the retaining straps over their midriffs.[41]

The quotes above describe the two worst incidents to occur to 6th AARR Hamilcars. In general, their landings were very successful, along with the other gliders on LZ 'N'. Wally Grimshaw was the troop sergeant of No.1 MMG Troop in 6th AARR's HQ Squadron. He recounted his memories of landing in a Horsa on LZ 'N' many years later, in the 1990s:

41 Tank Museum Library

We took up crash positions and a few minutes later felt the glider hit by small arms fire several times. Our Horsa glider seemed to stop suddenly as our pilot cast off and then banked to the left, swooped, did a tight turn and we landed. We had landed on our skids because we had previously jettisoned our wheels and struts as part of the DZ plan.

We quickly dismantled the tail of the glider and got our vehicles out of the body and loaded up the Jeeps. I rode a James motorcycle and led the way to the edge of the DZ, dodging the mortar bombs which had started to fall on the DZ and the odd bursts of MG fire.[42]

The mention of landing on skids is interesting, and confusing. Just about all the available photos of Horsas on landing zones during major operations show the undercarriages still on, and we have already noted that this was official policy. The explanation appears to be that the wheels fell off Grimshaw's glider by accident on take-off, an event recorded in 297 Squadron's records for one of the Horsas they towed on this mission. Sergeant Grimshaw's account notwithstanding, events on both landing zones 'N' and 'W' appear to demonstrate the wisdom of landing on undercarriages, permitting steering on the landing roll-out, rather than skids. This decision surely saved many accidents.

Landing zone 'W', where the airborne artillery and Devons company were arriving, was also the scene of a successful operation, but was generally judged to be rather more chaotic than 'N'. The approaching stream of towing combinations had become more spread out and less orderly. At one time, six combinations were observed approaching in line abreast. Even worse, whilst the official landing direction was west-east, some squadrons seem to have inexplicably got the idea that the landings should be south-north. Captain J.A.Morrison, commanding 'D' Squadron, Glider Pilot Regiment, was a participant:

We had been briefed to land from west to east, but as the Harwell gliders were landing from south to north I decided to lead my stream in, in the same direction. [...] Gliders seemed to be piling up in all directions...[43]

For Mallard as a whole, I have taken Allan Wood's figures of 256 gliders taking off with 10 lost en-route. Some accounts vary these figures by a glider or two but whatever figures we use, the airlanding reinforcement of 6th Airborne Division had been an outstanding success. Despite the vulnerability of this low-flying, slow-moving and densely packed formation, the main cause of casualties en-route turned out the be the parting of tow ropes. The operation had been an emphatic demonstration of the material superiority of the Allies, their air supremacy in this theatre, and of the dedication and abilities of all personnel involved.

Nevertheless, we have already seen that within this overall picture there was still room for chaotic events and tragic losses. Neither 'N' or 'W' was completely clear of anti-glider poles but in the event they did not turn out to be a serious problem, particularly to the higher-winged and heavier Hamilcars. Mostly they snapped the odd wing off of Horsas. 6th AARR's losses on landing were light. As we have seen, Staff Sergeant Heaton certainly knocked out one Tetrarch on his landing run, although the fate of his own load is not conclusively known. Accord-

---

42 Tank Museum Library.
43 Report contained in file 146, Museum of Army Flying.

ing to James Mrazek's book *The Glider War*, the crew of the overturned tank returned during the night and with the help of another tank they righted the overturned Tetrarch and returned it to action.[44] The collision between two Hamilcars as described by Trooper Darlington seems to imply only one of the two actually crashed, but other sources indicate both tanks were lost in the collision. However, the specially compiled report on the first 24 hrs in action which is contained in the war diary confirms only 2 tanks lost on landing, and we must take this as conclusive. One Hamilcar was hit by mortar fire on landing and was set ablaze, but the Tetrarch inside drove out successfully. It would seem no casualties occurred to 6th AARR's Horsas during the actual landings.

Unfortunately, as they drove across LZ 'N' towards their planned rendezvous, the tracked vehicles of the regiment encountered a serious problem. Cpl Sheffield, whom we last met playing football with officers of the regiment at Tarrant Rushton, described what happened:

> Most of us landed safely, and on leaving the glider I hitched up the three trailers to my tank. These contained petrol in the wheels and ammo in the large box between the wheels. We had very little opposition, a few mortars a distance away, when suddenly the tank stopped. The driver did not know why. I slid out of the turret to the ground, and found parachutes wound round the final drive. It was hard work cutting them off and, moving forward, we came across the Squadron Leader, in the same boat.[45]

Note that Tetrarchs as well as jeeps were tasked with towing the rota trailers. LZ 'N' had been, in the early hours of D-Day, DZ 'N', where the 5th Parachute Brigade had landed. It would seem that as well as anti-glider poles, parachutes were still present. It is also evident that this problem had not been encountered in exercises prior to D-Day. We can only assume that glider and parachute landing and dropping zones were kept separate during these exercises. Trooper Darlington provides a further description of what happened:

> The fields were hives of activities as gliders landed and unloaded. The problems, however, were not yet over for as the tanks disembarked, along with many other vehicles, they made for cover, running over the chutes left behind by the paras, who had been dropped to clear the DZ of any hazards, such as stout poles that had been dug in, and in some cases cemented, in our LZs. These chutes, however, became a bigger hazard than the poles, for as the tanks ran over them, the tracks picked them up, then wrapped them tightly round the driving sprockets, bringing the tanks to a halt either by slewing the tank round, or to a dead stop.
>
> The summary records that blow lamps were used. We had no such luxury, and even if we had, I would not have used them, as the heat would just have solidified them and been a permanent lock on the sprockets. The tank I ran to had one wrapped round the port track and I commenced cutting, firstly with my jack knife, then with my razor sharp fighting knife, whilst the tank commander and his gunner protected me from the small arms fire that had started. The task

44 Mrazek, *The Glider War*, p.183. This is the only reference I have found to the immediate recovery of the overturned tank. Mrazek is unreliable on many details in the course of his book.
45 Tank Museum Library

was made harder as not only was the canopy wrapped round the track and sprockets, but the rigging and harness as well. Finally we succeeded and there was a brief thanks and away it went to rendezvous. I do not know the tank commander's name nor, I suspect, did he know me. About half of my knife was lost from the point in this frenzied recovery and there were still a few more bogged down through the same problem. Others were freeing their vehicles, until finally all that was left on the LZ and DZ were the wrecked gliders, parachutes scattered round and the odd bursts of small arms firing. [46]

The report from the war diary indicates that 11 Tetrarchs were immobilised in five minutes. Exactly how long it took to free all the tanks is not recorded, but one source at least indicates it was dark before the awkward and frustrating job was finally finished.[47]

6th AARR's task was now to proceed to its harbour area and link up with the other elements of Parkerforce. This RV was at map reference 123734, which puts it just off the eastern edge of LZ'N'. The harbour area had been secured by the regiment's Parachute Harbour Party despite the loss of Lieutenant Belcher and his stick, as already mentioned. Something of the atmosphere during this period is captured in a report from a Captain Kew, of 12th Para Battalion, who in company with about 40 men was trying to rejoin his unit at Ranville. Passing through a British road block at around 2330hrs, he heard tanks behind. He thought at first they were German but they turned out to be 6th AARR vehicles 'moving into harbour'. He continued 'the fellows on the road block obviously had not been properly briefed regarding the fact that their own tanks would be in the vicinity behind them'.[48]

The other elements of Parkerforce, of course, had a longer journey than 6th AARR, having to cross the Caen Canal and Orne bridges. Crookenden records that 'A' Company of the Devons and the light battery reached their meeting with Colonel Parker 'without difficulty'.[49] It seems 211th Light Battery, RA, was in action north of Ranville within an hour of landing. They were making history as the first unit of the Royal Artillery to fly into action.[50] However, the Devons appear to have had more problems than Crookenden allows. The seven surviving gliders of the company became widely dispersed on landing and there were difficulties in removing the tails of some of the Horsas to offload the jeeps and trailers. Assembly was only complete at 2300, and on crossing the canal and river the company encountered enemy in Ranville. It seems to have been here that they heard Parkerforce was disbanded, and they were attached to 13th Parachute Battalion. The next day they were joined by the rest of their battalion which arrived by sea.

Even as the elements of Parkerforce were assembling, the decision to disband it was taking place. The division was desperately short of manpower, in particular because of the losses suffered in some very dispersed drops of the parachute units. The

46 Ibid, Darlington transcript. The 'summary' referred to is not the war diary, which is silent on these events. Darlington may have read one of the official wartime summaries such as 6th Airborne Operations Normandy, 6th June – 27th August 1944, held at the PRO (CAB106/1070).
47 The Sixth Airborne Armoured Reconnaissance Regiment (R.A.C.)
48 Report contained in PRO file WO106/4315.
49 *Drop Zone Normandy*, p.230.
50 *Go To It!*, p.76.

perimeter that the division was holding was also under pressure from German counter-attacks which had started before first light and had continued all day. In particular, 21st Panzer Division, despite serious delays caused by confusion over where the the main threat lay, had commenced counter-attacks against the airborne perimeter around mid afternoon on the 6th. Fortunately for the airborne soldiers, only one of the three kampfgruppen into which 21st Panzer had been divided attacked the airborne landings. This was Kampfgruppe 'Von Luck', which was based around Von Luck's 125th Panzer Grenadier Regiment of two battalions, along with a panzer battalion of about thirty Mk IVH's, the division's reconnaissance battalion and Assault Gun Battalion 200. They approached from the south towards Ranville along the east bank of the Orne, the area into which 6th AARR was supposed to probe. The Tetrarchs would have stood little chance against the Mk IV tanks and assault guns of Von Luck's command.[51] It is worth reflecting that, had the whole of 21st Panzer been employed (as their commander originally intended) in an attack against Ranville and the Orne bridges, this would have meant that 'in all, about 120 German tanks and 3000 infantry were pitted against three parachute battalions, a glider infantry company, some gunners and a few sappers totalling about 970 men, plus half a dozen 6 pounder and three 17 pounder anti-tank guns'.[52] While we might add the men and vehicles of 6th AARR to this list (and the omission is notable), Napier Crookenden's point is well made.

The 'tactical situation', to quote the conditions under which Parkerforce was to be deployed, clearly did not 'permit' the force's deployment. General Gale's own orders to the force, already quoted, give a strong indication that Gale had few illusions as to how risky the deployment of Parkerforce might be, with their talk of potential 'liquidation' and 'annihilation'. A trooper (John Banbery) who joined the unit in September 1944, talking to those who had been involved in Normandy, was left in no doubt that the mission was 'considered pretty suicidal by most people'[53] In a conversation with the author, Mr Banbery was also convinced that, no matter how strong the 'airborne spirit' may have been in the unit, there were many relieved men when Parkerforce was cancelled. Another member of the regiment, Norman Stocker remembered, 'Parkerforce was seen by many as unlikely to succeed and by some as a bit of a joke'.[54] The official sources indicate formal disbandment took place at 0300 7th June (the time it was originally intended it should be ready to move off). It would seem likely that General Gale made his decision well before that, perhaps even before 6th AARR had landed. We have seen how quickly 211th Light Battery came into action near to 6th Airborne's divisional HQ (rather than preparing to set off with 6th AARR), and the Divisional Headquarters war diary records that '211th Lt. Bty did not come under command Armrd Recce Regt as planned'.[55] This would appear to indicate a decision taken in advance of the evening landings not to deploy Parkerforce. Regarding his decision, Gale later wrote:

51 See Kershaw, pp.174-179
52 *Drop Zone Normandy*, p.234.
53 Bovington Library, transcript of Imperial War Museum interview with John Banbery, p27.
54 Letter to the author, August 2002
55 PRO file WO223/15.

I judged the situation to be such that I would not be justified in sending this force out. It would, however have been very interesting to have seen what it would have achieved in those first few days had the situation been more propitious. In view of our later experiences I believe, that once established in one of these villages [south of the perimeter], it might well have held its ground and paid a handsome dividend.[56]

So, as D-Day came to an end, it was clear 'Parkerforce' was not to be. However, the firepower and manpower the force represented would now be deployed to help hold the airborne bridgehead in the weeks to come.

56 *With The 6th Airborne*, p.91

Chapter 6

Normandy

Overnight, 6th AARR received their revised orders, which were to 'form a firm base in 8 Para area Bois de Bavent 1470 and carry out recce as far as road Troarn-Caen. No sp. arms. Protection at night by 8 Para Bn.'. The new harbour area was near to a road junction about two kilometres south-east of the village of Escoville. This put the regiment's home on the western outskirts of the Bois de Bavent, a wooded area which formed the south-eastern corner of the airborne perimeter, and which was held by the 8th Parachute Battalion. Setting off at first light the next morning the regiment had to deviate around Escoville which was still held by the enemy and from which elements of 'B' Squadron came under small arms fire. Contact was made with the paras at 0830, and patrols were pushed out immediately towards Escoville ('A' Squadron) and to the south ('B' Squadron). Enemy sightings commenced almost immediately, as the villages of Touffreville, Sannerville and Banneville were all occupied by the Germans. There were contacts as well as sightings, with some patrols encountering enemy motorcyclists, who were engaged. The Tetrarchs also encountered German armour: the diary records 'Light [tank] hit by enemy SP Gun at 135708 [just north of Touffreville], 1 cas x 1 Tank cas'. This would seem to be the action described in the following account by Sergeant Sheffield, which also describes a previous engagement with the enemy:

> We took up positions near a crossroads, a few miles from Ranville. Down one road, leading off from the crossroads, were German infantry in positions on the roadside. Our troop was detailed to do something about this, so Sgt. Knowles (ex Royal Hussars) in the leading tank, troop leader and myself in the rear, went like hell, machine guns roaring. But alas, the driver in the leading tank got knocked out somehow, blocking the road. It was very narrow, so the troop leader and I reversed out round a corner back to the crossroads. On inspection we had a bit of paint missing and bullet holes in the tool boxes. Once again we had been lucky.
>
> Not long after that sortie, an SP gun started giving trouble (88 or 105mm) shelling our infantry. Once again our troop (two tanks) were detailed to see what we could do. My tank leading, we moved off down another road when, coming to a bend, we came across this SP gun. My gunner fired, at the same time the SP fired, and it hit us hard just in front of the turret, setting us on fire, jamming the turret and twisting the machine gun. I was blinded at the time, my right hand and shoulder were useless and my face burnt. Somehow, with my left hand, I released two smoke rounds, ordered the driver to turn about and withdraw. The SP gun did not fire again. [1]

---

1 From The Airborne Light Tank Squadron – Sixth Airborne Armoured Reconnaissance Regiment

Sgt. Sheffield was returned to England for treatment which lasted 9 months, losing the vision in his left eye. On 8th May 1945, he was mentioned in dispatches for his actions that day as well as being awarded the Croix de Guerre with Bronze Star. The time of the action with the SP is not recorded, but it is interesting to note that at 1600 the diary of 8th Para Battalion records 'Armoured Recce reported that an SP gun was giving them trouble and would we deal with it'. A platoon was detailed but the German vehicle had gone. Assuming that these entries from the two diaries refer to the same incident, then we can see that, despite the courage of 6th AARR tank crews, they could end up relying on the infantry they were intended to support to deal with enemy armour.

Another example of an early tank combat was recalled by Sgt. Charles Elsey:

> Our first big punch-up came on the second day, when we were moving to another position. There were four Germans in a ditch with machine guns. I was the only one who saw them – nasty buggers – and they were shooting at us; even through the armour you could feel it. Now killing from a tank involves teamwork. I said to Ted, the driver, 'There's some on the left, turn left, go towards them – left, left, left!' Then, to the gunner, Bill, 'Traverse left, left, there's some jerries in a ditch, left, left, see them?' 'Yes, I've got them,' said Bill. 'Fire, fire,' I said. 'Go left Ted, towards them. You're hitting them Bill, you've got them. Drive over the ditch, Ted.' It was always like this, a combined operation – a driver to get you there, a gunner to fire, and a commander to find the target and say when to open up on it.[2]

The most significant sighting of the day was around late afternoon when 30 to 50 tanks and around 700 infantry were reported in the Troarn-Banneville area. These must have been elements of Kampfgruppe von Luck, and this demonstrates the wisdom of Gale's decision not to send Parkerforce out against such superior opposition. After many more sightings the regiment finished their long day by harbouring in their new location at 2230. One jeep and two Tetrarchs had been lost due to enemy action on the 7th: the jeep had been destroyed in an encounter with an enemy armoured car, and the other Tetrarch went up on a mine.

The unit now took up the two activities it was to be tasked with for the rest of the Normandy campaign, and which were to be the staple of its actions for the rest of the war. These were reconnaissance and the provision of fire support. At this time, and for some days to come, the front line was fluid and often ill-defined. There were opportunities for the regiment to penetrate into no man's land and even into what was thought to be German held territory. This situation would gradually change and the chances for vehicle reconnaissance steadily reduce.

As far as the recce function went, *Go To It!* summarises the regiment's activities in the following fashion:

> Initially it had been deployed with 8th Parachute Battalion in the Bois de Bavent where it had set up O.P.s watching the area bordered by Troarn, Caen, Ranville and Escoville. It had provided valuable information for the divisional commander, acting as his eyes and ears in the forward areas. As well as using 'B' Squadron's Bren carriers and Dingo scout cars, the regiment deployed patrols mounted on bicycles deep into enemy held areas. These obtained information on enemy dispositions, including vehicle parks and armour FUPs, which re-

---

2 *Men of the Red Beret*, p.176.

sulted in successful air strikes and bombardments by the cruiser HMS *Mauritius*.³

As has been mentioned, the author believes the reference to scout cars to be mistaken; however, the possibility that scout cars joined the regiment by sea at some time after D-Day cannot be entirely ruled out. It is likely the reference to bicycles refers to the use of motorcycles, although some bicycles were brought to Normandy by the regiment. The villages mentioned in these early days in Normandy are in the flat area of countryside south and south west of the Bois de Bavent, an area which was later to become well known as the starting point for Operation Goodwood, Montgomery's attempt at a great tank break-out which took place in July. Names like Sannerville, Touffreville, Cuverville, Demouville and Banneville appear repeatedly in the war diary. Probing the boundaries of the airborne perimeter brought constant contacts with the enemy and, of course, casualties. For example, a carrier was lost to a British-laid mine on the 9th, and on the same day an officer was lost in a contact with an enemy patrol. For most of the men it was their first time in action. One member of the regiment recalls that for the first few days, he continued to conscientiously close the field gates behind his troop vehicles, as he had been taught to do in English exercises in order to prevent the escape of livestock!⁴

The MMG's and 3" mortars were regularly called on for fire tasks against known or suspected enemy positions. We have already met Sgt. Wally Grimshaw, the Troop Sergeant of No.1 MMG Troop. His troop consisted of '4 Vickers MMGs, a range finder, 4 jeeps, 4 125cc M/cycles and 20 men'.⁵ We last heard of him heading for the edge of DZ 'N' on a motorcycle. His memories of his time in Normandy continue as follows:

> As we reached the shelter of the woods, I saw one of the regiment's DZ party who explained Col Parker's circus was off and to RV at the sawmills above Ranville in the woods. [...]
>
> We drove through the woods and finally met up with the rest of my troop with the Trp Cpl and two pilots. We made for the high ground. I was then ordered to put out my guns as local protection and within a few minutes engaged two six-wheeled armoured cars. After a few minutes firing they retired down the hill, followed by one of B Sqn recce troops. Our neighbours turned out to be 1st Canadian Para Regt, and I quickly liaised with them to make sure we did not receive any 'friendly' missiles.
>
> A perimeter was being mapped out and after a few hours, I went on a recce to a new position with one of the para bns, the 12th I think, plus one of the Independent Para companies. I had to select two front line positions and one to cover the rear in case the position was over-run because the paras were a little thin on the ground and we had to hold this particular front.
>
> For three days we were in these positions receiving all the crap they could throw at us, when my troop was relieved by our 2nd MG Troop who were in reserve in the brickworks in Ranville. The reserve troop were often called upon to give supporting fire on many targets by use of maps and compass. We found

3 *Go To It!*, p.91. FUPs = forming up positions.
4 Conversation with Brian Heape, March 2003.
5 'W.W. Grimshaw, 6th AARR', Bovington Tank Museum Library.

out that an OSS Div [*sic* – doubtless meaning an Ost Battalion, probably from 716th Division] were on our front and were prime targets, ready to desert when darkness had fallen. We therefore had guides out, ready to escort any deserters back to our lines. We used to have a 'Hate Hitler' 30 mins daily when we fired all our weapons on our front, and received a similar load of HE back in return.

We carried out our three days on, three days off until 18th August. We were then relieved by RM commandos who took over our positions.[6]

As for the light tanks, they would sometimes be used to 'beef up' a recce patrol, or to help the infantry with troublesome enemy positions. On the 11th, for example, two troops of Tetrarchs and a recce troop were sent to Escoville, which they found empty.

A member of 8th Parachute Battalion, Private Tony Leake, has left a memoir of his time in Normandy which includes passing mention of encounters with 6th AARR. In the early morning of 9th June he notes:

> Some Tetrarchs of the Divisional Armoured Recce Squadron came up to the woodyard that morning and lifted our spirits somewhat. A carrier from the same mob parked itself down the road from our platoon position.[7]

The woodyard was sited where the road from Le Mesnil joins the main Troarn-Escoville road. 6th AARR's efforts in the Sannerville area were indicated on the 10th when a patrol near Sannerville which included Pvt Leake 'found a jeep in a ditch near a farm. It was from the Armoured Recce and all its occupants had been killed or captured'.[8]

The vehicle which Cpl Sheffield encountered on the 7th may have been one of the conversions of old French Hotchkiss and Lorraine tracked chassis, altered to carry 75mm anti-tank guns and 105mm howitzers and which, as we have seen, 21st Panzer Division was using at this time. In this case, the 2pdr with Littlejohn converter carried by the Tetrarch may have had some chance of causing damage. Of course, against 'real' tanks and SPs like the Mk IV and Sturmgeschutz III, the Tetrarch was completely outclassed, and as has been noted the 3" howitzer carried by a small number of the Tetrarchs for infantry support was a poor weapon by 1944 standards. Consequently, when 'proper' tank support was called for, General Gale had recourse to armoured units from outside 6th Airborne. The first time this occurred seems to have been on 10th June when German counter-attacks were becoming particularly severe. 'B' Squadron, 13th/18th Hussars were summoned, with 8 Shermans and 5 Honey light tanks, the latter roughly equivalent to the Tetrarch in gun power and armour. The tanks, together with paras of 7th Battalion, were to start their attack from across DZ 'N', an indication of how dented was the paras hold on their perimeter at this time. It is interesting to note that, during this successful British counter stroke, at least one Honey was immobilised by parachutes exactly as 6th AARR's Tetrarchs had been.[9] Another example was the attack

---

6 Ibid.
7 Leake, 'Summer In Normandy', unpublished manuscript held at Museum of Army Flying, box no.441. p.10.
8 Ibid, p.10.
9 *Drop Zone Normandy*, p.257.

against Breville on 12th June, when a squadron of the 13th/18th Hussars in Shermans were again in support, but no Tetrarchs were used. It is worth mentioning that prominent in this latter attack was Colonel Reggie Parker, who had returned to his role of Deputy Commander 6th Airlanding Brigade. He was standing near the CO of his old battalion (12th Parachute) when that officer was killed, and despite a wound in the hand he took over the battalion and led them for the rest of the action.[10] According to General Gale, 'His leadership and example at this stage was a big factor in the success of the attack'.[11]

From the 11th of June, elements of 51st Highland Division crossed into the airborne bridgehead to take over the southern part of the perimeter. This put them into 6th AARR's sector and for a few days the regiment was under command 153rd Infantry Brigade. On the 13th the regiment was withdrawn to the Ranville area (quite close to landing zone 'N') and reverted to the command of 6th Airborne. The battle for Breville on the 12th had completed the stabilisation of the airborne bridgehead, and this stabilisation may have been a factor in the withdrawal of 6th AARR. All the brief histories of the regiment mention that, after 10 days 'in the line' the regiment was withdrawn for a rest, but that the Tetrarchs were recalled to service almost immediately to provide fire support to the hard-pressed airborne infantry of 5th Parachute Brigade, often being dug-in to perform this role. The move on the 13th seems to tie up (roughly) with this narrative, but the activities of the regiment over the next two months until the breakout commenced on 16th August were more varied and arduous than this simple account would suggest.

The extent to which the unit was 'resting' at any time during June is questionable. Starting from the 14th recce patrols were investigating new areas in the north and east of the bridgehead, such as Le Plein, Bavent and Sallenelles. A recce patrol investigating a strong point at Sallenelles was supported by two Tetrarchs which are recorded as expending '15 rnds 3in How, 10 rnds 2pdr and one belt Besa' against the enemy pillbox. The diary also records the use of the Tetrarchs to bolster the infantry defences. On the 16th two troops of tanks 'incl. 3" How.' were sent to defensive positions just south east of Ranville in the 51st Highland Division sector. The move to support 5th Parachute Brigade began on the 18th. For this, 'A' Squadron, four MMGs and the motorcycle-mounted assault troop were based at Le Mesnil. This village lies on a cross roads at the north west corner of the Bois de Bavent and was still very much in the front line at this time. It was also one of the key locations in Gale's defensive plan . 'B' Squadron, the HQ Squadron and RHQ were moved to a new harbour area on the Orne river just north of Ranville for rest, commencing on 21st June. These dispositions were broadly maintained until the last days of July. By 1st July, the force at Le Mesnil had been thinned out to two tank troops, Squadron HQ and four MMGs, the remainder joining the rest of the regiment in the rest area, with a system of reliefs which swapped three tanks every 48 hours from amongst those on combat duty. As we have seen in Wally Grimshaw's account, the MMG troops seem to have swapped over every three days.

The war diary records few details of combat for the Tetrarchs aiding 5th Parachute Brigade in the front line during this period. Whether this means they had a

10 *Go To It!*, p.87.
11 *With The 6th Airborne*, p.101.

relatively quiet time remains essentially unknown, although one light tank was recorded as hit by a 75mm round on 23rd June in this area with two casualties. Certainly the regiment continued to be regarded as a mobile resource which could be useful for all types of support. For example, late on 23rd June 'B' Squadron, one of the MMG troops and the RHQ tanks formed a potential counter-attack group with 8th Para Battalion at Le Bas de Ranville, returning on the 25th, whilst on 2nd July the mortar troop went to Le Mesnil to support an attack by 8 Para which was, in the event, cancelled. The war diary further records that a proposal to use the Tetrarchs to support another attack from Le Mesnil was not carried out. One rather unusual mission was detailed later by Sgt. Elsey:

> The Colonel asked me take out two tanks to protect the war correspondent Chester Wilmot, and his BBC wagon. It was the day of the 1000 bomber raid on Caen. [7th July – about 460 four engined bombers were actually used]. The Colonel told us to find a place where Chester Wilmot could see what was going to happen. So we prowled about and found a nice little hillock which gave us a good view towards Caen, no more than two miles away. It was an awesome sight – the bombers came over and the sky was black with them. Chester Wilmot was doing his recording, and I sat next to him.[12]

On the 31st July the whole regiment was placed under command 5th Parachute Brigade and moved to the area of the Orne bridges with responsibility for their defence, a move which took the entire regiment out of the front line. Even so, there was no question either of complete rest or complete safety. From 7th to 13th August 'B' Squadron was sent to the area north-west of Troarn to relieve 49 Recce Regt who were working there with 1st Special Service Brigade. The mortar troop went with them and stayed until the 16th. They were evidently busy as they recorded 840 rounds of 3" HE ammunition had been expended between 11th and 15th August. For the rest of the regiment, shellfire into the regimental area was a common occurrence, causing the occasional casualty. A divisional rest camp had been set up at Ouistreham, but even here there was no safety. When a German aircraft crashed on one of the houses being used for the camp, two members of 6th AARR's HQ Squadron were among the dead.

Elements of the regiment also got involved in a new area of combat, that of air defence. The war diary records a sprinkling of enemy air activity, particularly in July. Early in that month a self propelled German AA gun (an SdKfz 10/4, a single 20mm gun mounted on an unarmoured 1 ton half-track) was captured, and manned by Troopers C. Davies and L. Walden. On 4th July they claimed an Me109 shot down, and on the 10th an FW 190 was also claimed, though neither victory was officially confirmed.

It was, however, in August that a real change of role began to be planned, in readiness for the breakout from the Normandy bridgehead that was soon to occur. On 1st August two officers and forty three other ranks are recorded as detached to receive instruction on the Cromwell tank, and on the 6th this party returned to their unit along with eight of these vehicles. Some members of the regiment remember that the acquisition of the new tanks was primarily an initiative from the CO: the tanks were not intended for 6th AARR but somehow Colonel Stuart had

12 *Men of the Red Beret*, p.177.

Troopers Davis and Walden of 6th AARR with their captured self-propelled 20mm flak gun (IWM).

found them and thought they would be just the thing for his regiment. The new vehicles were taken on strength by 'A' Squadron and formed into two troops. It would seem that 'A' Squadron gave up most of its Tetrarchs at this stage, resulting in a drastic reduction in numbers made up for by the acquisition of genuinely effective tanks. Three Tetrarchs were retained in squadron HQ, and the light tanks in Regimental HQ were also retained, at least for the time being.

The breakout for 6th Airborne Division began on 17th August. The day before, Hitler had finally authorised a withdrawal of German forces from the Falaise pocket, signalling that he had at last admitted defeat in Normandy. It should perhaps be explained that the bridgehead east of the Orne had by this time expanded considerably, particularly as a result of the Goodwood offensive which was launched south-west from the bridgehead in July. 6th Airborne held the front from the coast to the Troarn area, with 49th Infantry Division on their right and 51st Highland Division south of the 49th. Besides the 1st and 4th Special Service Brigades of commandos who had been with the division since soon after D-Day, 6th Airborne had also been reinforced by the Belgian Brigade and the Royal Netherlands Brigade to provide it with the numbers necessary to hold its allocated stretch of front.

German withdrawals from their positions in front of 6th Airborne commenced as expected on the night the 17th. Gale's division would form the extreme left flank of the Allied push across France, moving along the coast as the left hand division of 1st Canadian Army (of which they were now a part) with 49th Infantry Division to their right. Their objective was to reach the Seine River. Against the advantage in strength provided by the reinforcing brigades, the division was disadvantaged by severe shortages of transport and bridging equipment. This was a particular problem as three major water obstacles would have to be crossed to reach the Seine: the Dives, Touques and Risle rivers. Of the two main routes available to him, Gale therefore chose the more inland route via Troarn and Pont Audemer as his main axis, as the rivers would be narrower on this route The road distance to Pont Audemer would be about forty five miles. The operation would very broadly be one of pursuit, and therefore one in which the division's Reconnaissance Regiment could expect a significant role.

The regiment was to take up position on the extreme right flank of the division, and on the 17th they moved south through Ranville to Banneville (south west of Troarn) where they briefly occupied holding positions. Trooper Darlington later recounted his own unconventional part in the initial moves. He had been one of the men detailed to collect the Cromwells, but at the start of the pursuit he was slightly wounded and unwell, and was asleep under a Tetrarch.

> I was once more rudely awakened and told we were breaking out. My only means of transport was the lopsided tank that I had slept under. The suspension on one side had collapsed, the 2pdr, Besa and radio had been removed but the engine worked. Another walking wounded arrived. 'Can you drive?' 'Yes'. Then he got in and I signalled to move, but with faulty suspension and a person unused to Tetrarchs, I soon had to change over as one could see that some of the ditches were mined. 'Traverse the turret to the rear and cover me with your weapon, and I will fire if need be out of the front'. We must have looked an incredible sight as we ambled off behind the heavies. It was either this, or walk, or be left behind.[13]

During the afternoon the regiment probed eastwards in accordance with their orders, keeping contact with the troops on both their flanks. They had 4th Special Service Brigade on their left, and their position on the southern flank of 6th Airborne meant they had troops of 49th Division on their right. They had reached St. Pair by the end of the day. They remained in this area until early on the 20th, waiting for a breakthrough by the infantry. A major assault was being put in by 3rd and 5th Parachute Brigades against the German blocking position around DozulŽ. At 0800 that day, they finally received orders to push all the way to the River Touque at Pont L'Eveque (over half way to Pont Audemer) and recce the bridges over the Touque there and to the south. During the 20th the unit seems to have been involved in difficult operations attempting to work round to the south of DozulŽ towards Rumesnil. The tanks of 'A' Squadron could not get across the bridges over the Dives and so it was left to 'B' Squadron to lead this effort. The squadron encountered German delaying parties at several locations, and lost two killed and five wounded during the day. The two killed may have been involved in the following incident, remembered by Norman Stocker (later to become a sergeant in the regiment), which reminds us that not all recce actions took place mounted in vehicles:

> I...recall vividly the occasion when on foot recce near to the village of Putot en Auge a number of us found ourselves coming under fire from a machine gun in a ditch at the far end of a small orchard through which we were advancing. Two

---

13 'A Darlington, 6th AARR', Bovington Tank Museum Library.

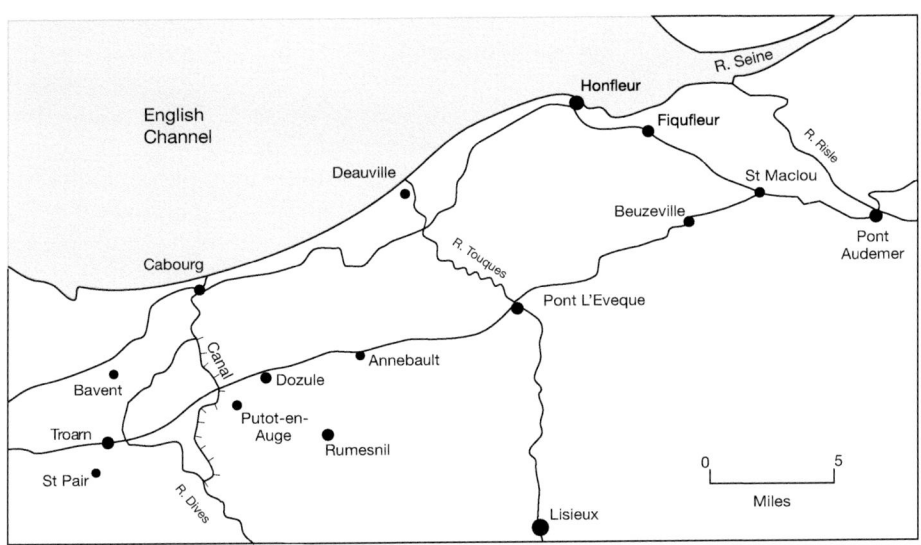

6th AARR in the breakout from Normandy, 17-26th August 1944.

of our number, Troopers Martin and Tonks were killed there, and are buried in the local churchyard.[14]

On the next day 1st Belgian Reconnaissance Squadron was placed under 6th AARR's command and this squadron passed through DozulŽ around 0820 and fanned out onto the roads to the east, with 'B' Squadron working to their south, still guarding the division's southern flank. The recce units now overtook the parachute infantry and led the advance eastwards. In General Gale's words,

> their primary task was to pursue the enemy, find out if he was going to hold any intermediate positions, and then discover his flanks. Their second and very important task was to keep in touch with the 49th Division on my right, whose progress was about the same tempo as ours, but who were moving on the Lisieux axis some ten to fifteen miles to my south. We might indeed be vulnerable on this open flank.[15]

The ground beyond Dozulé was close and hilly and afforded plenty of opportunities for further German delaying parties to hold up the advance. Contact with the retreating enemy was frequent during the 21st but progress eastwards was made, the various recce patrols performing their usual tasks of checking roads and villages and reporting enemy strengths and positions when encountered. 'B' Squadron was in contact with 49th Division's recce regiment on the right flank. By around 0900 on the next day (the 22nd) elements of the Belgian squadron were reporting on the state of the bridges in and around Pont l'Eveque. The town was strongly held on the east bank, however, and the recce units had to pull back whilst the town was assaulted by 5th Parachute Brigade. By this stage 'A' Squadron had

14 Letter to the author, August 2002.
15 *With the 6th Airborne*, p.138.

caught up and at 1600 1st Troop was ordered to take its Cromwell's to Pont l'Eveque to cover the bridging operations and then support 13th Parachute Battalion's advance into the town.

The River Touque ran through the town in two channels about two hundred yards apart. It would seem the small bridge over the western stream could not take the Cromwells, and they could not cross into the town until an armoured bulldozer had created a ford for them. Moving forward into the church square, they found that the Germans had set light to many of the buildings in the town creating a fierce blaze. Peter Harclerode's book provides a good summary of the action which followed:

> They engaged several targets and gave covering fire from near the church. They accounted for three enemy and destroyed one pillbox. Unable to cross the river, however, they were in positions vulnerable to enemy anti-tank guns and to the risk of catching fire from the blazing ruins of buildings around them. Shortly afterwards, one of the Cromwells was hit by a 20mm gun and was set on fire. The troop, which was commanded by Captain R.de C. Rennick, was then withdrawn.[16]

The war diary indicates the Cromwell hit by 20mm fire had its shock absorbers penetrated and rendered useless, rather than catching fire.

On the 23rd, 7th and 13th Parachute Battalions again attempted to take Pont l'Eveque. At 1245 a troop of Cromwells was again dispatched into the town to provide support. However, shortly afterwards the infantry were withdrawn due to fierce German resistance and the Cromwells were involved in covering this withdrawal. Overnight, the Germans themselves withdrew, and the paras were able to cross to the far side of the Touque during the next morning. At 1330 on the 24th 6th AARR was advised that it had first priority for vehicular crossing of the river, but a crossing at Pont l'Eveque was impossible as the the only way over the eastern channel was via a girder eighteen inches wide! Frantic searching for suitable bridges commenced, along with the construction of two class 40 bridges in the town by the Royal Engineers. Finally at around 1420 a crossing was found by patrols of the regiment well north of Pont l'Eveque and the regiment moved out. The Belgian Recce Squadron led the way to the northern bridge, followed by a forward RHQ, then 'A' Squadron and rear RHQ. 'B' Squadron with two armoured cars attached waited in Pont l'Eveque for the engineers to finish their bridges. However, by 1945 'B' Squadron was reporting that it would take twenty minutes to get two troops across at the town, and that the armoured cars would not be able to cross at all. They were ordered to follow the rest of the regiment, who had been checking routes eastward to Pont Audemer and northeastward to Honfleur, which was on the coast by the mouth of the Seine. Numerous contacts with the enemy took place during the evening but by 2230 it was too dark to do any more and the various parts of the regiment harboured for the night.

During the day 6th AARR had taken under command a troop from No.1 Canadian Centaur Battery, consisting of four Centaur tanks with 95mm howitzers and one Sherman tank. This battery was briefly mentioned in Chapter One, and theoretically consisted of three such troops.[17] It had been supporting 6th Airborne

---

16 *Go To It!*, p.104.
17 Details from war diary, No.1 Canadian Centaur Battery, supplied by National Archives of Canada.

Division since the second week in August, making up in particular for a perceived lack of 4.2" mortars in the counter-mortar role.[18] During the breakout phase, the battery had been having trouble with the Centaurs breaking down and had been operating at a much reduced strength. On the 24th itself, two of the Centaurs had broken down and the war diary of the unit indicates that it was suggested during the day that a six gun battery was all that could be maintained. The Centaurs of the battery were attached to 6th AARR for the next two days of combat, but it would seem unserviceabilities meant the unit operated in little more than troop strength.

The following day 6th AARR received orders to concentrate its efforts towards Pont Audemer. However, the regiment, with the Belgian Squadron still heavily involved, had become well spread out the previous day and and as it moved forward contacts were reported along an eight mile front, from Fiquefleur just south east of Honfleur to south of Beuzeville. The latter town was being held by the enemy in yet another delaying action, and once again No.1 Troop of 'A' Squadron under Captain Rennick were called on to give support. They were sent round to the south of Beuzeville and placed under the command of 8th Para Battalion, who were attempting an outflanking movement. The tanks first action was to support a company attack on a farm, for which they gave covering fire. As the tanks attempted to advance during the attack they encountered some sort of obstacle to their movement (the type of obstacle is not specified in the diary). In trying to find a way round, Capt. Rennick was wounded in the head by machinegun fire and Sgt. Cressy, the Troop Sergeant, took over command. The attack on the farm was completed successfully by the infantry.

The troop was then ordered to support another infantry attack on a farm, which was known to contain a 75mm gun. The leading tank came under fire by this gun but immediately returned fire, knocking the gun out. There was then a subsequent task where the troop gave fire support by shelling a German held wood. Following this, Lt. K.T. Robertson came up to assume command of the troop, following which the troop's busy afternoon continued. They supported a platoon of paras in occupying some high ground, meeting no opposition until the two leading Cromwells were actually on the objective, at which stage they came under fire from a machine gun which they subsequently knocked out. They stayed with the infantry for a while in case of counter attacks. Later, the troop was involved in covering the movement of other paras advancing towards the town down a track. After supporting the recovery of some wounded, the tanks advanced with the infantry for a mile along the track, silencing two machinegun posts along the way. As the light faded, the troop was further employed supporting another part of the battalion, shelling a house and a road block. Finally, with the light too bad for further fire support tasks, the troop returned to harbour with the rest of the regiment. In addition to Capt. Rennick, 'A' Squadron reported three men wounded by a mortar bomb during the afternoon's engagements. The Canadian Centaurs had also been involved at Beuzeville, firing 60 rounds per gun during an indirect shoot in support of 3rd Para Brigade at around 1900hrs. By this time they seem to have been reduced to a Sherman, three Centaurs and a 95mm Cromwell which their war diary

18 PRO file CAB106/970

indicates was borrowed from 6th AARR, though where the regiment had obtained this vehicle from in the first place is not known.

The regiment had not reached Pont Audemer during the day due to enemy resistance, but overnight General Gale had decided on a new course of action. Receiving a directive from 1st Corps for the next day's operations, 6th Airborne Division had been excluded from entering Pont Audemer and the task given to 49th Division. Gale, however, was convinced that he was better placed to take the town and reached the conclusion that, in his own words, 'by piling my soldiers on my tanks and by using every lorry I could lay hands on I was certain I could reach Pont Audemer first'.[19] He gave the van to the Royal Netherlands Brigade, who were mounted both in their own transport and on the Cromwells of 6th AARR, as well as the surviving tanks of the Canadian Centaur Battery. At some stage he appears to have received information indicating that the Germans were once again falling back and that such a dash had a good chance of success. He was proved right. 6th AARR's war diary indicated the regiment moved off at 0730 on the 26th August along the road leading from Beuzeville, through St Maclou to Pont Audemer. An hour later the leading elements entered the outskirts of the objective, finding all bridges in the town blown and the Germans gone. Around 0930 contact was made with elements of 49th Recce Regiment approaching from the south east. Gale had beaten 49th Division, but he does not mention what (if any) the consequences were of ignoring his previous orders.

'A' Squadron was ordered to block the southern approaches of Pont Audemer at 1140, taking part in what turned out to be the regiment's last action of the Normandy campaign. The whole squadron was involved, but it was the tank of Sergeant Thompson who encountered the enemy when he was ordered to cover a patrol of 'B' Squadron as they moved into a house. Advancing up the street, the tank was hit and penetrated by an anti-tank gun, the front gunner and the turret gunner both being wounded. Despite this, the tank got off three rounds of HE which silenced the enemy gun, before withdrawing to evacuate the wounded crew members. During the day, the Canadian tanks were also in action, firing in support of 6th AARR and the Belgian armoured cars from around 0930.

That same afternoon, 6th AARR was ordered to concentrate ready to withdraw into divisional reserve. The next day the Belgian Recce Squadron was returned to the command of the Belgian Brigade, whilst the Canadian battery remained in action for a couple of days before preparing to disband. 6th AARR withdrew westward and commenced resting and refitting, prior to returning to England along with the rest of 6th Airborne. It had been decided to bring the division home to prepare for further airborne operations, and the extended use of the division in the ground role was finally coming to an end. Of the performance of 6th AARR during the pursuit, the official summary stated:

> Once clear of the Dives valley the AARR with under command the Belgian and Dutch recce units [the latter are never mentioned in the war diary] was of the greatest assistance. Information provided was accurate and up to date and of great value. In addition to providing information they kept touch with 49th Di-

19 *With 6th Airborne*, p.148.

vision to the south and so provided a connecting link with the rest of 1st Corps.[20]

There is one particular uncertainty over the equipment of 6th AARR during the period of pursuit, concerning how many Tetrarchs remained with the unit by the end of the campaign. There are statements in two of the brief histories of the regiment, that during this period 'A' Squadron had 12 Cromwells, with four each in the squadron HQ and the two troops. There is no mention of the arrival of the four extra tanks in the war diary, but as the histories were written by ex-members of the squadron they must be given some credit. Therefore it seems quite possible that the Tetrarchs in Squadron HQ were at some stage replaced by four Cromwells. However, in the absence of any information to the contrary, it also seems possible that Tetrarchs soldiered on in the regimental HQ. One ex-member of the regiment remembered that the CO also acquired a Sherman from somewhere during this period, but when it broke down no spares were available.[21]

We should briefly note a few details regarding the fate of the glider pilots, tug crews and gliders associated with 6th AARR. It had always been intended that the glider pilots should be rapidly repatriated to England, as they were a resource too valuable to be frittered away in ground fighting. This was accomplished according to plan, and the pilots were back in the UK by D+2, having suffered generally light casualties. The tug squadrons quickly returned to smaller (but still hazardous) operations, including supporting SOE activities and dropping SAS groups behind enemy lines. One particularly interesting sortie by the Halifax squadrons involved successfully dropping six 6pdr anti-tank guns and their towing jeeps by parachute into the airborne bridgehead on 10th June. Of the 344 gliders landed in Normandy, only forty were eventually recovered. There had never been any prospect of recovering the Hamilcars due to their size, and as for the Horsas, the numbers damaged on D-Day had been joined by many more gliders damaged during the subsequent fighting. The forty Horsas were towed out by Dakotas, thirty nine reaching the UK safely, with one ditching en-route.[22]

An important conclusion for the future was noted in the report on 6th Airborne's operations. It read, '17pdr anti-tank guns were invaluable. Their arrival by air surprised the enemy and also enabled SP guns and tanks which 'stood off' to be engaged at long ranges'.[23] Subsequent airborne operations would see these guns being given priority in the Hamilcars over light tanks. As for the Hamilcars themselves, Brigadier Chatterton noted in his report that they had been 'an unqualified success'.[24]

Finally, since D-Day, 6th AARR had had a total of five officers and forty other ranks treated by 6th Airborne's divisional medical units. Total casualties for the period 6th June to 26th August were given as eight officers and forty four other ranks.

20 PRO file CAB106/970, 6th Airborne Operations Normandy 6th June-27th August 1944
21 *Men of the Red Beret*, p.177.
22 See Report on the British Airborne Effort in Operation Neptune by 38 and 46 Groups RAF, Museum of Army Flying, Box 146.
23 PRO file CAB106/970.
24 Chatterton's 'Appreciation for Mallard', Museum of Army Flying, Box 461.

This broke down into ten other ranks killed, six officers and twenty six other ranks wounded, and two officers and eight other ranks missing. A strength return for the 2nd of September gives 24 officers and 194 other ranks present in France. Trooper Darlington remembers that at the time of their final withdrawal, the regiment 'came out like Rag, Tag and Bobtail, extremely tired and dirty, and with memories as our cameras'.[25] Another trooper, C.L. Collins, concluded with a slightly different feeling, 'our casualties were light, and we arrived back at Larkhill feeling pretty pleased with ourselves'.[26]

By the second week in September, 6th AARR were indeed back at Larkhill, ready to commence a period of rest, retraining and reorganisation. They had embarked at Grays-sur-Mer on 4th and 5th September and had then sailed for Gosport. From there they drove to their transit camp at nearby Fareham, and from Fareham the regiment minus its tanks drove to Larkhill, the tanks proceeding by train. At Larkhill we will temporarily leave them and turn to the dramatic events which occurred later in September at Arnhem.

25 'A Darlington, 6th AARR', Bovington Tank Museum.
26 L. Collins, 'Tales Of Old Retold: Flying Tanks', *Pegasus Journal*, 1949.

Chapter 7

Arnhem and the Ardennes

Arnhem did not involve 6th Airborne Division or 6th AARR, so why should we include this famous airborne battle in our story? Our treatment of Arnhem will be brief, but is relevant for two reasons. Firstly, the Hamilcar was heavily involved and our story of the Hamilcar would be incomplete if its use here were not recorded. Secondly, the lack of a unit like 6th AARR at Arnhem requires explanation. We must look briefly at why 1st Airborne Division ended up with a different type of reconnaissance unit and why the Hamilcars at Arnhem carried loads which did not include light tanks.

Major General Urquhart, the commanding officer of 1st Airborne Division, received his orders for Operation Market (the airborne part of Operation Market Garden) on 10th September, soon after 6th AARR had returned to the UK from Normandy. Of the three airborne divisions involved (the two others being the American 82nd and 101st), his was to be dropped the furthest behind enemy lines, tasked with the job of seizing and holding the bridges at Arnhem until relieved by units of 30 Corps. A significant part of the eventual plan for the landing of 1st Airborne Division was that, due to reasons of local topography and the estimated deployment of German anti-aircraft guns, the drop zones and landing zones were situated up to 8 miles west of Arnhem, forcing the units of the division to make a lengthy march to their objectives. In this situation, the role of the division's recce unit, the 1st Airborne Reconnaissance Squadron (1st ARS), would be an important one. We have already briefly encountered this unit when we reviewed the formation of 1st Airborne Division, and we have also noted that it undertook joint training with the Airborne Light Tank Squadron in early 1943. It is now time to look more fully into the unit's background and organisation.

The Airborne Reconnaissance Squadron started life as 31st Independent Reconnaissance Company. This unit was officially formed on 8th January 1941, and was made up of men from the four battalions of 31st Independent Brigade Group, then based at Wheathampstead in Hertfordshire.[1] The four battalions in question were the 1st Battalion The Border Regiment, the 2nd Battalion The South Staffordshire Regiment, the 2nd Battalion The Oxfordshire and Buckinghamshire Light Infantry, and the 1st Battalion The Royal Ulster Rifles. All these units later became well known as airlanding battalions in both 1st and 6th Airborne Divisions, for reasons which we will see below. The formation of the recce company from these battalions should be seen in the context of the formation of the Reconnaissance Corps, which was created officially on 14th January 1941. Following the experiences of the campaign in France, each infantry division was to have its own reconnaissance regiment, including light armoured vehicles, normally to be formed from infantry units. The cavalry regiments which had previously carried out this role for the infantry (mainly using light tanks) were needed for the newly

---

1   Details from copy of 1st Airborne Recce Squadron war diary held at the Tank Museum.

forming armoured divisions. It was therefore appropriate that 31st Independent Brigade Group should form a recce company.

The Brigade Group moved to Wales during February to undertake training in the mountain warfare role. In October 1941 the brigade, now already used to 'travelling light', was selected to become the 1st Airlanding Brigade Group, soon to become part of the new 1st Airborne Division. During November and December the brigade group was moved as near as possible to Salisbury Plain, so that by the first week in December, 31st Independent Reconnaissance Company had become the 1st Airlanding Company, Reconnaissance Corps and was based at Newbury, Berkshire. In the same month, the unit was removed from 1st Airlanding Brigade and became part of divisional troops. On 22nd November the squadron had received a new commander, Major C.F.H. Gough. 'Freddie' Gough was to become a well known airborne personality, and led the unit into battle at Arnhem. During 1942 the Reconnaissance Corps adopted cavalry nomenclature for its units, and from 24th April 1st Airlanding Company became 1st Airlanding Squadron. The unit moved to Bulford on Salisbury Plain in May. The squadron was organised into an HQ Troop and four recce troops, 'A', 'B', 'C', and 'D', with the main vehicle used being the jeep, which could of course be fitted into the Horsa glider.

A detailed history of the squadron is not appropriate here.[2] It departed for the Middle East in April 1943, as part of the deployment of 1st Airborne Division to that theatre. The unit did not take part in the Sicily landings due to shortage of gliders, but was landed by sea to take part in the invasion of Italy where it performed distinguished service. The 1st Airborne Division (minus one of its parachute brigades) returned to England at the end of 1943, and 1st Airlanding Recce Squadron returned in December of that year. On 1st January 1944, the Reconnaissance Corps officially became part of the Royal Armoured Corps, so that 1st ARS and 6th AARR were now even more closely related. 1st ARS now commenced a period of intense training and reorganisation, particularly involving parachute training for many of its men, so that only the vehicles would have to arrive by glider. In recognition of this new capability the unit was renamed the 1st Airborne Reconnaissance Squadron in March 1944. General Browning had visited the unit in February 1944 and left the distinct impression that expansion to regimental size was only a matter of time, but this never occurred.[3] Although 1st Airborne Division stood by during and after the invasion of Europe for a number of operations which were subsequently cancelled, it was to see its next combat during Market Garden.

By the time of this operation, 1st ARS was organised as follows. It had an HQ Troop equipped with jeeps and motorcycles which included the usual administrative functions such as medical, supply and intelligence. There were three recce troops, each with three sections equipped with two jeeps each, usually with four to five men in each jeep. Each recce troop HQ also had two jeeps, so that each troop had eight jeeps and around 30 men. 'B' Troop had been lost in Italy and was never reformed, so that the troops were designated 'A', 'C' and 'D'. There was also a Support Troop with two 3" mortars and two 20mm Polsten cannon, the latter being for anti-aircraft defence but also useful against enemy ground targets. These heavy

2   Those seeking more detail should see Fairley, *Remember Arnhem: The Story of the 1st Airborne Reconnaissance Squadron at Arnhem* (Aldershot: Pegasus Journal, 1978).
3   PRO file WO171/406 War Diary, 1st Airborne Recce Squadron, Jan-Dec 1944.

weapons were also moved in jeeps and trailers, the cannon being towed behind the jeeps. Most of the recce jeeps had been fitted with Vickers 'K' machine guns, designed for use in aircraft but now obsolete for that role. The guns were lightweight and offered a high rate of fire and were used extensively to thicken the firepower of units like the Long Range Desert Group and the Special Air Service by being fitted to their vehicles, sometimes in twin mounts. With its lack of armoured vehicles, they were one way in which Gough could try to make his unit a little more potent. Total manpower of the unit was about 205 men at the time of Market Garden, with a total of 31 jeeps.[4]

As to why the unit had no armoured vehicles, the author has found no official records to provide any definite reasons. (We should note that the reference in some secondary sources to the use of 'armoured jeeps' at Arnhem is incorrect). The absence of tanks in 1st ARS can perhaps be explained simply by the course of events during the unit's development. The Airborne Light Tank Squadron, as we have seen, had actually joined 1st Airborne Division on being formed, but had been unable to follow the division to the Middle East as the Hamilcar glider was not available at that time. Thus the light tanks had, more by default than planning, eventually joined 6th Airborne Division. The absence of a significant expansion in the Hamilcar force between D-Day and Arnhem may also have been an obstacle to the expansion of 1st ARS into a regiment that included light tanks. Only the same two Hamilcar tug squadrons that had been available on D-Day were available for Operation Market. After Normandy, it is also evident that the carriage of light tanks had a much lower priority, and as we shall see in the second part of this chapter, 6th AARR itself was about to be reorganised with a much reduced complement of airborne light tanks. Thus the expansion of 1st ARS to include light tanks would have been counter to this trend and seems not to have been considered worthwhile. As for other types of armoured vehicle, the only reason for the continuing absence of some Dingo scout cars and universal carriers in 1st ARS seems also to have been the limited availability of Hamilcars, which were increasingly used to carry 17pdr anti-tank guns and supplies rather than light armoured vehicles. Dingos did finally begin to be issued to 1st ARS in January 1945, and some exercises with these vehicles, flown in Hamilcars, were conducted from Tarrant Rushton just before the end of the war in Europe.

For the drop at Arnhem, 1st ARS was assigned the role of dashing from the landing zones to the town in order to seize the vital bridges as soon as possible, relying on speed and surprise. Gough favoured dividing up his unit and using a troop of his squadron to scout ahead of each of the three parachute battalions which constituted the initial assault force, as they moved towards the town. This more conventional recce role was the role in which the squadron had been trained, but Gough was overruled, and the squadron was to be used as an independent formation to try to seize the bridges as soon as possible.[5] For his *coup de main* role, some armoured vehicles would obviously be preferable to the vulnerable jeeps, and Gough requested some help from 6th AARR. 'I wanted them to let me have three Hamilcar gliders, with a troop of light tanks from the 6th Airborne Armoured Reconnaissance Regiment, because I said that I didn't see how we could really do this

---

4 *Remember Arnhem*, pp.13-16.
5 *Remember Arnhem*, pp.26-27.

coup de main unless we had some armour'.[6] This modest and sensible request was, apparently, not acted on. 'I'm sure' said Gough 'that the boys from the 6th would have volunteered right away, but I don't think that any real effort was made to ask them'.[7] It should be born in mind that orders were issued to the commander of 1st Airborne Division only 7 days before the operation was to commence, and this could well have been a factor in preventing arrangements being made to borrow airborne tanks from another unit. Gough was also refused permission to upgrade his jeeps with twin mounted Vickers guns, on the grounds that sufficient ammunition could not be made available. These refusals to help a unit with a vital role seem, at least with hindsight, to have been a mistake. As it turned out, some elements of 1st ARS were ambushed on their way to Arnhem and so prevented from carrying out their mission, whilst other elements could find no way through. Only a small proportion of the unit (including, however, Freddie Gough) made it to the bridge. It would seem reasonable to conclude that some light armoured vehicles, whether scout cars, universal carriers or light tanks, would have improved the unit's chances of fulfilling its task.

A brief summary of the Hamilcar's role at Arnhem is now required. Lack of tug and para-dropping aircraft meant that 1st Airborne Division would have to be landed in three lifts, scheduled for the 17th, 18th and 19th September. The 1st Parachute Brigade and most of 1st Airlanding Brigade, plus various supporting troops were to land on the 17th. The gliders involved on this first day were to carry in the Airlanding Brigade and some of the supporting troops, and consisted of 307 Horsas and 13 Hamilcars. The 4th Parachute Brigade was the main part of the drop on the 18th, but gliders were also assigned to carry in further elements of the Airlanding Brigade and some supplies. For this 270 Horsas and 15 Hamilcars were assigned. The landing on the 19th was to consist mainly of the Polish Parachute Brigade plus a resupply effort. This would involve 35 Horsas and 10 Hamilcars.

Thus the original plan involved the use of 38 Hamilcars, only four more than on D-Day. Losses from D-Day seem to have been made up, as Alan Wood states that 64 Hamilcars were available to the RAF at the time of Operation Market. However, as we have seen, only the same two Halifax squadrons were available as tugs, although two more were forming, so that this limited the number of Hamilcars that could be deployed. Nevertheless, on all three lifts 298 and 644 Squadrons towed a mix of Horsas and Hamilcars, so that spare Halifaxes were obviously available, and it would seem therefore that more Hamilcars could have been used if the planners had been willing to assign them. All Hamilcars for Arnhem flew from Tarrant Rushton. It is worth noting that the vehicles of 1st ARS also flew from this airfield on the first lift, in Horsas towed by Halifaxes of 644 and 298 Squadrons.

Of the 13 Hamilcars to be flown in on the 17th, eight would carry 17pdrs of 1st Airlanding Anti-Tank Battery with their Morris towing vehicles, and the other five would carry ten universal carriers. Along with the vehicles the various crews totalled 90 men. The carriers were to supply transport for the 1st, 2nd and 3rd Parachute Battalions, the 1st Battalion the Border regiment and the 7th Battalion,

---

6   Quoted in *Remember Arnhem*, p.28.
7   *Remember Arnhem*, p.28.

King's Own Scottish Borderers.[8] Of the fifteen Hamilcars for the next day, eight were to carry another eight 17pdrs of the 2nd Airlanding Battery, and another four carried a total of eight carriers which were to provide battalion transport for the three battalions of 4th Parachute Brigade and for the 2nd Battalion, the South Staffordshire Regiment. The other three were packed with ammunition, engineers and stores. This was something of an experiment, as it was thought the Hamilcar would provide a more efficient way of bringing in stores than the relatively small Horsa. Once again, amongst the vehicle loads 89 men would be in the Hamilcars. The ten Hamilcars for the 19th were to carry in elements of the 878th US Airborne Aviation Engineer Battalion, who were to construct a forward airfield on landing zone 'Z' after clearing away the crashed gliders from the area. The loads were various bulldozers, cranes and graders along with engineering personnel. The British did not have an equivalent unit so the American engineers were borrowed for the operation. The rest of the American engineer battalion would fly into LZ 'X' in a grand total of 147 Waco gliders.

All of the 15 Hamilcars from the first lift arrived safely over the landing zone (LZ 'Z'), but two were sadly lost when they nosed over on soft ground, resulting in the loss of all four glider pilots on board when the gliders ended up on their backs. Three died, and the fourth was badly wounded and taken prisoner. The 17pdrs on board were also lost. The driver of one of the towing vehicles described his experience later:

> I can only describe it as a shuddering bump, a slight lift in the air and then a crash. We had overturned, and I was left hanging upside down, my right foot broken and trapped under the brake pedal, my head and face almost covered in what I thought was potato soil, and, to make matters worse, a jerrycan had burst, and petrol was covering me all over. I smelt awful and felt bloody awful. After some time, I felt someone touch me and ask what was wrong. I told him. He tried to release my foot, but I screamed in pain. So he came back with a hand spike and broke the pedal. He dragged me out and put me on a stretcher on the back of a jeep.[9]

The propensity to overturn on landing if the wheels dug in on soft ground was a weakness in the Hamilcar which seems to have first emerged at Arnhem. It was to cause problems during Varsity as well. The concentration of weight towards the front of the aircraft and the lack of a nosewheel were the main reasons. During training, landings on bad ground had obviously been avoided for safety reasons, so the problem had had no chance to emerge. One other Hamilcar came to grief in this lift when it overran the LZ and hit a railway embankment. The two carriers inside were catapulted out, one being driven away undamaged with the other being salvaged later. The glider pilots were unhurt.

On the next day, the second lift was delayed for a few hours by morning fog in the UK. En-route, one Halifax tug developed engine trouble and the Hamilcar with its 17pdr load cast off and landed at Chilbolton airfield. Another 17pdr Hamilcar ditched in the Channel when its tug also had engine trouble. One more 17pdr from this lift also failed to get into action, when its Hamilcar landed short of

---

8   Details of Arnhem loads from van Hees.
9   Quoted in Middlebrook, p.104.

the LZ ('X') after being hit by flak. Yet another Hamilcar was lost when one of the stores carrying gliders fell into enemy hands, possibly after being hit in the air and catching fire. The loads of the other two stores carriers were all recovered and were described as 'invaluable' to the hard pressed division.[10]

The third lift was delayed by continuing problems with the weather and the deteriorating situation on the ground as the operation began to go seriously wrong. Some Horsa resupply missions were flown on the 19th and 20th, but the Polish Brigade did not drop until the 21st, and in the end only one Hamilcar was used. This was the aircraft which had landed at Chilbolton on the second lift, but the attempt to carry in the 17pdr load failed again when the tow rope broke over Belgium. The glider made a safe landing near Gent. The ten Hamilcars carrying the American engineers would no longer be required as the situation on the ground had not developed as planned, and their lift was cancelled. They had been destined for LZ 'L', to keep them clear of landing zone 'Z' on which they were to create the forward airfield.

Broadly speaking the Hamilcars had been successful in their second major operation. The 17pdrs were to prove an important factor in allowing the division to hold on as long as it did, and the stores and carriers were also of great use, though the absence of a towing hook on the carriers (one of the weight saving features of the 'airborne' carrier) turned out to be a disadvantage. The Morris 30 cwt had suffered from unreliability problems during the operation, and would be replaced by the American Dodge 3/4 ton WC52 in the next big airborne operation, the crossing of the Rhine.[11] Why a few more Hamilcars could not have been made available to fly in some Tetrarchs or Locusts for the 1st ARS remains a mystery. The comments of Major Gough, already quoted, are the only reference to this idea that the author has found.

It is not necessary here to try to sum up the whole Market Garden operation, but as a final word it should be noted that both the glider pilots and 1st ARS were heavily involved in the desperate fighting that resulted, and both suffered (along with the other units of the division) very heavy casualties. Both would require large numbers of replacements before they were once again fit for battle.

Back at Larkhill, the men of 6th AARR who had returned from France were all granted leave between 11th and 24th September. The unit was also ordered to be ready once again for overseas service by 30th September. However, in the event the unit was to be given three months grace before it was once more in action, and during this period Lt. Col. Stewart took the opportunity to reorganise the regiment following its extensive combat experience in Normandy.

The changes took effect during the first week in October. The separate tank and recce squadrons disappeared and the regiment now consisted of two Recce Squadrons, a Support Squadron and the HQ Squadron. Each recce squadron ('A' and 'B') had four troops, the first being a tank or 'heavy' troop of four tanks, which would be Locusts when gliderborne or Cromwells otherwise. In addition the recce squadrons had three recce troops each with two universal carriers and two scout cars. The support squadron ('C' Squadron) had two MMG troops with four

---

10 PRO file WO219/5137 !st Airborne Division, Report on Operation Market.
11 See *Tugs and Gliders to Arnhem*, p.245.

Vickers each, mounted on carriers, and a 4.2" mortar troop with four mortars towed by jeeps. Also in the Support Squadron was the 'Blitz' or 'Infantry Support Troop', mounted on eighteen motorcycles with a scout car for the troop commander. Within the Headquarters Squadron was an Intercommunications Troop with ten motorcycles, an Admin Troop with various support services (for example, REME and RAMC) mounted mainly in jeeps, and a seaborne party of clerks, storemen, batmen etcetera mainly in three ton lorries. Regimental Headquarters was no longer equipped with tanks, but had two Daimler Scout Cars and three jeeps. The Squadron HQs were likewise mounted in scout cars and jeeps. The full establishment of personnel was set at thirty two officers and 326 other ranks.[12] In addition to this official complement of vehicles, it is clear from the war diary and memories of 6th AARR veterans that other vehicles were added to help the regiment function during the operations to come in north-west Europe. The White Scout Car (a wheeled, armoured vehicle from the USA with room for about six people) was used by squadron HQs and regimental signallers, whilst the medical officer acquired an M3 armoured half track to assist in casualty evacuation under fire. Additional three-ton trucks seem to have been attached to the fighting squadrons for resupply purposes. The regiment also acquired at least one Scammel Heavy Recovery Truck, for recovery of the heavier vehicles when damaged or bogged down, and a Sherman Armoured Recovery Vehicle for the same purpose. Trooper John Banbery, of 'B' Squadron, has a vivid description of the latter in action, following an incident in Germany towards the end of the war when his tank was bogged down with enemy infantry in the vicinity:

> They were extremely aggressive our REME, all paratroopers. [...] The fitters arrived and you could see them arriving because in the distance all sorts of things were going up in smoke and they came to us through a barn, not round the barn, they went straight through the barn with stuff going up in the air, and they had a Bren gun fitted at every corner and were firing the whole lot as they arrived. And they pulled us out quite easily.[13]

The drastic reduction in tank numbers which had occurred just prior to the breakout from Normandy was confirmed. The days of landing a whole squadron of twenty tanks were gone. Unfortunately, the reasoning behind the changes has not survived in records, but it is not unreasonable to assume that the large tank squadron was found to be rather unwieldy. If it consisted of all light tanks, there would be too many vehicles of little real use as battle tanks but which would also probably be too conspicuous and draining of resources for the reconnaissance role. On the other hand, a full squadron of Cromwells would be rather overdoing it for an airborne division, as even regular infantry divisions did not have an allocation of tanks. The practice in the British Army at this time was to attach tank squadrons from amongst the armoured divisions or from

---

12 Airborne Armoured Reconnaissance Regiment, RAC (1944), War Establishment, effective date 18th October 1944. My thanks to Paul Middleton for supplying me a copy of this document.

13 These are edited extracts from Mr Banbury's extensive taped interview with the Imperial War Museum regarding his wartime experiences, given in 1998. The transcript is a mine of information and will be referred to many times in the pages to follow. IWM Sound Archive 15205/7, Banbery, reels 1-7. Transcript provided by The Tank Museum, Bovington.

specialist tank brigades if the infantry needed armoured support. The reorganisation seemed to confirm the unit as one whose speciality was reconnaissance, with a move away from the tank orientated days of the Airborne Light Tank Squadron. The addition of the heavy 4.2" mortars is also interesting. These would be unusual weapons for a recce unit, but it should be remembered that after the experiences in Normandy the lack of this type of weapon, particularly for the counter-mortar role, had been mentioned. It would seem that the heavy mortars had been included in the division by allocating them to the recce regiment, and we shall see that 'C' Squadron was used very much as a divisional asset to provide fire support for various units of the division, not just for 6th AARR.

The rest of October, November and most of December were spent in training. This included all the usual items; exercises (including tank/infantry cooperation), work on the ranges, glider experience flying, and a 4.2" mortar course for some members of the Support Squadron. Exercise Beer, on 9th November, was a good example of how flying practice was incorporated into an exercise without taking the risk of off-airfield glider landings. The Hamilcars involved in the exercise flew from Tarrant Rushton, and after about half an hour in the air returned to land on the airfield. The loads then disembarked and proceeded by road to the exercise area.[14] The diary records one unusual event between 12th and 14th December when a recce troop of 'B' Squadron was placed under command of a company of 8th Parachute Battalion to aid in dealing with a suspected escape attempt from a P.O.W. camp. On the 14th the diary notes, 'Escape attempt did not take place but tp assisted in restoring order after arrest of the ringleaders'. On 19th December the division received a new commander, Major General E.L. Bols. Richard Gale moved up the airborne ladder to become deputy commander of XVIII Airborne Corps, of which 6th Airborne Division was destined to become a part. The round of training and exercises was finally brought to a halt on 20th December, when the regiment received orders to proceed overseas along with the rest of the division. Plans for Christmas leave had to be abandoned.

Three days previously, the Germans had opened their offensive in the Ardennes, and 6th Airborne were destined to supplement British forces already on the continent. It was on the 20th that Montgomery had been given command of all allied forces on the northern half of the 'bulge', as the German salient came to be called, and the bringing over of 6th Airborne mirrored Eisenhower's activation of the US 82nd and 101st Airborne divisions which had occurred on the 17th. Airborne divisions, waiting in reserve for an airborne operation to be ordered, formed a handy source of elite manpower, and the British in particular at this stage of the war were short of infantry resources. 6th AARR consequently spent Christmas Day loading themselves onto an LST (Landing Ship, Tank) at Tilbury Docks. The LST was anchored in the fairway fogbound until the morning of the 28th, so the regiment must have spent a very disappointing Christmas. However, by 1100 on the 29th the regiment was back on the continent, disembarking at Ostend a few days behind most of the division. The bulk of 6th Airborne Division had reached Ostend on Christmas Eve and by the 26th were already concentrated along the Meuse River between Dinant and Namur. 6th AARR caught up with the division on the 30th, and commenced patrolling the river in the sector Dinant-Givet.

14 PRO file WO171/425, 6th Airborne Division, War Diary, 1944.

The winter weather had made the journey to the Meuse something of a nightmare, and was to seriously affect subsequent operations. There was extensive ice and snow and nighttime temperatures were regularly down to -28° Fahrenheit. Icy roads had delayed the regiment, with the tracked vehicles being particularly badly affected. Digging in was hampered by the frozen ground, and simply surviving outdoors was a constant problem. Mist significantly reduced visibility on many days. Trooper John Banbery was a tank crewman with 'B' Squadron who had joined the regiment after Normandy, and later described some of the difficulties the unit had to deal with:

> We were given the tank suits just beforehand, the zipped tank suits. Excellent, very good for that time. That was all we had extra, nothing else. We didn't even know it was so cold out there. I went with Advance Party, Christmas Day. The other side of the Channel was very cold compared to here; the continental land mass was extraordinarily cold. I wore a jump smock on top of my uniform, just a bit more extra warmth. The main trouble was your feet, standing on metal.
>
> The only way we could get the tanks up hills was to put rocks under the tracks. Going up hills was quite a nightmare, because the tanks were all over the place. If you got a good rock you used to put it in at the front of the track and walk back and pick it up at the back and take it round to the front again, and it kept you walking. We were doing a walking pace a lot of the time. We had some trips where there were tanks all over the place, there were telegraph poles down and carriers slid into them and hit. It was quite chaotic at times.
>
> You had to be very careful where you stopped a tank, because on a slight camber on the road all of a sudden 28 tons would start moving. My particular tank went down a side road like that, sheered off a chunk of a bogie in the process. We had been standing there for about a quarter of an hour and suddenly it moved, nobody was in the way luckily. You learnt where to stand next to vehicles.[15]

Trooper Collins recorded that 'the height of one's ambition was to just to ride in a Bren Carrier next to its engine'.[16]

By the time 6th AARR arrived in the Ardennes, the German offensive had been halted and the allied counter attack was commencing. 6th Airborne Division had been added to the strength of 30 Corps.[17] The plan was for 30 Corps to take over the western tip of the bulge, relieving two American divisions which would be used in the counter attack role. Montgomery did not intend 30 Corps to take a leading part in the counter offensive, their job being primarily to follow up the retreating Germans and maintain pressure on them. This did not, however, prevent some sharp and sometimes bloody actions being fought by British troops, and 6th Airborne Division were to have their share. When 6th AARR caught up, the division was establishing itself in defensive positions on the far side of the Meuse, having taken over from the 84th US Infantry Division. The positions were located just to the west of the Marche-Rochefort railway which marked the German front line. The advance eastwards was to commence on the 3rd of January. By that date, 6th

---

15 Extracts edited from IWM interview
16 C.L. Collins, 'Tales of Old Retold', op cit.
17 Overview of British efforts in the Ardennes derived from Crookenden, *Battle of the Bulge 1944* (London: Book Club Associates, 1980), pp142-151

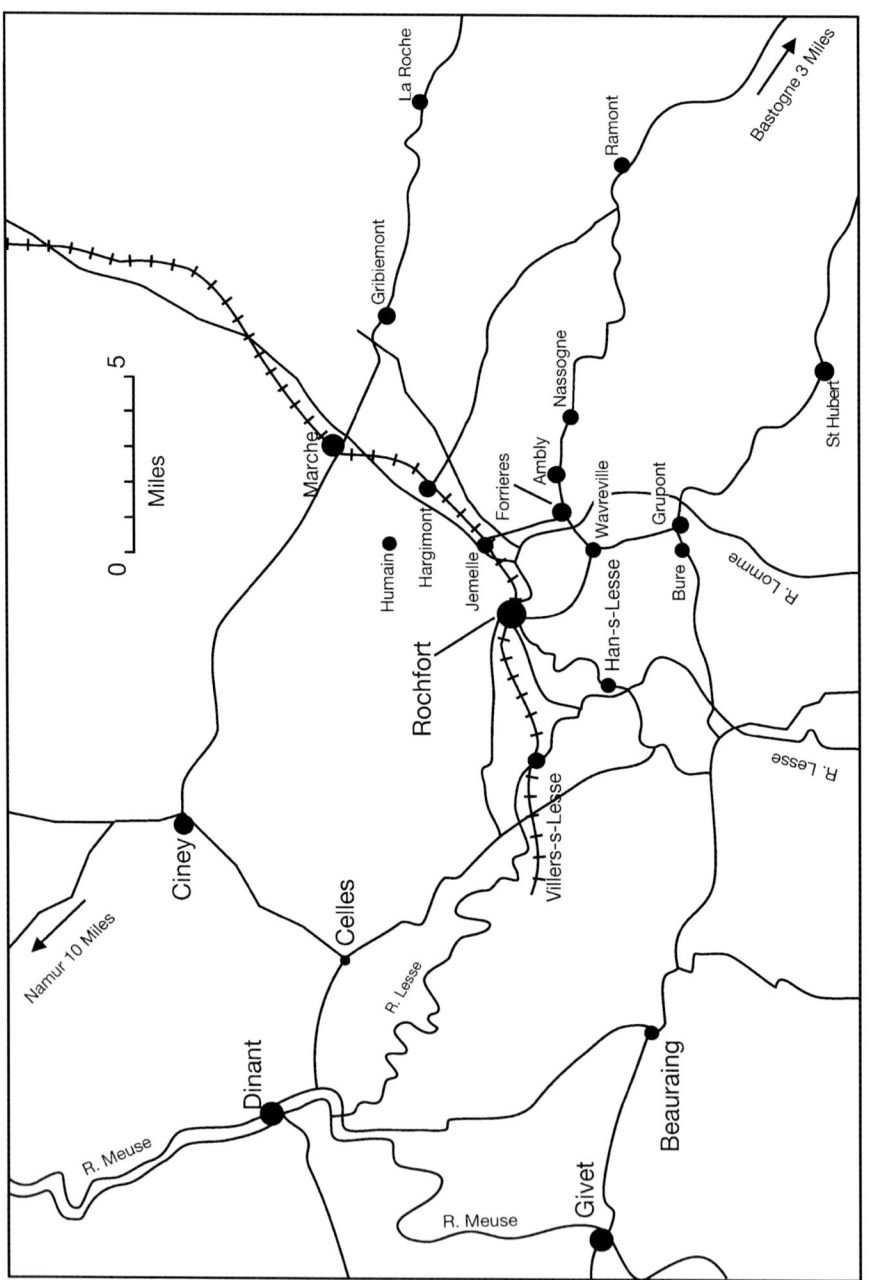

Ardennes, 30th September 1944-19th January 1945.

AARR had been ordered to occupy a small bridgehead south-east of the Meuse across from Namur, with responsibility for guarding the crossings in the area. This placed them in the rear of the division at the time the advance started.

The 30 Corps advance was to take place eastwards against the extreme western tip of the German salient, roughly from the direction of Dinant. 53rd Welsh Division was on the left of the advance with 6th Airborne on the right, and 51st Highland Division behind in reserve. The main, and most costly action by the paras was the vicious and bloody three day fight to capture the village of Bure by units of 5th Parachute Brigade, which took place from the 3rd to 5th January. Other parts of the division were more lucky, with the Germans withdrawing in front of them. The German units in the area were of high quality, most being from 2nd Panzer Division (elements of which were in Bure) or the Panzer Lehr Division. 6th AARR remained in their positions to the rear until the evening of 5th January when they were ordered forward to Hans-sur-Lesse. Regimental HQ was eventually established in a chateau just outside Villers-sur-Lesse, and for the next week the regiment was employed supporting the division as 6th Airborne probed eastwards in the direction of Bastogne, with the hope of meeting US troops advancing northwest towards them.

Initially the regiment was placed under 5th Parachute Brigade, and had responsibility for the local defence of Hans-sur-Lesse as well as patrolling the high ground east of the Rochefort-Wavreville road, around the villages of Jemelle and Forrieres. Constant difficulties were experienced due to ice and snow on the roads, and enemy mines. The first mine casualty was a scout car of 'A' Squadron on the 6th, and there were to be more to come. In these conditions, foot patrols were often undertaken. John Banbery's memories of his time in the Ardennes give a flavour of what the regiment experienced. He recalls the initial deployment in Han-sur-Lesse:

> It was a village, it was a tourist village even in those days and we were only on the edge of it – and then there was a wall of mist, and then there was nothing but the Germans through the mist somewhere. So we were always very edgy. Enough food but not a lot. Food was not coming through that well. Guard duties at night were pretty fiendish. You could only do an hour outside, it was so cold. Starting up tanks in the morning, you had to wear gloves because your fingers stuck to the metal. It was more the elements than the Germans, who were obviously retreating. It was very fluid. Our medical officer in his half track ran into a German tank on a road and they just turned him round and sent him back. You could meet anything down the roads.
>
> We didn't do much, but it welded us together. We had very few casualties because all the verges of the roads were mined by the Germans, so if you drove onto the verge – and you didn't know where the verge was because of the snow – some vehicles went up.[18]

His time in the town also included one unusual and unnerving encounter:

> We were sitting outside a cafe in Han-sur-Lesse and we had all our small arms in pieces – someone had decided they were getting a bit dirty and we'd better clean them. We were sitting at the cafe tables with bits of pistols, springs all round the

---

18 IWM interview.

place; and then round the corner came a Panther. People dived into holes, they dived all over the place. They picked up these bits of springs etc very quickly and the place vanished. In fact, it was a captured Panther but no-one told us it was coming round the corner. I think the Guards had it at the time. I've never seen people move so fast in all my life. Me included.[19]

On the 8th, 5th Brigade ordered one squadron of the regiment to execute a left hook via Rochefort and Humain (both already occupied by the paras), followed by a movement south towards Ambly, Nassogne and Forrieres, in order to cut the crossroads between the two latter villages and to see if it was possible to get round behind the Germans in this area. 'A' Squadron, with one MMG troop and one mortar troop from 'C' Squadron attached, executed the movement whilst 'B' Squadron kept up pressure from the west, with tanks of the latter firing on Germans in Forrieres early on the 9th. Later in the day the village was entered by 'B' Squadron, who found the Germans gone and the bridges blown. They were shortly afterwards relieved by infantry. In the meantime, 'A' Squadron had found their way south through Hargimont blocked by mines and more blown bridges. As they probed for alternative routes, an MMG carrier was lost to mines with three casualties. Even when vehicles did find a way over the small River Lomme, they found further progress blocked by deep snow (reported in the war diary as 12-15" deep) and only a foot patrol could make progress towards Ambly. All 'A' Squadron sub-units had been withdrawn west of Hargimont by the end of the day.

On the 10th, 6th Airborne Division was arranged into three brigade groups in order to push eastwards and clear the area south of Marche, in the area Marche-Gribiemont-Nassogne. 6th AARR was attached to 6th Airlanding Brigade and it would seem they were operating on the left flank of the division, with 51st Highland Division (who had taken over from 53rd Division) on their left. For the next three days they probed south-eastwards with 'A' Squadron in the lead, eventually reaching the village of Ramont. There were one or two minor brushes with the enemy but the movement took the form of following up a retreating enemy, with the main delays coming from roadblocks formed of felled trees, as well as the usual mines and snow. On the 11th, examples of road blocks included one using 13 trees over a distance of 200 yards, another of 12 trees over the same distance, with charges still attached to some trees. A crater on the road 15 feet deep and 18 feet long was also encountered.[20] On the 12th, 'A' Squadron's tanks were initially unable to leave harbour due to snow conditions. Finally, on the 13th, troops of 87th US Infantry Division were contacted a little west of Ramont, and this may have been the first contact (or at least one of the first contacts) between 30 Corps and 3rd US Army, who were advancing from their relief of Bastogne.

By this time, 30 Corps' role was coming to an end, as 3rd US Army from the south approached a link up with 1st US Army from the north. This link up finally took place at Houffalize (about 20km east of Ramont) on the 17th. Already by the 14th, all squadrons of 6th AARR had been returned to the Hans-sur-Lesse area for rest and re-equipping.

---

19 IWM interview.
20 Details from message log of 6th Airborne Division, contained in WO171/4157, War diary, 6th Airborne Division.

cleared of mines, and we had to form our own guard at night, and we did a night shoot. I should think the whole of Holland must have heard us, because if you start up four Meteors, which is followed by somebody accidentally standing on one of the gun triggers and firing the 75 into the back of the other tank ahead – without injuring anybody... That actually happened. It was loaded and the safety catch was on and somebody in the confusion in the darkness trod on the foot pedal and it went off! It was an HE shot not AP, luckily. Because we were going to fire HE. That was a good start. The Germans had fixed machine guns down some of the straight streets on the other side and as soon as we started moving they opened up with machine gun fire and we had a go at one or two factory chimneys and tall buildings on the other side, fairly effectively, I think. I don't suppose the paras were too keen as it probably opened up a lot of fire for them as well.[22]

The tanks employed both direct and indirect fire, the procedures for the latter having been learned at Larkhill during training.

Those members of the regiment not manning heavy weapons or tanks were also kept busy. The regiment was given responsibility for regular patrols of the wooded areas in their sector, and special searches were also laid on when enemy patrols were believed to have crossed to the British side. The boggy ground conditions, which followed the thaw mentioned earlier, often meant these had to take place on foot. On the 13th, ten Weasel tracked carriers were allocated to 6th Airlanding Brigade to help with transport tasks, who gave four of them to 6th AARR. These were American vehicles similar to the British universal carrier but with wide tracks which always made them particularly useful in boggy ground. The para and glider battalions were carrying out their usual policy of aggressive patrolling which frequently took them across the river onto the German side. As 6th AARR were officially in reserve, this dangerous task was spared them, although the war diary records that on the night of 15th/16th February an officer of 'B' Squadron accompanied a recce patrol of the 12th Devons over the river.

It was on the very next day that information was first officially received that the division was to return to England, following relief by 75th US Infantry Division. The movement order issued on the 19th records that at this time 6th AARR had a total of around 70 vehicles in all. On the 21st the regiment moved out, and over the 24th to 28th February were transported back across the channel to Tilbury, and thence once again to Larkhill. Personnel who had been on active service then received a well earned weeks leave during the first week in March. However, some elements of the regiment remained on the continent, and it must have occurred to many men that it would not be long before the whole regiment returned to the front. Indeed, the 'seaborne tail' of the whole division remained behind, meaning those supporting, reserve and administrative units which were not normally part of the division when it was committed operationally in its airborne role. These units would normally follow up an airborne deployment, moving by sea and road in order to join the rest of the division as soon as possible after the operation had started. The elements of 6th AARR which stayed in Europe were recorded in the war diary and consisted of a staff car, five 3 ton lorries, a medical half track, an armoured recovery vehicle and two Scammel recovery vehicles, the eight Cromwells and a jeep and

22 IWM interview

trailer. Two officers and 51 other ranks accompanied the vehicles, including skeleton tank crews of two men per tank. The other three crew members would man the airborne Locust tanks.

Suspicions of forthcoming operations were soon confirmed when on 9th March the regiment was told it would participate in Operation Varsity, the airborne part of Montgomery's massive operation to cross the Rhine into Germany. For only the second time, and also for the last time, the unit was to fly tanks directly into battle.

Chapter 8

Operation Varsity

The first phase of Eisenhower's plan to close up to the Rhine, prior to the final assault on Germany, had started before 6th Airborne left Holland. This was Operation Veritable, which opened on 8th February and involved 30 Corps, who attacked initially from starting positions well to the north of Venlo, under the command of 1st Canadian Army. The fighting to reach the Rhine in this sector was some of the worst of the North-West European campaign, and it was not until 11th March that the Germans retreated from their final bridgehead west of the Rhine at Wesel.

By this time the Americans were already across the Rhine at Remagen, and Patton's troops were to make a separate crossing at Oppenheim on the night of 22nd-23rd March. However, Montgomery did not modify his own deliberate and elaborate plan for crossing the Rhine in his own sector. When the assault across the river had been planned in January and February, Montgomery had every reason to expect that this last great natural obstacle protecting the heart of Germany would be bitterly contested. In Eisenhower's words, the crossing was expected to be 'the largest and most difficult amphibious operation undertaken since the landings on the coast of Normandy'.[1] In the event, the German Army was so weakened by the fighting prior to the Rhine crossing that the opposition was weaker than expected, and Montgomery drew some criticism from the Americans at the time for being overcautious.[2]

His assault was designated Operation Plunder, and the initial attack would involve two British and two American divisions, as well as a British Commando Brigade, attacking either side of the town of Wesel, supported by massive air and artillery resources and the specialised armour of 79th Armoured Division. To aid this attack, an assault by large airborne forces would take place just after the amphibious operation had started. This was Operation Varsity. Plunder was due to start on the night of 23rd/24th March. Varsity would take place on the morning of the 24th.

The forces for Varsity were those of XVIIIth US Airborne Corps, and consisted of 6th Airborne Division and 17th (US) Airborne Division. The Corps was commanded by Major-General Matthew Ridgeway, with 6th Airborne's old commander, Major-General Gale, as his deputy. Ridgeway had received outline orders for his corps on 14th February, and by 27th February had received the final plan with all necessary details. The task was 'to disrupt the hostile defence of the Rhine in the Wesel sector by the seizure of key terrain, by airborne attack, in order to deepen rapidly the bridgehead to be seized in an assault crossing of the Rhine by British ground forces, and facilitate the further offensive operations of Second

---

1 Quoted in Wilmot, p.681. The overall background to the events in this chapter is mainly drawn from this work.
2 Ibid, p.677.

Army'.[3] The key terrain chosen was an area of higher ground called the Diersfordter Wald, which lay north-west of Wesel, opposite the town of Xanten, and which overlooked the crossing points for the British 12th Corps. The Diersfordter Wald was a thickly wooded ridge which rose to around 200 feet above river level, in an area which was otherwise generally flat agricultural land. Just behind this ridge was the river Issel, which although only 30 to 50 yards wide was an obstacle to tanks. In addition, the local road net, including the crossings over the Issel, converged on the village of Hamminkeln, which lay between the ridge and the river. This village and the river crossings were therefore also included in the objectives of the airborne drop.

As with D-Day, the full details of Operations Plunder and Varsity are not required for this account, but an outline of the latter operation at least is necessary if 6th AARR's part in it is to be appreciated. The Diersfordter Wald feature was divided roughly in half, with 17th US Airborne Division responsible for the southern half, including some crossings over the Issel. 6th Airborne Division was responsible for the northern half, including Hamminkeln and the river crossings east of the village. The operation was shaped by the experience gained in previous large drops, and in particular the lessons of Arnhem. It would be a daylight drop to give the greatest chance of accuracy and concentration, a timing made possible by the overwhelming Allied air superiority. The target area was close to the start line of the ground forces: the Issel is only about 7 miles as the crow flies from the Rhine at Xanten, and much closer at Wesel. The link up between airborne and ground forces was therefore to take place on the first day. The objectives were also in range of Allied artillery support from the west bank of the Rhine. The whole corps would be flown in one lift, and the tactic of dropping and landing the troops at a distance from their objectives was not to be repeated. Six dropping and landing zones were selected for 6th Airborne Division which were all designed to place the assaulting troops on or very near to their objectives. The airborne landings would start at 1000 hours on 24th March, following the amphibious assault which would have commenced at 2200 hours on the 23rd.

As far as German opposition was concerned, the British report on Varsity concluded that "the Germans were never able to organise a strong defence to oppose the assault crossings of the Rhine".[4] They had sustained heavy losses in the fighting west of the Rhine and the general war situation meant that reinforcements were hard to come by. Almost all of 6th Airborne's assault area was in the sector of the German 84th Infantry Division, the right flank division of 86th Corps. On the 84th's right, and on the edge of 6th Airborne's area, was 7th Parachute Division, the left flank unit of 2nd Parachute Corps. All these units were part of 1st Parachute Army, which was a parachute formation in name only. Some of the units in this army were parachute trained Luftwaffe units but most were ordinary Wehrmacht units, and the designation 'Parachute" was honorary only. 84th Division had a total strength of only about 4,000 men. The Germans were, however, expecting an airborne assault. British intelligence estimated that on 17th March there were 153 light and 103 heavy flak guns in the triangle Emmerich-Bocholt-Wesel. A week later the estimate was 712 light guns and 114 heavy. Despite these

3   Quoted in Otway, p 299.
4   PRO file CAB106/1050.

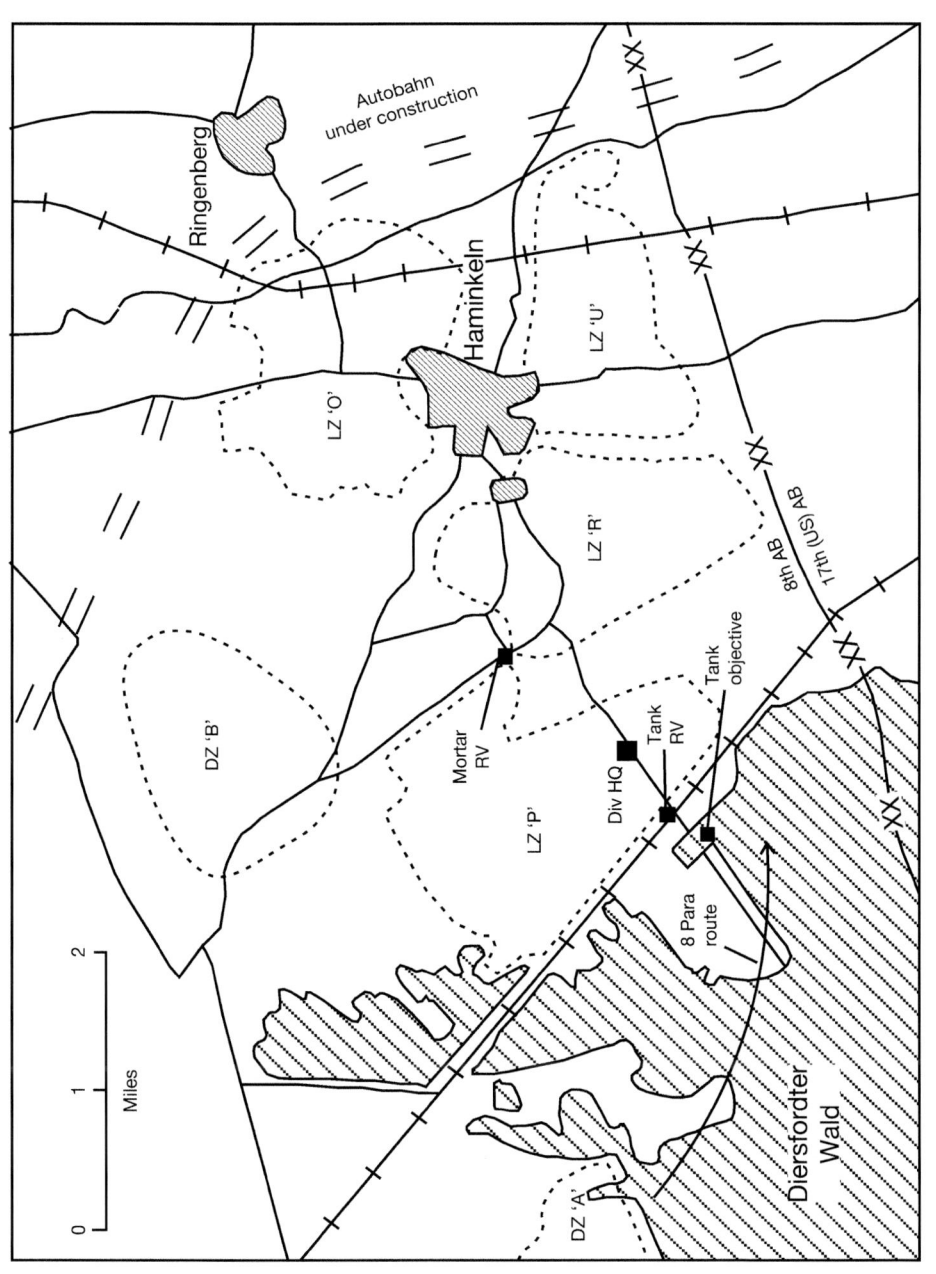

Operation Varsity, 24th March 1945.

preparations, the Germans were completely overwhelmed by the size and ferocity of the Allied air and amphibious assault when it came.

This would be the largest single lift of airborne troops in history. A total of 21,680 troops would be flown in, using 1,591 aircraft and 1,346 gliders for the whole corps.[5] For 6th Airborne, No.38 Group provided six Stirling and four Halifax squadrons, whilst No.46 Group provided six squadrons of Dakotas. These two groups provided all the glider towing for the British division, whilst all the parachute troops were carried by Dakotas of IXth (US) Troop Carrier Command. The lift was in all respects a maximum effort which taxed even the by now vast resources of the Allied air forces. The squadrons of 38 Group had to be increased in size from 24 to 34 aircraft each, with crew strength per squadron increased to 31 crews. The Operational Refresher Training Unit would also have to supply 20 Stirlings. No.46 Group had to employ aircraft and crews from the Operational Training Unit to provide the required number of tugs. In the end, 38 Group was required to provide 320 aircraft, 46 Group 120. Of the 440 gliders employed for 6th Airborne, 48 would be Hamilcars, the rest Horsas. As far as the Glider Pilot Regiment was concerned, the recent losses at Arnhem meant that a large number of RAF pilots (around 1,500 in all) had been drafted into the regiment to provide the glider crews required. This had caused some problems of integration, as some of the RAF pilots resented a posting to non-powered aircraft, and additionally had to submit to Army training to bring their battlefield skills into line with the rest of the regiment. In the end, though, their performance during Varsity earned nothing but praise from all concerned. The massive air armada, when finally joined up in the Wavre area (south of Brussels), would take two and a half hours to pass a given point.[6] The sheer mass of aircraft would mean that the landings, although a single lift, could not be completely simultaneous. The parachute brigades would come in first, followed by the airlanding brigade, and then the divisional troops. The gliders were programmed to land in a period of about 45 minutes, from P+21 to P+65.

Broadly, the plan for 6th Airborne Division involved using the two parachute brigades to capture the Diersfordter Wald, along with some of the ground around it and west of Hamminkeln. Hamminkeln and the bridges over the Issel were allocated to 6th Airlanding Brigade. In the centre of the three brigades, Divisional HQ would land along with some of the divisional troops on LZ 'P', which was north east of the Diersfordter Wald and west of Hamminkeln. Amongst these divisional troops would be two elements of 6th AARR, namely the eight Locust tanks of the two tank troops and the 4.2" mortars of the Support (or 'C') Squadron. The rest of 6th AARR would arrive by road, linking up with the airborne elements on D+1. The explanation for this limited involvement is fairly straightforward. In the first place, it was decided that the maximum infantry resources were needed on the ground to achieve the tasks in hand. To this end, additional gliders were allocated to the parachute brigades to bring in heavy equipment and stores, as well as ensuring that all anti-tank guns and the guns of the Airlanding Light Regiment were also flown in. The allocation of gliders to divisional troops suffered accordingly, and

5 Figures from *Glider soldiers*, p.320. The figures given in *Airborne Forces* differ only very slightly.
6 PRO file WO205/922. Other details in WO205/947, AIR 37/327 and CAB 106/1050.

only those considered essential were carried in. As all units were expected to go straight into action against known objectives, with the additional intention of early relief by ground forces, the presence of a full-blown reconnaissance regiment was obviously something of a luxury. General Bols therefore only called on those elements of the regiment which could offer a worthwhile advantage in firepower to his forces immediately on landing.

In terms of Hamilcar loads, the pattern established at Arnhem was continued. Only in Normandy were the majority of the Hamilcars allocated to lifting light tanks. For Varsity, the emphasis would once again be on carrying the 17pdr anttank guns and reserve stocks of stores, particularly ammunition. Of the 48 Hamilcars, 16 were allocated to the airlanded 17pdr anti-tank batteries, each carrying a 17pdr and a Dodge 3/4 ton truck as towing vehicle (the latter replacing the Morris 30cwts used previously). The next highest number, 12 in all, were allocated to 716 Light Composite Company, RASC. These were loaded with universal carriers with trailers and stores, the carriers to act as transport in collecting and distributing stores both from the Hamilcars and from re-supply drops. Eight Hamilcars were given over to transporting the Locusts of 6th AARR, then four to 53rd Airlanding Regiment, RA which appear to have been loaded with 44 stores panniers (almost certainly containing ammunition), each weighing 350lbs. Two were allocated to the Royal Engineers each of which carried a D4 bulldozer. Finally, the two parachute brigades were allocated three Hamilcars each. These carried universal carriers, one for each battalion HQ. All Hamilcars flew from Woodbridge in Suffolk, as the distance from Tarrant Rushton was too great. However, Tarrant Rushton was still the official Hamilcar base, and the gliders were loaded here and flown, fully loaded, to Woodbridge for the operation. As before, 298 and 644 Squadrons shared the towing task, each squadron taking 24 Hamilcars. Each of these squadrons was also allocated six Horsas to tow. Readers may be interested to know that two 25pdr field guns were flown in, mainly to fire purple smoke to mark targets for RAF ground attack sorties. Such guns would normally be considered a Hamilcar load, but they were shoe-horned into Horsas, although according to the records of 'B' Squadron, GPR, 'great difficulty' was experienced in both loading and unloading.[7]

Some comments about the overall effectiveness of the Hamilcars in Operation Varsity will be given at the end of this account. First, we should now turn in detail to the activities of 6th AARR, including both the airborne elements and the land based follow up. These activities were detailed by Lt. Col. Stewart in a report he submitted in April 1945. That this report has survived is largely due to the research efforts of Bob Bragg, an ex-Para, to whom I am indebted for passing the report on to me.

Lt. Col. Stewart organised his eight Locusts into two troops of three tanks and an HQ of two, and took command of what he termed this 'half squadron'. The Locusts used had the standard 37mm gun without the Littlejohn attachment. As we have seen, these tanks were given the role of divisional reserve. They were to assemble at the road/rail crossing on the south western edge of LZ 'P', and from there move to deny the enemy the use of some high ground on the eastern edges of the Diersfordter Wald which overlooked the site for divisional HQ. They had a general brief to render

[7] PRO file WO171/5129

support to any other troops they encountered on the way, if possible. The mortar troop, under the command of Captain O'Hanlon, consisted of the four 4.2" mortars and their jeep tows which were to be transported in four Horsas, plus an additional two Horsas each containing a jeep with two ammunition trailers. This troop was under overall command of the divisional CRA, and was to operate very much as an additional resource for the Light Regiment, Royal Artillery. The mortars were to be emplaced near a 'T' junction to the east of LZ 'P', on the western edge of LZ 'R' which was the LZ for 12th Devons. The troop was to provide an OP team which was to be capable of spotting for the guns of the light regiment if necessary. The OPs of the light regiment were in turn to be capable of shooting in the mortars if required. Manpower for the tank half squadron was three officers and twenty four other ranks, and for the mortar troop two officers and twenty six other ranks.[8]

To take the experience of the tanks first, loading at Tarrant Rushton took place over the period 17th to 20th March, and squadron records indicate the loaded gliders were ferried to Woodbridge on the 20th and 21st. Once at Woodbridge it is noted that 'engines were run daily' to ensure serviceability. Briefings for the troops took place on the 22nd and 23rd. Take offs from Woodbridge finally commenced at 0720 on the 24th. Glider pilots for 6th AARR's Hamilcars once again came from 'C' Squadron of the Glider Pilot Regiment. Weather conditions for Varsity were excellent, and all eight Hamilcar/Halifax combinations arrived in the vicinity of the LZ without incident. From this point on, however, the half squadron suffered a number of misfortunes and tragedies.

The first of these occurred to the Hamilcar containing the Locust of Sgt Dawson. Whilst approaching the Rhine, the glider appeared to disintegrate and the tank fell to the ground. Descriptions of this event differ over the cause: either enemy fire or structural failure. According to the account of Trooper C.L. Collins, the floor of the glider gave way and the Hamilcar made a safe landing with most of its floor missing. The tank and its crew were found some months later in the mud at the edge of the Rhine.[9] The signals sent from Tarrant Rushton giving the first reports of Varsity have a slightly different story to Trooper Collins. These indicate the Hamilcar 'exploded' or 'disintegrated' just after casting off to the west of the Rhine, at around 1035. The glider then 'crashed to the ground', rather than landing safely.[10] An ex-member of 'A' Squadron, in a letter to the Pegasus Journal written as recently as 1998, maintains the damage to the Hamilcar was due to enemy fire.[11] However, the glider raid report for this combination (a 298 Squadron Halifax and Hamilcar chalk number 262) survives and would seem to provide the most accurate answer to this minor mystery. This records that the glider broke away five miles west of the Rhine, ten miles south west of the LZ. The report continues, 'tail gunner saw tail and fin break off, and glider immediately dropped – rope broke and two seconds later whole glider appeared to disintegrate. Nothing of any solid appearance seen to fall after that'.[12] A report from another eye witness has also re-

---

8 These figures from CAB 106/1050, appendix 'D'.
9 'Tales of Old Retold', op.cit.
10 These signals can be found in PRO file AIR37/327.
11 Letter from A.H. Watson, *Pegasus Journal*, June 1998
12 PRO file AIR27/1651.

cently come to light which supports this account. Peter Davies was flying another Hamilcar close by:

> Just before we crossed the Rhine, the tank being carried by a Hamilcar flying on our port side shot out through the tail of the aircraft complete with its shackle chains and the crew still sitting on its side. The tank seemed to stand still in mid air then slowly turned over, [whilst] the rest of the glider began to break up on the tow rope which was eventually released, presumably by the tug aircraft.[13]

No German flak would be encountered five miles west of the Rhine, so structural failure would appear to be confirmed as the cause, possibly caused by the tank breaking from its moorings. The position given for the incident also throws doubt on the story that the tank was indeed found in the Rhine at a later date. Whatever the full details, Brigadier Chatterton stated later that this was the 'only known instance' of a Hamilcar breaking up in the air.[14]

The problems faced by the remaining seven tank-carriers as they reached the vicinity of the LZs had two basic causes: firstly German flak and secondly the obscuration of the landing areas by smoke, dust and haze. These problems they shared with all the gliders that landed that day. The poor visibility was the result of the Allied artillery and air bombardment, which had started fires and raised clouds of smoke and dust, added to in some areas by the firing of smoke shells to mask the Allied assault. Part of this massive bombardment had been intended to suppress enemy flak positions, but in this it had only been partly successful, and the gliders made excellent targets for the surviving German weapons as they flew in. In addition, the gliders followed so closely behind the parachute troops that the latter had insufficient time to destroy the flak positions that remained. Most tug crews lost sight of their gliders in the smoke and haze before they landed, and the glider crews themselves experienced considerable difficulty in identifying their landing areas and even judging their height.

The CO's glider lost a wheel, probably to flak, before landing, but landed safely although off its LZ. The glider with the tank of Lt. Davies made a successful landing on the LZ despite being hit three times by flak. Lt. Kenward's glider landed safely on the LZ 'without mishap' according to Stewart's report, but surviving film of Kenward's Hamilcar shows he had to drive out through the nose door which must have become jammed. Of the remaining four Hamilcars, three crashed. One tank seems to have survived more or less intact except for damage to its machine gun, whilst another ended up crashing through a house on landing which put its wireless and 37mm gun out of action. This latter problem was realised when the first round caused the gun to splay open, although the co-axial machine gun was still working and was used to support American troops who were in the area. These Americans were probably members of the 513th Parachute Infantry Regiment of 17th Airborne Division, who had landed in the wrong place but went into action against any Germans they could find.[15] The third crashed glider had landed close to the CO's (and so off the LZ), but encountered a ditch on the landing roll-out and tipped onto its nose. The tank broke loose and somersaulted through the air,

13 Letter to *The Eagle*, December 2003.
14 *The Wings Of Pegasus*, p.221.
15 *Airborne Forces*, p.308.

landing on its turret, and was completely written off. An account of the flight and landing of this tank has been left by one of its crew, Trooper K.W. Dowsett:

> Our ETA at the LZ was 1040 hrs and as we approached we secured ourselves into our seats. The guns were loaded (37mm and .30 coaxial machine gun), the engine started and we were all set. I heard one of the glider pilots say, 'Hang on chaps. We're going in now.' A very short time later we seemed to be going around and around and then, with an almighty crash, we came to a halt upside down suspended in our safety harnesses. It transpired later that, after casting off, we had glided down very close to a light flak position which took part of the Hamilcar's wing off. In the resulting crash both our pilots were killed and the tank, propelled by its own movement, tore loose from the securing shackles and somersaulted through the air, landing upside down on its turret.
>
> We eventually, with great difficulty, released our harnesses and were able to crawl out from under the tank. We were a pretty sore and sorry crew. My personal weapon was a Sten gun which, due to insufficient storage space inside the turret, was strapped to the outside – this was bent and totally unserviceable. A somewhat uninspiring descent into Germany – I didn't even have a weapon!
>
> As the three of us lay alongside the wreckage, keeping our heads down and wondering when it would be practical to move on foot towards our RV, we heard the sound of tracks and thought this was the end for us. But, unbelievably, it was our commanding officer's Locust rattling up with the commanding officer himself, bedecked in his brightly coloured cavalry forage cap, sounding his hunting horn as he stood upright in the turret! We climbed on to the back of his tank and set off to the RV where defensive positions in the vicinity of divisional headquarters were being established.[16]

All vehicle and gun crews flying in Hamilcars wore seat belts during take-off and landing, which probably served in this case to save three lives. The final Hamilcar landed safely but north of the LZ. All forty eight Hamilcars landed between 1046 and 1100.

To summarise, then, the situation immediately after landing was that six tanks had made it onto the ground in running condition. Unfortunately, two more of these would never make it to the RV. Lt. Kenward's tank, one of those completely undamaged, went to the assistance of some American paratroops who were in action against a farm. Within five minutes of landing, this vehicle had been knocked out by a German self-propelled gun. The Americans helped rescue the crew, two of whom were wounded. The war diary attributes this casualty to an '88'. Another tank, that of Corporal Ward, was the tank that had landed safely but well north of the LZ. The tank broke down whilst attempting to tow a jeep out of a crashed Horsa. This resulted in the tank being immobilised in an exposed position that was apparently forward of the leading troops, who in this area were the 12th Parachute Battalion. This vehicle was gallantly kept in action for the whole day, and is the vehicle which some accounts say killed over a hundred of the enemy.[17] Lt.Col. Stewart limits himself to reporting that the vehicle 'accounted for a considerable number of Germans.' This Locust was never able to join the rest of the unit as, by

---

16 *Go To It!*, pp 140-141.
17 See, for example, *The Glider Soldiers*, p.326.

A Locust is captured on film crossing LZ 'P', 24th March 1945. Horsa glider behind (IWM).

Lt. Kenward's Locust knocked out close to its landing point. The glider by which it arrived is seen in the background. Note absence of Littlejohn adapter (IWM).

nightfall, enemy soldiers were infiltrating around the tank's position and the crew were forced to destroy it.

In the end, then, four Locusts reached the RV, and these had assembled by 1230 hrs. Of these, one had an unserviceable main armament and a broken wireless. Another had an unserviceable machine gun and was also without a working radio, leaving only two tanks fully fit for action. As we will see later, this level of losses amongst glider loads, and particularly for those gliders carrying vehicles and heavy equipment, was not unusual for Varsity. Nevertheless, regardless of his unit's losses, Stewart set about carrying out his orders.

He established communications with divisional HQ both personally and by wireless, and then sent two tanks forward onto the high ground which was his objective, with the intention of denying it to the enemy. The advance was covered by the two other tanks which remained in hull down positions behind the embankment of the railway. The high ground was crossed by the forward (eastern) edge of the Diersfordterwald, which turned out to be occupied by the enemy. The two leading tanks came under fire almost immediately and a platoon of the 12th Devons was sent to support them. One company of Devons ('C' Company) had been sent to LZ'P' to protect divisional HQ so once again this unit and 6th AARR were associated. Through the rest of the afternoon a stalemate appears to have reigned, with both the forward and rear elements of the small force drawing both sniper and machine gun fire. Any movement to get into improved fire positions was met by well aimed machine gun fire which broke several periscopes. Some 75mm infantry guns further back in the wood also engaged the tanks. One of the tank commanders, Sgt Hardwidge, was wounded during this period. Around 1800 the enemy fire increased and now included mortars. The two leading tanks seemed to be attracting a lot of fire which was causing casualties to the Devons and so these tanks were withdrawn slightly. Shortly before dark, a reinforcement of fourteen glider pilots arrived which were sent to thicken up the positions of the Devons. Stewart also moved his two rearward tanks forward and arranged his little battlegroup to form a strong point. The infantry borrowed the AA Bren guns from the tanks to increase their firepower.

Contact was expected with 8th Parachute Battalion during the night, which Stewart was hoping would advance towards him from their dropping zones to the west. However, the only firm contact that night was with the enemy who made two attempts to infiltrate the British positions, resulting in one German being killed. Movement heard in the woods shortly after these attempts was engaged with a 2" mortar, but the return fire seemed to be from the same type of weapon so fire was ceased in case the noises were coming from elements of 8th Battalion. Later, the Germans appeared to have withdrawn and at 0430 word was received from divisional HQ that 8th Battalion were remaining inside the woods until daylight. First contact with supporting forces in fact came a little after first light when some tank destroyers appeared along with a squadron of DD Shermans from 44th Royal Tank Regiment. At 1030, the first elements of 6th AARR's land party made contact, led by Lt. Rollason.

We can now turn to examine how the 4.2" mortars had fared. These had proceeded by road to the airfield at Great Dunmow, six and a half miles east of Bishops Stortford and fifty miles from Woodbridge, which did not make last minute coordination of the two parts of 6th AARR particularly easy. The airfield was now home to 190 and 620 Squadrons who had moved in from Fairford for the operation. These squadrons were still equipped with Stirling IVs. It is not possible from surviving records to say which squadron towed the Horsas which carried 6th AARR's mortars, or if it was tugs from both squadrons. Certainly, the glider pilots were drawn from 'G' Squadron of the Glider Pilot Regiment, and the Horsas were the new Mk IIs with hinged noses. Take offs for Varsity from Great Dunmow commenced earlier than from Woodbridge, at around 0630, mainly because the airfield was further from the target area. The Horsas carrying the mortars of 6th AARR were, however, landing on LZ'P' at about the same time as the Locusts, starting at 1057. They experienced the same problems of flak and poor visibility which once again resulted in inaccurate landings and significant casualties. Most of the troop landed east of the intended area, in the western outskirts of Haminkeln, where they had to contend not only with AA fire but small arms fire from German units close to their points of landing. The detachment commander, Captain O'Hanlan, found himself under 'intense small arms fire' as soon as he landed, and together with the men in his glider he joined with troops from the 12th Devons to clear the enemy opposition from the immediate area 'with the bayonet'.[18] Only then could the jeep and mortar trailer disembark. On the way to the RV further enemy fire was encountered from houses along the route. In Lt. Williams glider, the jeep was destroyed by flak before the glider even reached the ground. Once again, small arms fire was encountered as soon as the detachment landed and Williams was wounded. The crew was ordered by an officer of 53rd Regiment to leave the mortar and report to their command post. During the afternoon the crew returned with a borrowed jeep to retrieve the mortar, but once again came under small arms fire and had to withdraw. Only after dark could the mortar finally be recovered. The Horsa carrying Sgt Cresswell and his crew landed safely and this mortar detachment had only to contend with some inaccurate mortar fire as they disembarked. They moved off successfully to the RV. The fourth mortar was, however, completely lost. The Horsa carrying it was shot down 'very wide of the LZ close to a German Para HQ'.[19] One occupant, Lance Corporal Rothwell, was killed, and the remainder were all taken prisoner after being disabled in the crash. Of the two jeeps with ammunition trailers, one made a good landing, although east of the LZ, and made it to the RV. The other was never traced, and its driver, Trooper Freebury, was posted missing.

As with the tanks, only about 50% of the mortar troop was available for action immediately after the drop. Three jeeps, one mortar and two ammunition trailers were destroyed, and one mortar only reached the RV after dark. No record of shoots by the mortars on the 24th has survived, but we may assume that those available were in action throughout the day. Stewart noted in his report that during the 25th and 26th:

> The mortars carried out several shoots by Capt O'Hanlon from a precarious position in Haminkeln Station. This OP was under observed fire and he deserves great credit for his persistence in occupying it.[20]

---

18 Quotes from Lt Col Stewart's report, p.2.
19 Ibid, p.2.
20 Stewart's report, p.4.

Before leaving the airborne action and recording the progress of 6th AARR's ground element, we should give some attention to the success or otherwise of the Hamilcars used in Varsity. All forty eight Hamilcars departed successfully from Woodbridge, but there were many losses prior to landing. Official analysis after the operation indicated that thirty eight Hamilcars had landed in the divisional area, with some in the wrong LZs and others outside any of the designated LZs.[21] Records of 298 and 644 Squadrons show that seven Hamilcars seem to have been lost en-route, varying from one which had to cast off as early as 0740 (i.e. a few minutes after take off) due to engine failure in the tug, to the loss of one of the tank carrying gliders just before the target which has been examined above. In most cases the glider is recorded as having 'cast off' and landed safely in a field somewhere. The most likely reason for casting off would be either a broken tow rope or problems caused by turbulence from the massive formation of aircraft within which the Hamilcar combinations were flying. It would therefore seem that three Hamilcars were destroyed by enemy fire over the LZs, where they made tempting and vulnerable targets. One source gives only twenty three Hamilcars 'arrived safely'.[22] This phrase is not defined in the source, but may refer to gliders which made normal landings and ended up undamaged, as opposed to those which made some sort of crash landing. Certainly, losses were significant. Of the sixteen 17pdrs, nine were lost along with their tows. In combination with the losses of 6pdrs (10 lost from 34), this seriously weakened the anti-tank defences available to the division. The RASC Hamilcars also suffered heavily. The use of these gliders as bulk carriers of stores and the universal carriers to transport those stores was still something of an experiment for Varsity, building on the smaller scale trial at Arnhem. Of the twelve, eight landed in the divisional area, from which seven carriers were eventually recovered. However, when the planned resupply drop by Liberator aircraft occurred at 1300 only two RASC carriers and a handful of personnel were available to collect them. By late afternoon, six carriers and three trailers were available.[23] Stores were collected from only three of the RASC Hamilcars. The conclusion was that the use of Hamilcars as stores carriers should only take place if the gliders landed a few hours after the assault landings, once the LZs were properly secured. Details of the fate of other Hamilcar loads are incomplete, although 8 out of 18 carriers were apparently lost which would mean three of the carriers meant for the battalion HQs were not available. Those that did arrive were evidently a welcome sight, at least according to the following quote from the CO of 8th Parachute Battalion in his report:

> At 1115 hrs the Hamilcar glider of 8 Para Bn made a perfect landing [...] This was very good news as it held the carrier which was soon being used, spare mortars, MMGs and wireless sets.[24]

The two RE bulldozers evidently landed successfully. They are both recorded at work on the 24th, one helping to dig in divisional HQ and the other digging in the 75mm guns of 53rd Airlanding Regiment.

21 See PRO files CAB106/1050 and AIR37/327.
22 PRO file WO205/947
23 WO205/947
24 Quoted in CAB106/1050

Hamilcar and Universal Carrier (probably belonging to 12th Devons) on LZ 'P'. The glider's undercarriage oleos have been lowered. (IWM).

The tendency of Hamilcars to nose over when encountering obstructions was again in evidence in the destruction of one of 6th AARR's Locusts. Stewart added in his report that where ditches or similar were expected on the LZ, the Hamilcars should land on skids which would prevent this problem. He also pleaded for the Hamilcars to be fitted with the means of lowering the undercarriage from the cockpit, to speed up unloading and prevent risk to the glider pilots. A final recommendation was that Locusts should be carried with their guns traversed to the rear (which apparently was not possible with the Tetrarch) in order to prevent damage to the guns during crash landings.

Overall, the losses for Varsity were within the numbers expected, and all objectives were achieved on time. The operation was therefore judged a success. Of the 440 gliders allocated, 402 reached the LZs, a loss rate of 8% which was thought acceptable. However, only 88 landed without damage.[25] As we have seen, losses in vehicles and heavy equipment had in most cases averaged about 50%, which had severely hampered some aspects of the operation – as a further example, jeep losses had been 46%. The limitations of gliders during the assault phase were thus being exposed. Often laden with ammunition or vehicles full of petrol, they were vulnerable targets, and if the glider was lost the whole load went with it. Within the overall success, the severe losses to the RASC Hamilcars caused this aspect of the operation to be judged a failure. Of all the massive glider force, only 24 Horsas were eventually recovered. These were dismantled, shipped to airfields west of the Rhine and then towed home. Some of the Hamilcars were also dismantled and some of the sub-assemblies and vital parts were shipped home to assist in the production of further aircraft. As a final footnote on the use of large gliders, a report

25 *Glider Soldiers*, p.323.

from 1st Allied Airborne Army regarding Varsity recommended that 100 'large-type' gliders be available for each US airborne division, to carry guns and trucks of up to one and a half tons. As this was the last large scale airborne operation of the war, the recommendation could not be acted on, but the intended glider was probably the Waco CG-13A or a similar type (for a description see chapter 11). There was no mention of any requirement to land tanks.[26]

As far as the Locusts were concerned, they had been unfortunate to suffer so severely before getting into action, and despite fighting hard all day it is clear they were unable fully to take their objective before dark. On the plus side, their presence seems to have kept the Germans occupied and away from divisional HQ, although the rear divisional HQ (which was nearer to the area where the Locusts were fighting), suffered from sniping and mortar fire and ended up moving to join the main HQ during the evening of the 24th. The limitations of the main armament of the Locust had been demonstrated as recently as 13th March when, following practice firing on a Salisbury Plain range, the war diary had noted, 'the bursts of 37mm HE were so slight as to render observation difficult'. This was hardly a weapon likely to provide useful supporting fire for the paratroops and glidermen. The lack of effectiveness of the airborne light tanks in a full scale 1945 battle had been clearly demonstrated, even in a situation where it appears enemy tanks and anti-tank guns were locally absent.

When the main part of 6th AARR started out once again from England, it had two link-ups to make, the first with the party that had stayed behind in Europe after the actions in the Ardennes and Holland, and the second with the airborne parties. Before setting out, the land elements removed the airborne flashes, formation signs and any other identifying marks from their uniforms and vehicles for security purposes. They set off on 15th March, under the second in command Major J.C.G. Dunolly, using the cover identity of 'Stewart's Horse'. At their transit camp near Tilbury they were somewhat dismayed when a tannoy announcement referred clearly to the unit by name, rather spoiling their security arrangements, but they made a protest and the mistake was not repeated. The unit embarked on four LSTs on the morning of the 16th, and arrived at Ostend around the middle of the next day. According to Stewart's report, 'no one in authority appeared to know where our Cromwell tanks were or whether they had received any orders of an impending operation'. He also noted 'OC Div. Land Elements in N.W. Europe did not appear sufficiently in the picture. At no time were we adequately briefed and operational maps non existent'. The advance to the Rhine was obviously plagued by administrative problems. In addition to the above, the CO's report also noted problems with the organisation of the road moves:

> In spite of the protests of the 2nd i/c, the halt orders were always 10 mins to every hour only. This does not give sufficient time for essential maintenance on a long march. Also P.O.L. [petrol, oil and lubricants] requirements were invariably overlooked, it not being appreciated the amount required to move this regiment. We frequently moved on "black market" petrol procured by individual initiative from formations which were not warned to supply us. It was a credit to

---

26 PRO file WO205/952, Report from HQ 1st Allied Airborne Army on Operation Varsity.

the regiment that we made the link up less one motorcycle. In 11 days we had travelled in 5 countries – England, France. Belgium, Holland and Germany.[27]

In the event the first link up took place in two stages. All except the tanks joined up at Divion, near Bethune in France, on the 19th. The regiment then continued through Belgium and Holland where they crossed into Germany via the bridge at their old stamping ground of Venlo. Between Venlo and the Rhine they stopped at the town of Geldern and here on the 24th they linked up with the eight Cromwells that had stayed on in Holland. The tanks must have travelled from their base at Helmond, a town about 12km east of Eindhoven where they had been staying for the last month. Trooper John Banbery was one of the tank crewman who had stayed with them.

They sent the Cromwells with two man crews to a town called Helmond, which was a British military town with many different units there. I recall it was quite an amazing place. It had just about every tank there you could find or know of, battered. Our red berets were put away and we were given black berets and RAC badges, and we were attached to them. They looked upon us with great suspicion. We were something very odd and we kept our mouths very shut. We spent from then until just before the Rhine crossing working on the tanks and of course we soon got pretty tired of the tanks, we had a lot to do hanging around. [...] And we then got orders to move up to the Rhine.[28]

The reluctance of Trooper Banbery and his comrades to answer questions and the discarding of their red berets was of course part of the same security process as the main body was undergoing. As we have seen, an advance party crossed the Rhine the next day and met up with the airborne tanks on the morning of the 25th. On the 26th the main body of the regiment crossed the river, and the Locusts were handed over to REME recovery teams. The Cromwells were crewed up and the regiment was once again complete. The movement order for the crossing of the Rhine has survived and gives a good idea of the vehicle strength of the regiment at this time. It records 8 Cromwells, 1 Sherman (probably an armoured recovery vehicle, but possibly Stewart's command tank), 20 Daimler scout cars, 3 White scout cars, 20 Universal Carriers, 16 lorries (mainly 3 tonners), 1 M3 half track, 2 Scammel recovery vehicles, 26 Jeeps, 2 staff cars and 29 motorcycles, making a total of 99 vehicles plus various trailers and the motorcycles.

The land elements of all divisional units rejoined 6th Airborne Division after Varsity. In the same way as during the breakout from Normandy, 6th Airborne was to become part of 21st Army Group and fight in the ground role, as British forces advanced across Germany in the last six weeks of the war. Until midnight 27th/28th March, however, the division still fought as part of XVIII Airborne Corps. The division then became part of VIII Corps, which had been held back as the reserve corps of 2nd Army during Plunder. Now VIII Corps was to lead the break out: 'it would advance on the right of XII Corps and pick up the 6th Airborne Division and the 1st Commando Brigade as it went through'.[29] VIII Corps at this time contained 11th Armoured Division and 6th Guards Armoured Bri-

27 Stewart's report, p.11.
28 IWM interview
29 Ellis, p.294.

gade. On the 11th of April it was supplemented by 15th Infantry Division. Throughout the advance across Germany, 6th Airborne would usually have elements of 11th Armoured to its left, or else units from XII Corps, which commonly turned out to be from 7th Armoured Division. Just to confuse matters, 7th Armoured was itself under command 8th Corps for a while during late March. To the right of 8th Corps and 6th Airborne Division would be American troops from XVIIIth Airborne Corps, operating as part of the US 9th Army.

Before describing the advance across Germany, it is worth pausing briefly to describe the situation of the Germans so that 6th AARR's activities may be seen in proper perspective. The German divisions which had opposed Operations Plunder and Varsity were part of 1st Parachute Army, which as we have seen was an airborne formation in name only. As the American formations to the south of 2nd British Army drove through the Germans to commence their part of the encirclement of the Ruhr, the left flank of 1st Parachute Army was wide open and it began to retreat to the north-east. The Army received a new commander (General Gunther Blumentritt) in late March and he has left a graphic account of the state of his forces:

> Once the Rhine had been crossed the situation, with the forces at our disposal, was past repair. When I took over my new command on 28th March I found that there were great gaps in my front, that I had no reserves, that my artillery was weak, that I had no air support whatever and hardly any tanks. My communication and signal facilities were entirely inadequate and there was one corps under my command that I was never able to contact. The reinforcements that came to me were hastily trained and badly equipped, and I never used them so that I could save needless casualties.[30]

The superiority of the Allied forces by this stage was so great that the only sensible options were retreat or surrender. German soldiers did surrender in increasingly large numbers as the days and weeks went by, but their commanders felt compelled to at least make the pretence of fighting on. Therefore Blumentritt tried to conduct an orderly withdrawal, attempting to keep casualties to a minimum.

The Ruhr was encircled on 1st April, and on the 18th 325,000 soldiers within the resulting pocket surrendered. With the crossing of the Rhine and the collapse of the Ruhr, the possibility of any overall plan for defence in the west ceased to exist. The German forces gradually disintegrated as the Allied armies rolled east. As Martin Shulman put it:

> Baffled, disorganised, lost, the scattered remnants of the Wehrmacht hid in the woods until they were overrun, fought until they were overwhelmed, or waited until they were overtaken, depending upon the ability, fanaticism or common sense of their officers.[31]

The German Army, then, was beaten, but under Hitler's influence refused to entirely lie down. The war was effectively won but tragically it would cost thousands more lives before the final German surrender came. Some of those lives would be lost from the ranks of 6th AARR.

30 Quoted in Milton Shulman *Defeat In The West*, (London: Pan Books, 1988) p.311. This is the paperback edition of the original first published in 1947.
31 Ellis, p.316

Chapter 9

Across Germany

On the morning of the 27th March 1945, 6th AARR was under orders to advance east from the Rhine bridgehead, carrying out reconnaissance ahead of the advance of 5th Parachute Brigade, whose objective for the day was the town of Erle. By 1100 both 'A' and 'B' Squadrons were over the Issel, where 'A' Squadron contacted enemy troops estimated at company strength. However, these troops were obviously not prepared to offer determined opposition as by 1215 'A' Squadron were on the move again. By early afternoon 'A' had been ordered to take the left flank and advance towards Raesfeld whilst 'B' Squadron continued east towards Erle. However, about 8000 yards west of Erle 'B' Squadron were halted by enemy who meant to make a fight of it. Initially they received fire from 20mm flak guns, but at 1600 they reported losing a tank to a self-propelled (SP) gun. They were already down one tank which had run off the road and needed recovery. The opposition was eventually estimated as five SPs supported by infantry and 20mm flak. Nevertheless the squadron made determined attempts to overcome this opposition, but whilst trying an outflanking move two Cromwells were lost. The crews were later praised by their CO for showing 'great courage and devotion to duty'.[1] John Banbery was involved in this action and these are his memories of it:

> We attacked a farm, which we didn't realise was extremely heavily protected at the time. On the way in we hit a self-propelled gun. We were very lucky. We hit the self-propelled gun which was inside a rubbish heap on the outskirts of the farm, camouflaged beside it. The Germans baled out, and we didn't fire at them. We let them bale out, and I think that saved us as well afterwards, because they could have fired on us. [Banbery's tank was rapidly hit and disabled, but he had no idea where the fire that hit his tank came from]. There was an awful lot of stuff flying about, and we were very near the German tanks. We could see that we were so near that the flash was almost touching our tanks at times. We were that near.
>
> We baled out. We ran across a ploughed field. I was expecting to be shot in the back any moment, but we weren't. So we got back to our own unit.[2]

The second tank of the outflanking move was knocked out a little further on, with the crew captured and the driver injured in addition. That driver was Bob Walklett, and he has also recorded his memories of that day:

> We were a young crew. I was nineteen. The gunner was also nineteen and our newly-joined wireless operator was just one month from his nineteenth birthday. My commander and the bow gunner were both in their mid-twenties.[3]

1 Stewart's report, p.4.
2 IWM interview.
3 Walklett, pp.30-31. Along with his three brothers, Bob founded and became Managing Director of the specialist car makers Ginetta after the war.

Regarding the outflanking move he remembers:

> Once we had commenced the manoeuvre it was not going to be easy to extricate ourselves should the opposition prove too strong. It was necessary then for us to cross a newly ploughed field in order to penetrate the enemy gun area. Our unexpected angle of approach, together with a continuous stream of HE shells from our 75mm gun and machine gun fire from our Besas, was making it difficult for the German gunners to respond effectively to our forceful advance. Unfortunately, once we were inside their gun area it became clear that we had stirred up a real hornet's nest – there was a host of guns with infantry support – and whilst dealing with an SP gun we were hit by anti-tank gun fire...
>
> The force of the explosion lifted the tank violently and blackness descended upon me. When I came to I was on fire. A superhuman effort extricated me from the driving compartment. I dropped to the ground. I heard shouts: 'Over here', and I ran towards the voices. Rifles cracked and short bursts of machine gun fire accompanied my exit. I made the ditch. My crew beat my burning uniform out with their bare hands and I passed out. We were captured and became prisoners.[4]

Bob was sent to a German hospital, but about ten days later was liberated by men of 6th Airborne Division and returned to hospital in England.

John Banbery's crew somehow managed to take four German prisoners (from the 48th Flak Regiment) whilst getting back from their knocked out tank, and these prisoners reported three of their guns had been knocked out by 'B' Squadron that morning. John continues:

> We sat waiting for the Paras to come up, they were all on foot at that time. While we were waiting, the troop commander's tank must have been visible to these Germans because suddenly it was hit twice, went up in the end but nobody was hurt. The rest of the squadron was behind us, spaced out. We moved back a bit when the troop leader's tank was hit to somewhere slightly more secure. There were carriers and other vehicles turning behind us, or getting into ditches out of the way. We were slack. We shouldn't have been caught like that, there is no doubt about it. What we should have realised was on the way along we'd run across several SAS jeeps coming out from there, and the farms in the distance were smoking. They'd got the Germans hopping about there, so we were going into a bit of a hornet's nest I think. We should have realised better that they'd stirred it up a bit with a big wooden spoon.[5]

The enemy was finally cleared from the axis of advance by 7th Parachute Battalion, who attacked using information passed on from 6th AARR. The area was not secured until midnight, and in the end the battalion killed or captured 80 men and 11 guns.[6] The Cromwells of 6th AARR had unknowingly bitten off more than they could chew, but had attacked with great verve. Before continuing with the story of the advance, John Banbery's comments on how the losses to 'B' Squadron's tanks were made up are worth repeating:

---

4 Walklet, p.31.
5 Account edited from IWM interview.
6 *Airborne Forces*, p.311.

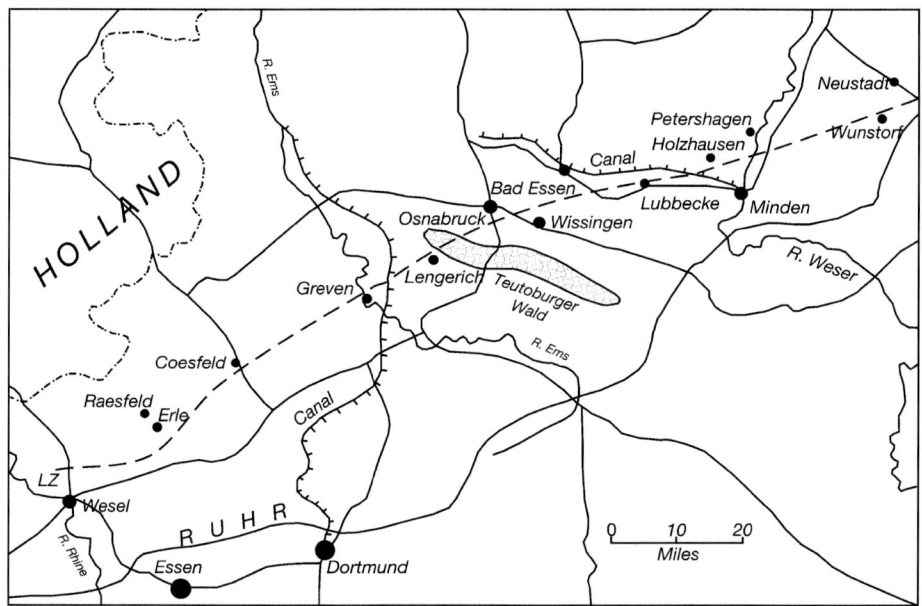

Across Germany 1, 27th March-11th April 1945
(dashed line shows line of advance, 6th Airborne Division)

We went around on the squadron 3-tonner for a bit, we sat on the back of that with a Bren gun. We used to join the squadron every night to refill, replenish fuel, etc. [After a short while] we went back to this unit that we'd stayed with at Helmont. Unfortunately, the tanks they gave us were the ones we'd cannibalised, so we picked up tanks that were less than 100% by a long way, and there was nothing we could do about it at all. We had some very very poor tanks after that. The tank I was on, the gunner couldn't fire the main armament. I had to fire it with a spanner on the firing mechanism. Each time we fired I used a spanner and kept my hand out of the way of the recoil. It worked.

One of the other vehicles had a wireless that didn't work properly, and another had a turret that wouldn't turn and you had to turn the tank to put the gun on line. The fourth tank was pretty well OK – that was our surviving tank.[7]

Trooper Banbery's crew eventually disposed of their own faulty tank by exploiting its tendency to overheat. They continued to allow it to do this until the engine seized, in an example of what John Banbery calls 'constructive maintenance'!

The 27th of March had been the first hectic day of many hectic days to come. That night, as we have seen, 6th Airborne Division came under 8th Corps and in the next six weeks kept up an almost continuous advance that took it to the Baltic at Wismar. Until the 11th April, the division was the spearhead division of the Corps, despite an initial lack of transport. The general pattern was for the three brigades of the division to alternate in leading the advance, or when the division ad-

7 IWM interview.

Cromwells of 'B' Squadron, 6th AARR at Bekowitz near the Baltic coast, May 1945 (John Banbery).

vanced 'two up', to take turns as the reserve brigade. 6th AARR was often well to the fore carrying out a classic reconnaissance role, checking out routes, road junctions and bridges and probing for the enemy. The armoured support that 6th AARR could provide with their Cromwells was important but obviously limited, and so it was strongly supplemented by the 4th Tank Battalion, Grenadier Guards whose Churchills were attached to the division and distributed amongst the battalions and brigades as required for specific actions. Also attached to the division was the Inns of Court Regiment, another reconnaissance regiment mainly equipped with the usual complement of armoured cars, carriers and scout cars. Indeed, during its advance to the Baltic, 6th Airborne Division was transformed by the addition of attached supporting units from a relatively lightly armed airborne division into an elite infantry division. As well as those elements already mentioned, two field artillery regiments, a medium artillery regiment, a self propelled anti-tank battery and three platoons of troop carrying transport were more or less permanently attached during this period.[8]

On the morning of 28th March, the division received orders to advance to Coesfeld, a town about 35 miles north east of Erle. The 3rd Parachute Brigade would be leading, but ahead of them 'A' Squadron of 6th AARR carried out the reconnaissance role, with additional orders to make contact with American units on the right flank as well as 11th Armoured Division on the left. That day there were several contacts with the enemy, including one around midday on the road to Lembeck which resulted in two scout cars knocked out and Lt. Renny being

8 *Airborne Forces*, p.315.

wounded. The squadron eventually reached the outskirts of Lembeck, a town about 5 miles east of Erle, at 1630. Here they were halted by strong enemy resistance, including some of the seemingly ever-present 20mm flak guns. Troops of 3rd Parachute Brigade took over to assault the village, but were assisted by fire support from 'A' Squadron's tanks and 'C' Squadron's heavy mortars. During the evening 'C' Squadron of the Inns of Court Regiment came under the command of 6th AARR and orders were received for the following day's reconnaissance, which was to take place on a broad front from Lembeck towards Coesfeld, using all three available recce squadrons.

Throughout the 29th, 6th AARR pushed towards Coesfeld. All the problems that might be expected were encountered – blown bridges, soft going and bad roads, groups of enemy putting up resistance, and other groups of enemy giving themselves up as prisoners. Sub-units were constantly leapfrogging each other, or looping round to find alternate routes, but by evening Coesfeld was reached. Whilst it was taken by 6th Airlanding Brigade, the recce units tried to work around the rear of the town, but found the enemy too strong and retreated to harbour for the night.

For the next two days 6th AARR, with the Inns of Court Squadron still with them, continued to head the division's advance beyond Coesfeld towards the towns of Greven and Lengerich. Between these towns was the obstacle of the Dortmund-Ems canal. Once again, they were in constant contact with the enemy, and in addition to the two recce squadrons, 'C' Squadron of 6th AARR was also in action. The mortars were required for supporting fire against enemy positions and the assault troop was also called on to assist in dislodging some of the more stubborn enemy resistance. From the night of 30th/31st March, 22nd Independent Parachute Company was also under command of 6th AARR to provide additional infantry resources. The reader will remember that this company were the pathfinders for the division when operating in the airborne role. John Banbery recalled them as 'very tough indeed. I suppose if there was anybody you wanted to have with you to help you they were about the best'.[9]

By early evening on the 31st, the Inns of Court squadron was able to report that the bridges over the Dortmund-Ems canal were blown. By this time, the war diary was reporting that 'A' Squadron was down to an effective strength of two troops, each with only two vehicles. They had, for example, lost a carrier to a panzerfaust when the squadron got mixed up in 6th Airlanding Brigade's attack on the town of Billerbeck, about five miles north east of Coesfeld. In another typical action on the 31st, 'B' Squadron with 22nd Independent Company in support, destroyed an 88mm gun and took eighteen prisoners at the village of Gimbte, a little south of Greven.

During 1st April, there was a chance of a less busy day as the division was held up whilst crossings over the canal were constructed. However, elements of 6th AARR still saw action as they moved up from their harbour area west of the canal to help cover the movement of 6th Airlanding Brigade up to and eventually over this obstacle. The war diary records examples of the regiment providing fire support, with 'C' Squadron using its MMGs to cover a road junction and bridge in the area. 'B' Squadron had a troop of MMGs and one of mortars under command from 'C'

9   IWM interview.

Squadron, and whilst covering a party of Royal Engineers used mortar fire to clear a house of enemy troops, taking 48 prisoners. The 1st appears to have been the last day that the Inns of Court squadron operated with the regiment, though their departure is not formally recorded. By the morning of the 2nd, the regiment was able to cross the canal and carry out recce duties, with particular attention to be paid to the state of the roads, towards Lengerich and the high, wooded ground of the Teutoburger Wald beyond. This was found to be occupied by the enemy. All squadrons of the unit met the enemy at some point during the day, and it would seem that almost anything could be encountered. Enemy forces of up to 100 infantry were reported in the diary, along with armoured cars, scout cars, SP guns and transport vehicles in small groups. No sub-unit knew when it might be shot up by MG fire or encounter an anti-tank gun positioned to delay the allied advance, and these conditions applied throughout the advance across Germany.

What were living conditions like for the men of the regiment during their advance? John Banbery recalls that with luck the men would find a building to sleep in during night stops, with the sleeping bags that were standard issue to airborne troops being particularly welcome. If not, 'we had a fair sized tarpaulin that had fastenings on it, and we could fasten it to the back of the tank or the side, and we slept under that'.[10] As for food, once in Germany the crews had no scruples about living off the land, taking whatever food they could find. Ham and the bottled fruit which could sometimes be found were particularly popular. Otherwise they had the standard ten-man ration packs, which would last a five man tank crew two days:

> There were about half a dozen packs, and they were all lettered and you knew the ones you liked best. And whoever went to collect the rations was given instructions, for God's sake, get some C ration or B ration. Some had more puddings in and some had more bacon and things like that. We used to fry the puddings. Treacle pudding and ginger pudding fry very well. And quickly of course, because otherwise you've got to put them in hot water and wait. The food was quite good.
>
> When we stopped in an evening, after we'd refuelled and re-armed, immediately somebody had to start getting food ready. So there was food quite quickly in the evening, [and then] you could be briefed for the next day. By that time your troop leader had been to the 'O' (orders) group and come back with what was going to happen the next day. While you were eating, we sat and talked about it, so you could get a good night's sleep in.
>
> We had five open necked thermoses and one very large one, per vehicle, and in the morning before we set off, we always filled the big one with hot tea, and the co-driver used to sit there with cheese, biscuits and various tins, and he used to feed us during the day. That was his job. He hadn't got much else to do and he'd got more room than anybody else. The rations always included cigarettes, there was always a tin of 60 cigarettes. Most people smoked.[11]

Crews washed and shaved every day, but clean clothes were harder to come by:

---

10 IWM interview.
11 Ibid.

MMG carrier of 'C' Squadron with carrier from 2 Recce Troop of 'B' Squadron (John Banbery).

We had string vests, that was another airborne issue, which rolled a lot of the dirt off you. We didn't get much chance of washing clothes ourselves, it was only when we got to a field bath that we got any clothes, any fresh ones. We probably only had about one spare shirt for ourselves. But people were pretty clean. On the sanitary side we used whatever loo was around to find, carefully because it was a favourite time to get potted by a German sneaking up, so you were pretty cautious about that. It was a rush out and rush back, usually. I didn't have any lice or anything like that. People were clean, no problems at all.

On 3rd April rapid progress began to be made by some parts of the division. 'A' Squadron of 6th AARR was under command 5th Para Brigade, with 'B' Squadron under command 3rd Para Brigade. The rest of 6th AARR, including 22nd Independent Company, were under command 1st Commando Brigade (which was operating with the division around this time) and were responsible for right flank protection. Both parachute brigades also had support from squadrons of the 4th Grenadier Guards. Their objectives for the day were Osnabruck (5th Brigade and the Commandos) and Wissingen (3rd Brigade). 5th Para Brigade encountered considerable opposition on their route and did not reach Osnabruck until midnight on the 4th. 'A' Squadron had, however, managed to recce ahead and had reached the outskirts of this major town by the evening of the 3rd. The Commando Brigade was given the task of clearing the town. Overall, Wissingen, a few miles south east of Osnabruck, turned out to be the easier objective. Nevertheless, during the morning advance 'B' Squadron encountered 20 to 30 enemy in a house which had eventually to be cleared by elements of the squadron with the help of

22nd Independent Para Company. Meanwhile, the leading troop of the squadron had looped around this opposition only to come under shellfire from at least one heavy gun firing from high ground to their north. There were further contacts as the squadron pushed on through the afternoon: at 1455 the diary records one of the tanks hit four times by a 'bazooka' without being damaged. However, it seems that by this time the pace of the divisional advance had really got going, with 3rd Para Brigade 'travelling on the backs of tanks and in half-tracks and armoured troop carriers': by early afternoon they were moving so fast that 'B' Squadron could not keep ahead of them.[12] The paras were in Wissingen well ahead of their attached recce unit, which had taken up the role of flank guard.

From Osnabruck the division turned east towards Minden and the Weser river. The next day (4th April), in the push for Minden and the crossings over both the Weser and the Weser-Ems canal, 6th AARR would have what the CO described as 'undoubtedly the red letter day of the campaign'.[13] It would see the town of Minden falling to the British in the early hours of 5th April, but would involve 6th AARR in the most costly day's combat of their short but active history. Therefore it is worth recounting the events of the day in reasonable detail, especially as information from participants allows the main fighting to be reconstructed.

For this day, 'A' Squadron came under command 6th Airlanding Brigade, whilst 'B' Squadron stayed with 3rd Para Brigade, along with 'C' Squadron and the RHQ. 6th Airlanding was on the right according to the 6th AARR war diary. This is slightly confusing, as 6th Airlanding's eventual objectives were crossings over the Weser in the Petershagen area, which is to the north of Minden and hence on the left flank of 3rd Parachute Brigade. It would appear in fact that 6th Airlanding were in general following up behind the paras on the 4th rather than moving on their right flank, although their initial route may have been more to the right.[14]

'B' Squadron moved off at 0800, leading with their tank troop and with an MMG troop and mortar troop from 'C' Squadron under command. Once again, a squadron of Grenadier Guards Churchills was with each brigade as well. Behind them came 22nd Independent Company, who had the rest of 'C' Squadron with them. RHQ moved with brigade HQ. River crossings at Bad Essen, although ready for demolition, were taken intact at 0915. A little further on, at the village of Harpenfeld, some enemy were encountered but were by-passed by 'B' Squadron, who nevertheless took the opportunity to shoot up some flak and half-tracks which they saw to the north of the road. The enemy in the village were dealt with by 22nd Independent Company who took 133 prisoners. 'B' Squadron, under orders to push on with all speed (as was the whole regiment) continued towards the town of Lubbecke. Just before they reached it they were able to 'bounce' another intact bridge at the village of Blasfeld, in the process shooting up the officer and NCOs detailed to demolish it. They continued their headlong advance but the next bridge they had been detailed to check, just to the north of Lubbecke, was blown as the leading troop came into view of the German demolition team. Alternative crossings were evidently found, as 'C' Squadron were ordered to take over at these two bridges whilst 'B' continued their advance. At this stage, the commander of 3rd

---

12 Quote from *Go To It!*, p.162.
13 Stewart's report, p.7.
14 *Airborne Forces*, p.313.

Para Brigade decided to split off 'B' Squadron as part of his plan to secure the river crossings at Minden. Whilst the parachute brigade, with a squadron of Churchills from 4th Grenadier Guards, headed into Minden using the main road, 'B' Squadron would route around to the north via Holzhausen. With the German's attention focussed on the main attack, it was hoped 'B' Squadron could slip into the town from the north and capture the bridges over the Weser.

As they advanced on their 'left hook', the troops of 'B' Squadron were twice more involved in a desperate competition with German engineers who were attempting to blow the bridges along the route before the British arrived. One bridge was demolished before they could reach it but at another the tanks of the heavy troop surprised a force of retreating Germans, which included infantry, vehicles and horse drawn artillery. Lt. Col Stewart recorded that 'many infantry were killed, the remainder making good their escape across country, but all the artillery (5 guns), an armoured car, an SP and some half tracks were brewed up where they were and pushed off the road'.[15] This took place at around 1330: about an hour later radio reports from 'B' Squadron indicated that a different force of Germans had taken an opportunity to inflict severe casualties on 6th AARR.

What happened in this latter action can be reconstructed in some detail, thanks in particular to one of the German participants, Walter Schroder. After the war he managed to contact some members of 'B' and 'C' Squadrons, and in a letter written in 1988 gave his account of the fighting, which can be linked with the information in the CO's report and the war diary. Following the earlier actions, it appears the two squadrons on this flank had reformed with 'B' Squadron leading and 'C' following. As 'B' Squadron left Holzhausen, they saw a battery of 12 88mm flak guns in some fields to the north of the road. The guns were pointing skyward ready to engage aircraft. The sound of the approaching Cromwells was at first assumed by the Germans to be that of retreating friendly forces, but this impression was soon violently altered when the tanks opened up with their machine guns. Beyond the German battery was a further unit of 8 88s manned by Italians. 'B' Squadron kept going, shooting on the move, and by the time the enemy guns had lowered their barrels they were safely past. However, the flak guns were now ready for 'C' Squadron following behind. This is how Walter Schroder remembered it:

> Slowly the barrels of the 88s came down, one by one, based on commands of the individual gun chiefs. The first rounds got off as the second tank was just past our position on the way to Minden. Maybe the Italians fired on them too, but that I do not know. At any rate, the tanks kept heading down the road, paying little attention to us. Next came a column of soft vehicles. I remember the front wheel of a motorcycle being hit by a panzerfaust shell fired by the fellow next to me (we had dashed up to the road by then), then I saw at least two (maybe three) small trucks – of the 3/4 ton type and also a bren carrier.
>
> All these vehicles got it bad, nowhere to go but stand there and wait to be hit. The kids on the guns – and they were all what were known as 'Luftwaffenhelfer', i.e. auxilliarists 16 to 17 years old that had been drafted right out of high school – as a unit, just blasted away. Also fired a round into the farmhouse at the edge of town where the column was coming from, when the

---

15 Stewart's report, p.8.

farmer showed the white flag. I saw a fellow near the bren gun carrier using smoke pods/grenades to obstruct our view. [16]

John Banbery was in one of the Cromwells, and his memories 55 years later were succinct:

> We got to a battery, a German battery; there were 12 88s and about 8 manned by Italians, and the squadron leader was making for this bridge, so we fired at the battery and then went past. Unfortunately by the time the support squadron came along, they blew the squadron right off the road. We lost the whole squadron virtually; not many killed, but we lost the whole squadron.[17]

The tanks of 'B' Squadron assisted in allowing the remaining troops of 'C' to escape towards Minden, minus the Assault Troop who were behind guarding one of the bridges taken earlier. The war diary reports the losses as one White Scout Car, and four jeeps from the mortar troop, plus one entire MMG troop reported missing. We must assume Schroder's 'small trucks' were the jeeps. The number of men killed or wounded is not recorded in the available reports, but it seems the number was mercifully low: nevertheless a significant proportion of 'C' Squadron's vehicles were lost. According to the CO most vehicles, even if not destroyed, had to be left behind. His report also states that 'the MMG troop remained in action until all its vehicles were destroyed and was taken prisoner while trying to rejoin the assault troop'. Three men of 'C' Squadron were recommended for medals, Captain O'Hanlon, Trooper Harvey and Trooper Pilcher. O'Hanlon had gone forward with a PIAT to try and engage the Germans and had continued to fire the weapon until he was severely wounded in the neck. Harvey continued to fire his MMG from his damaged carrier until it was knocked out and he was himself wounded. Pilcher's carrier received a direct hit, but he went to another carrier in an attempt to withdraw it, until this too was hit and he was blown out.[18]

Captain O'Hanlon was eventually rushed by jeep to Minden in an attempt to get him to a doctor in the town, which was still in German hands. He was attended by one of the German speaking members of the regiment and a German lady, who managed to get him the help he needed. Another member of 'C' Squadron was Trooper George Firth. He was travelling in the last of four carriers in No.2 MMG Troop of 'C' Squadron. The three carriers ahead of him were all destroyed or damaged, but George was able to get away with the survivors to a nearby house, where they were taken prisoner. He was a POW for three weeks until eventually freed by US forces in Hannover.[19] 'C' Squadron as a whole was now obviously badly disorganised and temporarily out of action.

Subsequently, the assault troop moved up to observe the German position, and were eventually joined by 1st Platoon and Company HQ of the Independent Parachute Company, who as we have seen were attached to 6th AARR at this time. This combined force then assaulted the enemy position around dusk (Schroder remembers about 1700) with complete success, killing 40-50 men, capturing all the

16 Schroder letter. A copy of this document is held at the Tank Museum, Bovington.
17 IWM interview.
18 Citations preserved in the papers of Major Charles Kent, OC 'C' Squadron, Tank Museum archive.
19 Conversation with the author, July 2002.

88s along with some 20mm guns, and capturing three officers and 171 other ranks. The war diary and the CO's report are silent on British casualties in this attack, but one of the brief histories of the regiment notes that casualties were 'severe'.[20] Walter Schroder remembers it in these terms:

> [22nd Independent Company personnel] sniped at us from the trees near the edge of the village. They got a fellow in the stomach who was about 10 metres from me. Your men next charged across the field firing from the hips and before long, were on top of the dugouts ordering our personnel out of the emplacements. I'd say it was a short and sweet engagement, and the war was over at this site.

Meanwhile, 'B' Squadron continued their advance into the outskirts of Minden where they encountered yet another damaged bridge. However, they managed to get the tanks across it only to find themselves facing an enemy held roadblock of concrete blocks. They engaged the enemy here until forced to withdraw by the arrival of two SP guns and additional infantry with panzerfausts. They eventually harboured, along with the remains of 'C' Squadron, at the damaged bridge. John Banbery has described in his interview how damaged bridges were sometimes 'jumped' by simply driving the Cromwells over them at high speed. He also recalled the events of the night and following morning:

> We had a fairly rough night, people crawling around with panzerfausts. I got my hair parted that night by a panzerfaust. I was on guard sitting in the turret. And the next morning we decided that we'd try the tank, and we got over the bridge. By this time the locals weren't firing at us, they'd gone into their holes, and we got down to the main bridge which was completely blown in the middle. There was no way we were going to get over it. The squadron leader came in our vehicle to have a look. We went right up to the bridge to have a look, but it was impossible. Sniper hit the padding on the hatch cover, and a sniper just missed my ear by a quarter inch. They were in the big buildings on the other side of the river. And then we moved back from there.[21]

There had been a number of casualties overnight due to enemy snipers. Members of both squadrons continued to patrol on foot during this period, attempting to scout the town and make contact with troops from the southern prong of the advance. Contact was finally made at 0900 on the 5th when the Medical Officer appeared, having come through the town from the south. Due in no small part to the activities of 'B' and 'C' Squadrons, 3rd Parachute Brigade had been able to make a rapid advance towards Minden during the 4th, and the town was taken by a night attack after some fierce fighting, being declared clear of opposition by 0230 on the 5th (although evidently some Germans still remained in the town).

For 'A' Squadron, the 4th had been a little less fraught. According to the diary, the squadron bumped an enemy position after advancing two miles and lost a tank to a 75mm anti-tank gun. This opposition was overcome by 6th Airlanding Brigade supported by the Grenadier's Churchills in a 'fierce fight', which did not allow the squadron to recommence its advance until 1300. After this, the squadron continued without opposition but were soon ordered to swing left onto the axis of

---

20 Outline History of the 6 Airborne Armoured Reconnaissance Regiment (RAC).
21 IWM interview, p.32.

3rd Parachute Brigade, and ended up harbouring for the night well to the west of the rest of the regiment. As we have seen, 6th Airlanding Brigade were in fact following up 3rd Parachute Brigade rather than advancing on their right flank, and ended the day concentrated north of the town of Lubbecke, roughly 15km west of Minden.

Lt. Col. Stewart proudly summed the day up as follows:

> Distance of advance 38 miles. An advance of this distance, carried out in the face of opposition, reflects the very greatest credit on all concerned. It was unfortunate that several vehicles and men were lost, but in a seize and hold role losses must be accepted and they were out of all proportion to those inflicted on the enemy and the distance gained.[22]

Indeed, the whole division had done well, pushing hard to the east despite enemy resistance which, though patchy, could be sharp. As an example of how hard the division was working, 3rd Parachute Brigade had advanced 36 miles in seventy hours from Greven to Minden during the period 2nd to 4th April.[23]

The next day, the fifth, the only significant move was that of 'A' Squadron who moved forward to Petershagen on the Weser north of Minden. 6th Airlanding Brigade were forcing a crossing of the river in this area on the 5th, but 6th AARR were ordered into divisional reserve on this day and 'A' Squadron seem to have been backing up the airlanding troops rather than scouting for them, as no action is recorded in the regiment's diary. On reaching Petershagen the squadron stayed in harbour, as the other elements of 6th AARR had done throughout the day, for 'much needed maintenance and reorganisation', as the CO put it. Throughout the 6th and 7th the regiment remained in divisional reserve and enjoyed a period of comparative rest, while the main work of the division was the establishment of a secure bridgehead over the Weser river. The reconnaissance regiment of 15th (Scottish) Infantry Division took up the recce task for 6th Airborne during this period. By the evening of the 7th the lead elements of the division were over the River Liene in the vicinity of Neustadt and Wuntsorf, a good twenty miles east of Petershagen.

The rapid advance of the division meant that considerable clearing up of by-passed enemy troops was likely to be needed. From the 7th up to the end of 11th April 6th AARR's main job was to assist in this task. In pursuance of this, they crossed into the area east of the Weser on the 8th of April, but it seems there was little or no contact with the enemy in the succeeding three days. It was on the 11th April that 15th (Scottish) Division took over from 6th Airborne as the spearhead division of 8th Corps, with 6th Airborne Division being assigned the task of clearing up the axis of advance. The official history of the campaign has this to say about 6th Airborne's rate of advance in the period up to 10th April:

> It is worth noting that in this long advance the 6th Airborne Division moved faster than the 11th Armoured Division. [...] This was partly the result of poor roads and bad going across country but also because the strength of the German defence was lightest on the British right[24]

22 Stewart's report, p.8.
23 *Go To It!*, p.162.
24 Ellis.

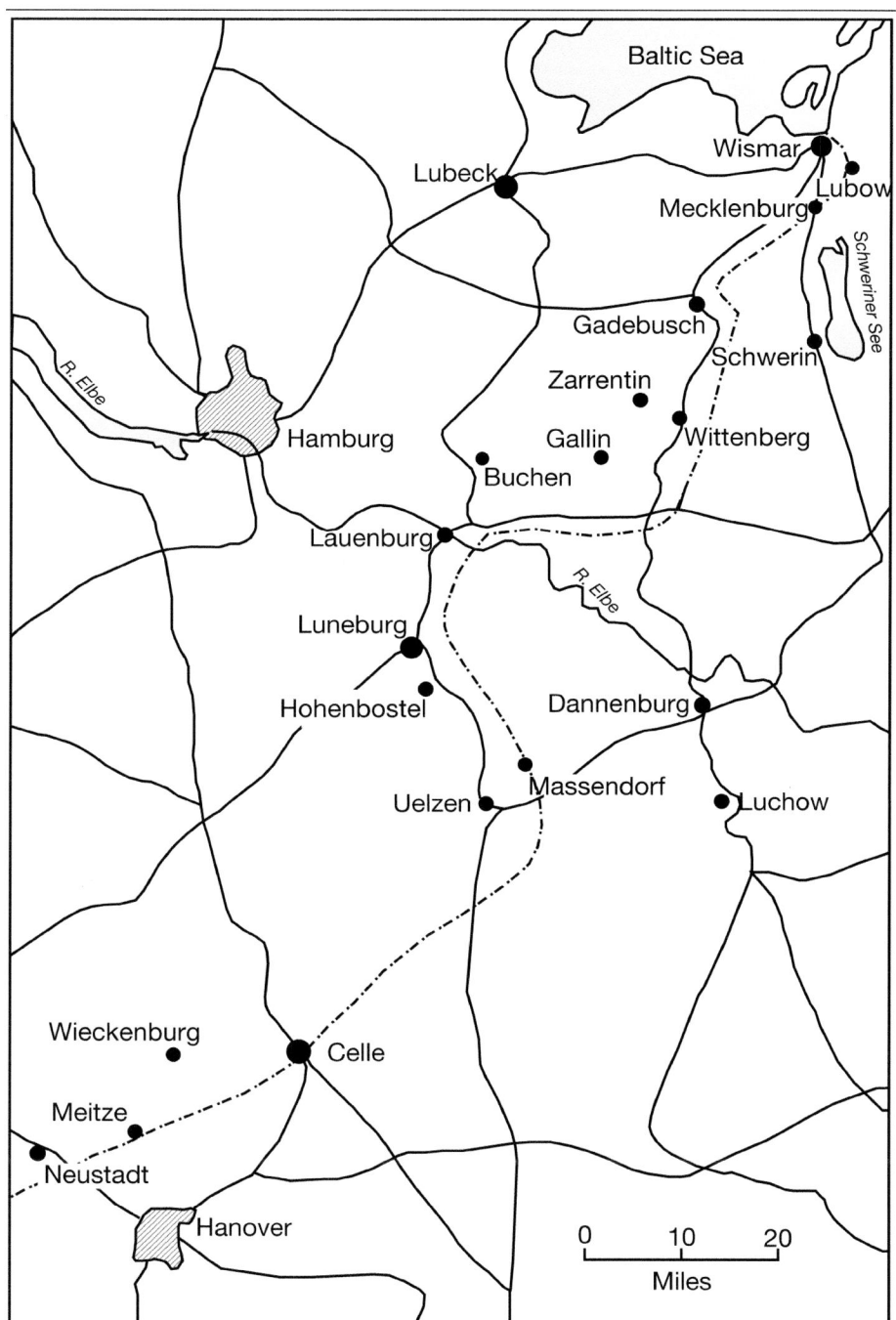

Across Germany 2, 12th April–3rd May 1945
(dashed line shows line of advance, 6th Airborne Division)

Doubtless the men of the 6th Airborne would have said that their own determination and aggressive spirit should be added to this list of reasons.

Despite the division losing the role of spearhead, on the 12th April 6th AARR once again had a 'real' recce mission given to it. The division was pushing on through the town of Celle towards another German town, Uelzen. On the 12th, 'A' Squadron was ordered to clear the area north of the road towards Celle, in company with 8th Para Battalion. This time, the enemy were encountered, and in particular were holding the village of Wiekenberg. One troop of the squadron worked round the village to the east and north-east, helping a company of paras. Sadly, the troop leader, Sgt Roberts, was killed in the fighting. The village was not finally cleared until early evening, at which point 'A' Squadron withdrew to harbour in the village of Meitze. Over the next two days there was a further opportunity for the regiment to rest, and the CO notes in his report that it was around this time that Lt. Ingall and seventeen other ranks from the MMG Troop, who had been taken prisoner at Holzhausen, returned to the unit.

On the 15th the move towards Uelzen recommenced. German resistance in this area had temporarily stiffened, and 15th (Scottish) Division was due to assault Uelzen on the 18th. Meanwhile, units of 6th Airborne, including 6th AARR, were to work around to the far side of the town to cut off the enemy's retreat. Peter Harclerode records that 'resistance in the area of the town was the most determined that 6th Airborne Division had yet encountered east of the Rhine and the enemy artillery, mainly self propelled guns, was particularly troublesome'.[25] The German troops causing all the trouble in Uelzen were from Panzer Division 'Clauswitz', a recently improvised formation including elements from the 233rd Panzer Training Division from Denmark.

For 6th AARR the 15th and 16th were fairly uneventful, with further investigations of wooded areas behind the line of advance the order of the day. On the 17th, however, the regiment, still with 22nd Independent Company under command, was ordered into the area south and east of Uelzen to support the advance of the division into this area. Orders for the move were received at 1300, but even before anyone had a chance to get going the Sherman Armoured Recovery Vehicle belonging to the regiment was hit by a panzerfaust in the area of the overnight harbour. One of the troops in 'A' Squadron investigated but the enemy had gone. The regiment began to check the villages and roads east of Uelzen, and had many sightings of the enemy. One tragic action on this day serves to illustrate the pressures and dangers that were still being faced by the regiment. The war diary states the basic facts: a troop of 'B' Squadron came under fire and had two scout cars knocked out, Lt. Turpin being killed. The troop had faced an advance down a straight stretch of road. With the squadron under orders to press on a s fast as possible, the usual cautious advance by bounds, where the movement of one vehicle could be covered by others from stationary positions, was abandoned. The troop set off down the road and what were believed to be SP 75mm guns picked off the two leading scout cars. Trooper Brian Heape, in the third vehicle (a universal carrier) had the awful experience of seeing Lt Turpin's driver suffering badly in one of the burning vehicles. He turned his carrier round and retreated to avoid becoming the third victim of the German SP, but on encountering a paras' medical jeep, he

25 *Go To It!*, p.166.

boarded it and led it forward under cover of a red cross flag to give assistance. The Germans had gone in the meantime, and the driver survived, though badly burned.[26]

Most of the regiment harboured at the village of Massendorf overnight, about 7km north-east of Uelzen, with 'B' Squadron in a small village a little further east. On the 18th, as the successful assault of Uelzen went in, the regiment was once again out on the roads east, north-east and south-east of the town. They were both searching for the enemy and providing 'protective recce' (i.e. acting as a screening force) for the activities of the infantry brigades of the 6th Airborne. These brigades were securing the area in an attempt to trap German units retreating from Uelzen, and also trying to effect a link up with 11th Armoured who were attacking around the north of the town.

The British had broken the resistance of the Germans in the Uelzen area during the 18th, but a regimental group from 'Clausewitz' had escaped from the town on the night of the 17th. The retreating enemy still occupied a number of the villages to the east of the town. British attention was now turning to the major river barrier of the Elbe, which lay at its closest only about 35km (as the crow flies) north-east of Uelzen. During the 19th and 20th of April, 6th AARR assisted in 6th Airborne Division's task of probing east towards Dannenburg and Luchow on the way to the river. They soon found the enemy holding many of the intervening villages and by the end of the 20th it had been decided to use 5th Para Brigade and 6th Airlanding Brigade to attack east to clear this area. Both recce squadrons of 6th AARR stood by during the 21st to assist this effort but they were not needed. As 8th Corps closed up to the Elbe over the next two days, 6th AARR were able to take a back seat.

The chosen location for the formal assault crossing of the great river was Lauenburg, which lay on the Elbe due north of Uelzen. Consequently, 6th AARR moved into accommodation in the Hohenbostel area, roughly halfway between Uelzen and Lauenburg, to await their turn to cross. D-Day for the assault, which was to be led by 15th (Scottish) Division, was the 29th, and 6th AARR were allocated to 6th Airborne's divisional reserve, expecting to cross on D+2. They were therefore able to enjoy a few quiet days, and it would seem that it was during this period that the CO wrote his report on Varsity and the days after, which has been used extensively in developing the above account. The last day recorded in the report was the 23rd of April, and it was on this day that the whole of 8th Corps was finally deployed on a 38 mile-wide front along the west bank of the Elbe. For the record, at the crossing of the Elbe, 8th Corps consisted of 11th Armoured Division, 5th Infantry Division, 6th Airborne Division, 15th (Scottish) Division, 6th Guards Armoured Brigade and 1st Commando Brigade.

This pause provides an opportunity to review the impressive rate of advance of the regiment during the post-Varsity period. According to Otway, the overall rate of advance from the Rhine to the Elbe by 6th Airborne Division was 11 miles a day, and operations for the division and 6th AARR during this time had been close to continuous. The greatest advance in one day by 6th AARR had been the 38 miles covered on 4th April. The CO kept a record of distance covered for some of the days of the advance in his report, and it is clear that when the regiment was

26 Additional detail from conversation with Brian Heape, June 2003.

tasked with its true recce role at the head of the division, advances of 10 to 20 miles a day against opposition were typical. Since leaving the Rhine bridgehead on the 27th of March, 6th AARR had covered around 250 miles along the divisional route to the Elbe.

Major Charles Kent of the regiment took the opportunity of this lull to write to his father on 22nd April:

> Frankly this party hasn't been by any means a picnic and has been by far the worse operation in many respects. I have been shot at more this time and conditions in general have been a little more exacting. Operating in enemy country can be a bit of a strain, however we shall get over it no doubt... We have had quite a lot lately – I can do with it and I am sure the chaps can also. They are grand chaps, Dad – I shall never tire of singing their praises. They have been truly magnificent – it would take too long to relate half the things they have done.[27]

As the regiment entered the last week of hostilities in North West Europe, there was one more spectacular day's advance ahead of them before they reached their destination on the Baltic coast.

The plan for the crossing of the Elbe was for 15th (Scottish) Division to lead the assault and establish a bridgehead on the far side of the river. Following this, 6th Airborne, with 15th Infantry Brigade of the 5th Infantry Division under command, would move across the river to widen the bridgehead by taking over and extending its eastern half. This process went largely according to plan, and 6th Airborne were in position across the river by the evening of 30th April. German resistance was nearly at an end and there was little serious fighting. The American troops operating to the right of 8th Corps were once again the XVIII US Airborne Corps, and once 6th Airborne had established themselves on the east bank of the river they again came under command of this Corps. The airborne corps was placed back under 21st Army Group control at this time to provide reinforcement for the tasks ahead. VIII Corps was to swing to the west and north towards Lubeck and Kiel, whilst XVIII Airborne Corps (6th Airborne, 82nd US Airborne, 8th US Infantry) was allocated the Darchau – Wismar sector.

6th AARR had crossed the Elbe on the night 30th April/1st May, with the tanks having to use a different bridge to the rest of the regiment due to their greater weight. On the morning of the 1st, the enemy was still reported to be holding two bridges over the Elbe-Lubeck canal (which ran north from Lauenburg) at the town of Buchen. Buchen was about 10km north of Lauenburg. 6th AARR were ordered to secure the crossings using all three squadrons and the Independent Parachute Company. The tanks would not be available as they had been delayed during their crossing of the Elbe. The regiment would approach Buchen from the south and east as they were already in the eastern half of the bridgehead and east of the canal. 'B' Squadron, with an MMG troop and the Assault Troop under command, was to take some high ground just to the north-east of the town at the village of Brothen. Once this was done, 'A' Squadron would move to seize the crossings, with 'C' Squadron and the Independent Para Company following up with RHQ. Elements of 15th Scottish would be attacking the same area from the other side of the canal.

27 Charles Kent collection, in 6th AARR file, Tank Museum archives.

Orders were issued at 0830, and by 1325 Brothen was reported clear of the enemy. Soon after Buchen was also reported clear and RHQ entered Buchen at 1420. There is no report of any fighting in the war diary so it seems the enemy had departed. That evening the tanks rejoined the regiment.

That same evening, orders were issued for what was to be 6th Airborne Division's final advance of the war in Europe. The division was to advance with all speed to the Baltic at Wismar, with the intention of heading off the Russians who were approaching from the east. The Russian entry into Denmark was to be prevented. The advance was to be led by 3rd and 5th Parachute Brigades. They were to move 'embussed' (i.e. in troop-carrying trucks), with 3rd Brigade on the right supported by a squadron of Churchill tanks of the Royal Scots Greys, and 5th Brigade on the left supported by 6th AARR. Orders were issued on the evening of the 1st May. 'B' Squadron, less its tank troop but with a troop of MMGs under command, would recce the centreline of the advance. 'A' Squadron, also less their tanks but including 22nd Independent Company, would initially protect the left flank, supported by 'C' Squadron. The Cromwells of both squadrons were collected together to form a half-squadron and were to move with the leading infantry battalion (12th Para Battalion), thus putting them behind 'B' Squadron. The second troop would carry infantry of the 12th Battalion on the tanks as they advanced.

The regiment moved out of harbour at 0630. By 0705 'A' Squadron had already taken the regiment's first prisoners of the day, and the influx of prisoners was to become a torrent as the day progressed. By 0745 the leading troop of 'B' Squadron received some fire from the small town of Gallin, but resistance was brief and the Germans here were soon surrendering. At 0900 'A' Squadron linked up with 'B' as planned and from here the two squadrons leapfrogged their way forward. At midday 'A' Squadron reached Zarrentin, about a third of the way to Wismar. They by-passed the town leaving 'B' Squadron and the Independent Company to clear it. This was quickly accomplished; by 1230 'B' Squadron were reported as 'pushing on at top speed' and were temporarily out of radio contact.

At this point, the advance was marred by tragedy when a troop of the squadron were attacked by friendly fighter aircraft at around 1300hrs. They were displaying their orange recognition panels, but the situation was extremely fluid and the troop was out on its own. They spotted some Typhoon fighter-bombers, which to their dismay commenced to dive down and attack. Only one fired its rockets, the others appearing to realise their mistake at the last minute. One carrier was hit. Of the four men on board, the driver and vehicle commander survived but the two men in the rear, John Hayes and 'Ginger' Hasler, were both killed by blast. They appear to have been the last fatal casualties of the war suffered by the regiment and this was a particularly tragic way for these casualties to occur.[28]

However, the Germans were disintegrating before the eyes of the advancing troops. Any pretence of resistance had been dropped and the advance quickly assumed the form of a race between 3rd and 5th Brigades for the prize of being first in Wismar. The key was the town of Gadebusch, where the parallel routes of the two brigades converged and from which there was only one good route to Wismar. In the end, it was 3rd Brigade which won the race, first to Gadebusch and then to

---

28 Additional details of this incident from one of the survivors, Mr Derek "Mick" Hood. Conversation with author, June 2003.

Elements of 6th AARR in Schwerin, early May 1945. Scout car in foreground, carriers behind (Norman Stocker).

Wismar itself. By the time 5th Brigade HQ was holding an orders group at Gadebusch (at 1350), 3rd Brigade had already passed through and were entering Wismar. The 5th Brigade was ordered to Mecklenburg, about 10km south of Wismar, from where it would exploit south to reach the north end of the Schweriner See, a large lake which extended for around 20km to the south. Hence the division would block the Russians with one flank on the Baltic and the other on the lake.[29]

From early afternoon, the war diary records both 'A' and 'B' Squadrons advancing at full speed. The main obstacles seem to have been the vast numbers of Germans trying to give themselves up and the assortment of German transport blocking the roads. At 1400 'A' Squadron took 200 prisoners along with their horses; during the next hour they took 200 more in the same area. However, the concept of 'taking' prisoners was rapidly becoming redundant as thousands of Germans, usually still armed, lined the route of advance trying to surrender. The diary states that 'it was impossible to count the number of POW and often difficult to disarm them all'. The usual reaction seems to have been to simply drive past whilst waving the Germans to the rear. 'B' Squadron had been ordered to push north then swing east to the line between Lubow (about 5km south-east of Wismar) and Hohen Viecheln (on the north shore of the Schwerin See). They were to attempt to contact the Russians who were believed to be in this area, but no Russians were

---

29 In *Go To It!*, Peter Harclerode has the two brigades commencing their advance on 1st May. This does not agree with the war diaries of the two brigades or the diary of 6th Airborne Division, neither does it tie up with the diary of 6th AARR. I therefore believe the account I have given to be correct. See *Go To It!*, p.167.

Members of 3 Troop, 'A' Squadron in front of a scout car, near Luneberg Heath, late April 1945. L to R: Tpr Bevan, Lt Scott-Martin MC, Tpr Smith, Tpr Gray, Sgt Lornes. In front, Cpl Wattam MM (Ian Waters).

found. By 1900 the squadrons of the regiment had withdrawn and were harboured. 3rd Parachute Brigade had already encountered the Russians east of Wismar during the afternoon, and after some confused and uncomfortable initial contacts the Russians accepted that they had been beaten to it and settled down as uneasy neighbours to the British. The official history records that XVIII Corps took 100,000 POWs on 2nd May, and 150,000 on the 3rd.[30] These are suspiciously round numbers, but they indicate the scale of the collapse. Montgomery himself summed up the day in a report filed on the evening of 2nd May to the Chief of the Imperial General Staff, Field Marshall Alan Brooke:

> There is no doubt that the very rapid movement from the Elbe bridgeheads northwards to the Baltic was a very fine performance on the part of the troops concerned. There is also no doubt that we only just beat the Russians by about 12 hrs.[31]

Early on the 3rd, 'B' Squadron were once again sent out to the same area to contact the Russians. This time they were successful, reporting contact at 0911hrs in the vicinity of Lubow with members of the Stalingrad Armoured Division. This day was the last that 6th AARR were officially recorded as on 'operations'. From the 4th, although hostilities had yet to officially cease, their role was one of establishing military government.

For the next few days, 6th Airborne Division as a whole was engaged in sorting out the various unit boundaries for this role, processing prisoners and establishing

30 *Victory in the West*, p.338.
31 *Monty*, p.610.

relations with the local Germans and the Russians. 6th AARR were allocated an area bordering the coast to the west of Wismar. Still supported by 22nd Independent Company, they set about establishing check points to control the flow of local civilians, displaced persons and German soldiers. There was a curfew to be policed between 2000 and 0500, and (as per their parent division) relations to be established with local authorities, through whom it was preferred to work in all administrative arrangements. Contacts with Russian units also continued at all levels. Field Marshal Montgomery arrived on 7th May for a meeting with Marshal Rokossovsky at HQ 3rd Parachute Brigade. The rather more basic nature of contacts with the Russians as experienced by 6th AARR has been described by John Banbery:

> We were very wary because they were pinching everything they could get their hands on. If anybody went in a vehicle over to their side, they let you go and kept the vehicle, so people were extremely wary and no DRs [Dispatch Riders] were allowed across, because they took the bikes straight away. The same with scout cars and anything like that.
>
> I think nobody quite trusted them. They were obviously a different sort of soldier from us, because you'd only got to say to the Germans 'the Russians are coming tomorrow', you couldn't see their feet for dust. It was an easy way of getting billets. The Russians were staggering back from the farms and camps clutching all sorts of things – radios, massive bits of household machinery that they didn't know how to work. But they were carrying them just the same. People were getting away from the Russians as fast as they could so there was a lot of movement. The Germans were very scared of the Russians, there was no doubt about that.[32]

Fred Murray, Squadron Sergeant Major of 'B' Squadron, remembers an attempted visit to the Russians. He set off in a jeep with the squadron CO and second-in-command, armed with some bottles of liberated champagne. However, the Russians refused the party entry into their lines. The British were concerned to see that the Russians were using local Germans to help them dig in their tanks, in positions sited to cover the British forces in the area.[33]

In the early hours of the 5th, 6th AARR were advised by divisional HQ that hostilities had officially ceased, following the unconditional surrender of German forces in North West Europe the day before. On the 8th, they were informed of the momentous news of the capitulation of all German armed forces – 'V.E. Day'.

The task of military government seems to have proceeded quite well. The following is a quote from the unit's war diary for 10th May:

> The job of Military Government in this area proceeds quietly and smoothly. The local people show a certain willingness to co-operate and so far no deliberate defiance of the laws enforced has been encountered. All except one of the Squadron Leaders have fixed office space where local people can go with their complaints and requests.

The good news was that it had been decided to bring 6th Airborne Division home quickly. On the 14th, an advance party from the recce regiment of 5th Brit-

---

32 IWM interview, p.36.
33 Conversation with author, October 2002.

Members of 6th AARR meet with soldiers from the Stalingrad Armoured Division, 3rd May 1945. The tank is a T-34/85 (Norman Stocker).

ish Infantry Division arrived in 6th AARR's area, and preparations began for the journey home. The tanks and carriers were handed in to the local ordnance depot on the 16th, and the next day the regiment was officially relieved by 5th Reconnaissance Regiment and started back the way it had come, towards Gadebusch and then Luneburg. They were supplied with eight ex-German transport vehicles by their parent division to help them on their way, and were initially accompanied by 22nd Independent Company. From the airfield at Luneburg, about 185 men of the regiment flew back to the UK on the 18th and 19th. The remainder of the regiment continued to Ostend, and from here a small party returned home via Tilbury. Most of the land party drove on to Calais and returned via Dover. The regiment was complete at its Larkhill home by the 26th of May, almost exactly two eventful months since Operation Varsity.

On their return from Germany, most of the unit enjoyed 28 days leave. Unfortunately however, the war in the Far East was still in progress, and 6th Airborne Division was initially earmarked for a role in the South-East Asia theatre. Some men had a shortened leave allocation in order to take part in preparations for this role. John Banbery remembers being recalled for training on Sherman tanks. On 26th June, the regiment was ordered to provide an advance party of twelve for dispatch to South-East Asia to be trained in jungle warfare techniques. In the event, a party of 21 is recorded as departing for this role on 13th July. For most of the regiment, however, July saw the resumption of the usual round of training. The diary hints that some sort of reorganisation was taking place, but details are absent, although it seems that in general personnel in the division were changed around as long service soldiers were demobbed and younger replacements took over. One important change took place on 16th July when Lt.Col. C.P.D. Legard, from the 5th Dragoon Guards, took over as CO of the unit. The take over is baldly stated in the diary, but it must have been an emotional farewell for Lt. Col. Stewart who had commanded the regiment throughout its combat operations in Europe.

Plans for the use of 6th Airborne Division were changing constantly around this time. It was first to be used in Malaya, then Singapore, but with the cease fire in Asia and the Pacific on 15th August and the official Japanese surrender on 2nd September, the situation changed again. World War Two was now effectively over, and only one airborne division was to be retained in the immediate post-war period. First Airborne Division was still recovering from the Arnhem operation, and remained weak in numbers and state of training. Therefore, despite being the junior of the two divisions, it was 6th Airborne that was retained whilst 1st Airborne was disbanded. As might be expected, there was some switching of units between the two divisions to accommodate the demobbing process and to retain the best of what was to be kept, but the details need not concern us. The important fact was that 6th Airborne was designated part of the 'Imperial Strategic Reserve', and was to be posted to the Middle East. Between 15th September and 6th November the division departed for Palestine. On 10th October, it was 6th AARR's turn to leave Larkhill, and to commence what was to be their final operational deployment.

Chapter 10

Postwar

Both 6th AARR and Britain's glider-borne tanks survived into the post war period, but only for a short time. The post war story separates into two strands, as 6th AARR's deployment to the Middle East cut them off from developments in the UK, and the latter continued to be the only place where Britain's Hamilcars, Tetrarchs and Locusts were based. Firstly, then, 6th AARR's tour in Palestine will be briefly described, at the end of which the unit disbanded. Secondly, the story of the winding down and final disappearance of the Hamilcar-tank combination in the UK will be told.

The ship carrying 6th AARR docked at Haifa on 22nd October. Judging by the war diary, the unit took very few or no vehicles with it, as it is recorded that the unit was lorried to its camp near Gaza El Bureij the next day (a journey of about 100 miles to the south) where it began to draw new vehicles. These included 11 Sherman tanks, and more vehicles were issued the next day. They were distributed equally to the three fighting squadrons so that the previous organisation disappeared and a new structure, evidently thought more appropriate to the new campaign, was introduced. Each squadron had two tanks, two 4.2" mortars, two MMGs and a number of jeeps. These new arrangements seem to have been completed with commendable speed and energy: by the end of the 24th, the new CO reported the regiment complete and ready to move off at 20 minutes notice.

What role had 6th Airborne Division been assigned, and what situation awaited them in Palestine? The Palestinian location had apparently been chosen 'due to its superior training facilities and airfields'.[1] However, the division had very little parachute or airlanding training during its stay, a position made worse after the RAF began to reduce its strength in the country due to terrorist activity. Aircraft for the division were provided by 283 Wing RAF, which contained the division's old friends 644 Squadron and 620 Squadron, both with Halifaxes. Horsas were also taken to Palestine to work with the airborne division, along with 'A' and 'D' Squadrons of the Glider Pilot Regiment as well as a detachment from 'G' Squadron. Horsa flying took place throughout 1946 and 1947, but no Hamilcars were taken to the Middle East. Consistent with their 'total soldier' ethos, members of the GPR were also involved in various ground operations. As far as parachuting went, most of the airborne drops made were refresher courses for paras already entitled to their wings, although some basic courses were run. The highest level exercises that could be managed were battalion drops.

In fact, the division was to be occupied mostly with internal security duties. At this time, the British held a mandate (originally issued by the League of Nations in 1923) to administer Palestine, which had a majority population of Arabs and a Jewish minority. With the end of the Second World War, and following the Holocaust,

1 *Go To It!*, p.178.

there was increased pressure for Jewish immigration to Palestine and Jewish hopes of making a homeland in the area. When 6th Airborne arrived, the British position was that further Jewish immigration was to be halted until the consent of the Arab population was obtained. As a result, British troops were seen very much as the enemy by the Jews, and the more extreme elements had formed terrorist groups which engaged in military action and civil disobedience directed against the British. Peter Harclerode has summed up the division's reception in the country as follows:

> When 6th Airborne arrived in Palestine, it was met by a hostile reception from the Jewish press which referred to its troops as 'Gestapo'. This was highly objectionable to the division, many of whose members had been Jewish and many of whom, during the advance to the Baltic, had seen the results of the Nazis' treatment of Jews. [...] Small wonder then that, in the main, many of its members sympathised with the Arabs.[2]

John Banbery was one of the members of 6th AARR in Palestine and in his interview with the Imperial War Museum, he confirmed this general feeing of sympathy with the Arab side. He also indicated that Jewish members of the unit were sent back to England to spare their feelings, although a few apparently 'hopped the regiment while we were there and joined the Jewish forces'. Other members of the regiment remember that the Jewish members of the unit were never taken to Palestine in the first place.

In short, the political situation was as complex and intractable as it is today, although different in structure. Peter Harclerode indicates that significant training was given to help the men of the division in their new role, but Banbery's memory is that very little training in security operations and rules of engagement was given to 6th AARR. This may have been due to the regiment's limited involvement in security operations compared to other units of the division. Nevertheless, he has strong memories of a hostile and frustrating environment:

> You couldn't go into the towns because the people disliked you. All the jeeps had wire cutters because they used to put hawsers across the roads to cut people's heads off, and the DR's heads off. People were just seeing their time out because by that time everybody had got a demob number, and you knew when you were going. We weren't attacking anybody, but people were very very alert. We'd had people killed. They machine gunned tents, so we'd had a few casualties dotted about. I think [the regiment] were at the time a little bit surprised that they were firing at us. We felt we'd been trying to release them previously. It was more surprise, a sort of 'Well, that's a funny way of saying thank you'.[3]

Although initially based in the Gaza area, the regiment's main area of operations was the area to the south-east of Tel Aviv, where the roads and railway ran from Tel Aviv to Jerusalem and where Lydda Airport was also located. First to be detailed was 'B' Squadron who moved out to Latrun on 1st November. They commenced recceing the roads in the area, and set up patrols to check on any unusual traffic. In an emergency, they would be tasked with keeping the road from Latrun to Jerusalem open and escorting convoys along it. On the 6th of November, 'C' Squadron moved out to Gedera, about 12 miles west of Latrun, engaged in similar

---

2 *Go To It!*, p.178.
3 Edited extracts from IWM interview.

duties. Also on the 6th, 21st Independent Parachute Company came under command of 6th AARR. This company (from 1st Airborne Division) had replaced 22nd Independent Company during the shake-up that occurred when 1st Airborne had been disbanded. On the 10th came orders for the tactical RHQ to move to Lydda airport, which they did on the 12th accompanied by the tank troop of 'A' Squadron. The airport was an important British base, and apart from the RAF, 6th Airlanding Brigade already had their HQ here. Presumably this move was to help coordinate the activities of 'B' and 'C' Squadrons, and also coordinate the additional work that the regiment received on the 11th. This latter was responsibility for patrols of the railway from Latrun to Majdal, particularly at night. For this role, 21st Independent Company would help, and the regiment was provided with what the diary described as 'two armoured rail trolleys', though exactly what these were I have not discovered. Attacks on railways, for example by cutting the lines with explosives or attacking signal boxes, were a favourite way for terrorists to cause disruption at this time. One noteworthy incident during the time at Lydda was when Lieutenant George Warburton of 'C' Squadron was kidnapped along with two other officers from the officer's club at Tel Aviv. They were taken away in coffins on board a lorry and were held for about 10 days before being released.[4]

Shortly after this period, on the 14th, serious riots broke out in Tel Aviv as a result of further political developments, revolving around British reluctance to back a Jewish homeland in Palestine and continuing restrictions on Jewish immigration. The riots were serious and continued over two days. To restore order, the whole of 3rd Parachute Brigade was eventually committed, and to maintain control they received various reinforcements in subsequent days. Amongst these was the tank troop of 'A' Squadron 6th AARR, which assisted in patrolling roads and were detached from 17th to 21st November. Another large scale British operation was mounted during the last days of November following attacks on the coastguard stations at Sidna Ali and Giv'at Olga, which lay on the coast roughly half way between Tel Aviv and Haifa. The British 'cordon and search' operations which took place in an effort to apprehend those responsible sparked off additional disturbances, which eventually consumed the equivalent of eleven infantry battalions (from both 1st Infantry Division and 6th Airborne Division) before the operations were complete and order restored. From 6th AARR, a troop from 'C' Squadron, and 'A' Squadron less its tank troop were deployed to Sidna Ali on 26th November. 'A' Squadron took over protection of the police post at the coast guard station whilst repairs were completed.

With all the sub-units of 6th AARR operating well away from Gaza, it was evidently thought time for the rest of the regiment to move, and on 3rd December RHQ and the HQ Squadron moved to Sarafand, within the main area of operations assigned to the fighting squadrons. On the same day 'C' Squadron moved the roughly 10 miles from Gedera to Ramle, and the regiment as a whole was additionally made responsible for the road from Ramle to Jerusalem.

On the 11th December, the war diary records a Squadron Leaders conference, with the first item on the agenda being 'Amalgamation with 3H to commence from 1.1.46'. 3H were the 3rd, The King's Royal Hussars, an armoured reconnaissance regiment which had been in Syria when 6th Airborne arrived in Palestine, but had moved down to come under command of the Airborne Division soon after

---

4 This story via Geoff Campbell of 'C' Squadron.

6th AARR Shermans at the Ra'Anana police post, Palestine, January 1946 (Geoff Campbell).

its arrival. They had worked alongside 6th AARR on many occasions, and now the continuing shrinkage of Britain's forces meant that 6th AARR was to amalgamate with this regiment, losing its identity in the process. On 15th December, 21st Independent Company left 6th AARR and moved to Quastina, coming under command 3rd Parachute Brigade. The regiment itself seems to have continued with its duties during January, and it was not until 1st February 1946 that 6th AARR officially ceased to exist, handing over all its operational duties to 3rd Hussars. It was around this time that 6th Airlanding Brigade also left the Division, being replaced by 1st Parachute Brigade. The airlanding troops were redesignated 31st Infantry Brigade and remained in Palestine until they were disbanded in November.

The amalgamation of the two recce regiments was obviously made possible by the continuing process of demobilisation. A considerable number of men from 6th AARR transferred over. The Hussars history indicates about 400 joined them at this time, but this included men from 22nd Independent Company as well.[5] 3rd Hussars would continue as the armoured reconnaissance regiment of 6th Airborne Division until that division was disbanded. John Banbery was himself demobbed about this time, but his personal impression of the amalgamation was not very positive. Asked what the feeling about being wound up was in 6th AARR he replied:

> Hated it. No doubt. I wasn't there, but talking to them now, none of them liked it. 3rd Hussars were very pro-Hussar so anybody who'd come from Airborne, their chances of promotion were pretty poor. They had more of the old Army discipline. We had discipline without it being obvious, so people didn't like it.[6]

5 Bolitho, p.306.
6 IWM interview, p.43.

One of the NCOs, Ted George, remembered the amalgamation in these terms. 'After our rag tail lot it was very nice, but we never really did mix'.[7]

With the end 6th AARR as a regiment, it is not necessary for us to continue the story of 6th Airborne in Palestine. Suffice to say that the division, with 3rd Hussars as part of it, stayed in the country for another two years after 6th AARR's demise, and continued to carry out a difficult and often dangerous task in an atmosphere of increasing unrest. Originally the division was scheduled to return to Europe to become part of the British Army of the Rhine in March-April 1948. Sadly, in February of that year, the division learned that their withdrawal from Palestine was to coincide with their disbandment. It had been decided that Britain's regular airborne force was to shrink to just a single brigade group in 1948. The elements of the division left Palestine in a phased withdrawal during May and June of that year, with the 3rd Hussars one of the last units to go on 30th June. It is now time for us to return to the UK and see what had become of the force of Hamilcars and light tanks that had been left behind when 6th AARR moved to the Middle East.

On 23rd August 1945 a conference was held at HQ 6th Airborne Division to discuss the future of the unit in the immediate post-war period. The division was to become essentially all parachute, with three parachute brigades forming the basis of its fighting strength. Two passages from the report on the meeting are worth quoting, the first relating to the future of gliders in airborne operations:

> Development has already made the parachuting of moderately heavy equipment far more economical in air lift than transport by glider. Furthermore, as there is always likely to be a shortage of aircraft, the transport of troops by glider is too expensive except for special tactical reasons, when a concentrated coup de main force is required.[8]

The writing was evidently on the wall for the military glider. Whilst the high glider casualties in Operation Varsity had obviously been of concern, the reasoning in the quote above is not absolutely clear: a Stirling or Halifax towing a Horsa could still deploy more men than if they were used on their own to drop parachutists. Only with a new generation of transports (in the British case the Handley Page Hastings) would the balance change. But preserving a force of gliders in the climate of post-war rationalisation was evidently considered an expensive luxury.

Thoughts on the future usefulness of the division's reconnaissance regiment were also committed to paper:

> There is little requirement for a recce regiment in an airborne op when a quick follow up is likely and ops are taking place within artillery support of ground formations. When operating at a greater distance there may be a small requirement for a recce element to be air transported. In both cases, a complete recce regiment will be required to enable the division to function as an ordinary division in the ensuing battle.[9]

This confirmed the procedure the division had adopted for Operation Varsity. For Varsity itself, there had been little requirement for a recce unit, but in the subsequent advance across Germany the support of a conventional recce regiment had

---

7 From a letter of November 1996, Tank Museum archive.
8 WO171/4158, Appendix 'A'.
9 Ibid.

been found essential. With the division now in Palestine, the special conditions of that deployment meant that 6th AARR retained a non-standard establishment suited to its role in that theatre. Meanwhile, in the UK, the official organisation for a recce regiment attached to an airborne division had been the subject of discussion and standardisation.

The RAC monthly liaison letter for December 1945 outlined the changes. Essentially, every infantry division was to have a recce regiment organised on standard lines, to be equipped with tanks, scout cars and armoured personnel carriers. The recce regiment selected to be attached to an airborne division would have the same organisation for operations in the ground role, but it would have additional airportable equipment allocated to it so that it could adopt a different establishment for airborne operations. The regiment in the airborne role would have an HQ squadron and three recce squadrons, but the important point was that the only armoured vehicle would be the scout car, supplemented mainly by jeeps. The scout cars would go in by glider (the Hamilcar being the only possibility at this date) or be paradropped. Neither 6th AARR nor 3rd Husssars ever had time to adopt this organisation before 6th Airborne Division was disbanded.

A parallel report from a conference held by the Director (Air) at the War Office in January 1946 confirmed that the Locust and Tetrarch were considered obsolete, but with the growth of the concept of airportability, looked forward to the introduction of new armoured cars or light tanks which could be useful in an airborne role. It is not the intention of this chapter to stray into a history of post-war airportable armour. Sufficient to say that the RAC and D(Air) documents taken together indicate that the Locust and Tetrarch had been rapidly dropped from airborne forces after the end of the war. Taking into account their very limited battlefield capabilities as tanks, and their unsuitability for pure reconnaissance, this was surely an entirely sensible decision.

Post-war plans for airborne forces were constantly changing, usually resulting in a reduction in strength. One last change is worth mentioning here, and forms perhaps a final postscript to the story of 6th AARR. The year before the regular airborne force was reduced to brigade strength, a Territorial Army (TA) airborne division was formed, designated 16th Airborne Division (TA). The officer in charge of putting together the recce regiment (though not its eventual commander) was none other than Lt.Col. Stewart, the old CO of 6th AARR. He contacted all his old officers, encouraging them to join if they could. How many joined is not known, but I owe this information to one of the ones who did, Geoff Campbell, who had been a subaltern in 'C' Squadron 6th AARR, having joined in November 1944. The unit selected as reconnaissance regiment for 16th Airborne Division was the North Somerset Yeomanry, who were the TA unit affiliated with the 3rd Hussars. They were based in the Bristol/Bath/Weston-super-Mare area, and many of the officers involved in the initial organisation came from 3rd Hussars. The regiment used Comet and Centurion tanks, which of course were never intended to go by air, but had a parachute squadron for airborne deployments, much in the spirit of the December 1945 reorganisation mentioned above. 16th Airborne Division (TA) was reduced to a brigade group in 1956.

We have seen that in the UK, the Locust and Tetrarch were considered obsolete by the end of 1945. The Locust seems in fact to have been declared obsolete as early as July 1945.[10] Some reports indicate the Tetrarch may have soldiered on for a few years for use in demonstrations and tests. Alan Wood, the author of Glider Soldiers, was involved in glider flying post-war and himself flew a Hamilcar from Fairford in 1947. He states, 'the Tetrarch remained in airborne service (3rd Hussars) at Fairford and Netheravon until the Hamilcar was redundant'.[11] Exactly why the older Tetrarch, which had been replaced by the Locust as it was in such short supply, once again entered service as an airborne tank is something of a mystery, but the same story appears in a letter written by the then librarian of the Museum of Army Flying (John Cross) in response to a research enquiry in 1982. The letter has been kept, and states:

> Tetrarch remained in use until 1949. A Hamilcar flight was maintained at Fairford till 1948 and the 3rd Hussars kept on a troop for working with them. However, the closure of that flight and the cessation of all glider training in early 1950 put paid to the concept and the tanks were withdrawn from service.[12]

Unfortunately, these statements have to be taken on trust as no documents appear to survive describing tank activities in this period. The 6th AARR war diary covers only Palestine, and neither the 3rd Hussars diary or their museum has any record of any flying activities in England at this time.[13] Perhaps they were crewed by a small cadre of RAC personnel on an informal basis, possibly including some old 6th AARR men, but no definite information has been found. Exactly when the last Tetrarchs were retired also remains to be discovered. A few more details are available on how the relatively large number of Locusts in the UK were disposed of. It would seem most remaining Locusts found their way into the hands of Belgian scrap dealers, but some also joined the Belgian Army as command tanks in Sherman regiments (minus their guns, as with the tanks supposedly issued to the Royal Artillery). Some also served with the Egyptian Army during the early conflicts with Israel around 1947-1950. Units of at least company (i.e. squadron) strength were fielded, but the source of the vehicles is unclear. There may be a tie up here with rumours that a few Locusts were issued to the RAF in Palestine for airfield defence after the war. In the USA, some Locusts escaped scrapping by being sold as agricultural tractors, after having their turrets removed.

The demise of the airborne tanks did not of course mean the immediate demise of the Hamilcar, which continued to be useful for carrying outsize loads for the surviving airborne force, especially as long as this remained at divisional size. Initially, the main base continued to be at Tarrant Rushton. By November 1945, post-war adjustments resulted in 190 Squadron (now equipped with Halifaxes) moving in to Tarrant Rushton to become the main towing squadron, and 'G' Squadron the Glider Pilot Regiment replacing 'C' Squadron who had done all the Hamilcar flying during the war. On 31st December 1945, 64 Hamilcars are still recorded as being on charge at Tarrant, along with 21 Halifax VIIs and a single stray Halifax III.[14] Routine training and continuation flying was taking place,

---

10 'M22 Locust Light Tank', p.100.
11 *Glider Soldiers*, p.106.
12 Museum of Army Flying, Box 425.
13 See also Bolitho, pp 304-313.
14 RO file AIR28/818, Operations Record Book, Tarrant Rushton, May 1943 - August 1946.

along with the odd transport operation for bulky loads and occasional movements to other airfields to provide aircraft for demonstrations and air displays. On the 30th December, seven Halifax/Hamilcar combinations departed for Rennes, Bordeaux and Istres in France carrying 'Babs' equipment, returning during January. 'Babs' stood for Blind Approach Beacon System, a bad weather landing aid which was one of the forerunners of the modern Instrument Landing System.

It was during January 1946 that the disposal of 'surplus' Hamilcars began. It was apparently considered that the number on charge was more than were required, and by the end of the month 44 had been moved out for disposal, leaving twenty on strength. Up until the end of July, routine flying continued, with new glider pilots still being converted onto the Hamilcars. However, the end was in sight as in that month six more Hamilcars were 'offered for disposal' due to glue deterioration, with 13 remaining at the end of the month (a further Hamilcar had been written off in an accident in April). During August 1946, sixteen Hamilcars are recorded being flown out from Tarrant to Netheravon and Brize Norton for disposal: perhaps three extra gliders previously not airworthy were made flyable to make moving them easier. Tarrant was being closed down as an operational station, and by the end of August the last Halifaxes had moved out, these now being operated by 297 Squadron, although the change in squadron was more apparent than real as 297 were a re-numbered 295 Squadron, who in turn had been re-numbered from 190 during post-war re-structuring.[15] In February 1947, Transport Command reported 18 Hamilcars still held by 38 Group, although eight were about to be written off due to their condition.[16]

It would seem 297 Squadron moved to Fairford from Tarrant Rushton, and Fairford now became the main base for the surviving Hamilcars as well as for the 'Hamilcar Flight' of the Glider Pilot Regiment. In April 1947, four RAF Transport Command squadrons were at Fairford: 47, 113, 295 and 297, each with 6 aircraft. The Operations Record Book for the station is rather thin on details of flying activities, but glider towing, including Hamilcar flying, was taking place, though how many Hamilcars were on strength is not recorded. By this time, however, such flying was hardly intense. By July 1947, out of a monthly total of 420 hours Halifax flying, only 1 hour and 15 minutes was glider towing, and until the station closed in December 1948 glider towing hours per month were mostly in single figures. By the time of the closure of the station, only 295 and 297 squadrons were present, and both were about to convert to the Hastings.

As far as Netheravon was concerned, by 1946 the airfield was not a squadron base but No.1 Heavy Glider Servicing Unit was situated there until June of that year, with Hamilcar 1 and Hamilcar X aircraft present. The airfield continued to be a venue for trials and demonstrations of airborne equipment, and in September 1947 nine Hamilcars are recorded landing there as part of an exercise. A Hamilcar from Abingdon is recorded in the Operations Record Book as making a heavy landing and subsequently receiving repairs at Netheravon as late as January 1950. In March 1950 a Hamilcar towed by a Hastings was once again damaged on landing during a 'Transport Support Demonstration'. Hamilcars were also occasional visitors to airshows and Battle of Britain Days; one was present at a Farnborough display in July 1950.

15 Lake, p.91.
16 PRO file AVIA15/2369.

Despite all the post-war cut backs, there was still some official support for the Hamilcar. In January 1948, an Air Ministry memo confidently stated, 'there is very little doubt that a further production of Hamilcars will be required'.[17] This prediction was ill-founded, and another memo from March 1950 in the same PRO file describes the Hamilcar as 'virtually obsolescent'. I have found no definite records of Hamilcar flying after 1950, but a copy of a policy statement by the Land/Air Warfare Committee survives from February 1951 on the subject of 'Operational Gliders'.[18] This states that 10 Hamilcars and 20 Horsas were to be retained in case of emergency for coup de main operations, as their silent approach continued to render them useful. However, the use of gliders in large scale operations was ruled out. It is also interesting that development of a glider larger than the Hamilcar was also ruled out as no tug of sufficient power was available. This was one of the reasons such a large glider had been considered impossible 10 years previously.

Flying may have continued in some form into the 1950s, as a few Hamilcars may have remained scattered at various transport, maintenance and trials bases in the south of England. Michael Bowyer notes the last two Hamilcar 1s as being 'sold off' (presumably for scrap) on July 1954 and April 1956.[19] One report is that the last Hamilcar was burnt on Old Sarum airfield (home at the time of the Army Air Transport Development Centre) in 1960.[20]

One special version of the Hamilcar deserves a mention. In 1947 the Hamilcar fuselage still had the largest cross section of any RAF aircraft, and in August of that year a Hamilcar X was converted for use in Airborne Early Warning (AEW) trials. A radar scanner with a diameter of 7 feet 6 inches was fitted in the cargo bay along with a suite of radar equipment, and a special one-off glazed nose was also fitted. The conversion was done at the Telecommunications Research Establishment at Defford, and trials took place for about a year, tracking targets such as the TRE's Bristol Beaufighter. The trials were apparently 'very successful'.[21] The trials were, however, only trials and there were never any plans to use the Hamilcar X as an AEW aircraft. The airframe was disposed of in September 1948 by being blown up in a simulated attack at Defford's Battle of Britain Day display. The glazed nose, however, apparently lived on for a while at Defford as a greenhouse!

GAL did briefly try to market the Hamilcar X after the war as a possible large capacity freighter (in conjunction with appropriate tug aircraft), as contemporary advertising shows.[22] The attempt came to nothing: both the market itself and the proposed solution may have been too specialised to offer any commercial reward. However, it is worth noting that GAL's experience with the Hamilcar was the starting point for the production of the RAF's first true heavy lift transport, the Blackburn Beverley. A post war Air Ministry specification for a short range, heavy lift aircraft was met by the company with their GAL 60 Universal Freighter. This was a four engined high wing aircraft with a massive box-like body and a tail boom

17 AVIA15/2369.
18 PRO file AIR20/8685.
19 'Hamilcars in Action', p.536.
20 This information from Alistair Mellor of the present day Airborne Forces Project Team at Boscombe Down. Alistair also provided me with information on the New Medium Glider.
21 Jarrett, 'Nothing Ventured …', in *Aeroplane Monthly*, February 1992, p.22.
22 See for example *The Aeroplane*, December 7th 1945.

carrying the tailplane, with large doors at the rear of the main fuselage giving access to the load bay. The aircraft was built at Feltham but before it was complete, GAL merged with Blackburn Aircraft. The GAL 60 was dismantled and taken to Brough, were it was first flown in June 1950. The design was developed and improved by Blackburn, and a Mk.2 aircraft which became the Beverley was flown in 1951. Eventually, 47 Beverleys were built, serving with 6 RAF squadrons from 1955 to 1967 until replaced by the C-130 Hercules. A payload of 44,000 lbs (19.6 tons) could be carried for 200 miles by the Beverley, which, with a wingspan of 162 ft, was a large aircraft even by modern standards, and which had the capability to operate into short, unprepared airstrips.[23]

The final postscript to the British glider story was the New Medium Glider, proposed by GAL in 1946. It was a rather more capable replacement for the Horsa, being a high wing, tricycle undercarriage wooden glider with a span of 93 feet and a length of 73 feet. It was designed to be capable of being being towed by the twin engined Vickers Valetta, the new medium transport aircraft of the RAF, at speeds up to at least 200kts. Maximum useful payload was to be 9000 lbs (4 tons), and loads could include a Daimler scout car, a 17pdr anti-tank gun and a 25pdr gun, the latter two without their towing vehicles which would have to be carried separately. The glider was obviously tailored to the requirements of the re-organised post war airborne forces, including the recce regiments which would have scout cars as their heaviest air transportable vehicles. A mock up was constructed, but as has been already indicated, gliders were fated to disappear from the British Army's inventory.

Naturally, the rundown of the glider force also meant the rundown of the Glider Pilot Regiment. By 1948 there was a headquarters and training squadron at Aldershot, and two operational squadrons, 'A' at Waterbeach and 'B' at Netheravon. It was a flight of 'B' squadron which was based at Fairford to operate the surviving Hamilcars following Tarrant Rushton's demise. Late 1948 saw a pause in glider pilot training as all tug aircraft were required for the Berlin Airlift, but training was resumed afterwards. However, in September 1950 the GPR was reduced to a single squadron, and at this stage training of new glider pilots ceased. The regiment did not disband until 1957, but by then the main role was flying Auster light aircraft in the liaison role. The two main histories of the GPR seem to indicate that Hamilcar flying ceased in 1949-50, and Horsa flying soon afterwards, but once again precise information is absent.

As the above paragraphs demonstrate, some details of the demise of the Hamilcar, Locust and Tetrarch in the post-war period are missing. However, the reasons for their disappearance are straightforward enough. In the case of the tanks, they were already of doubtful use even during the war, and were quickly judged obsolete when it ended. Their battlefield capabilities were so limited that to keep them on as part of the standard establishment in a rapidly shrinking airborne force was not worthwhile. The glider itself was doomed by the developing technologies of paradropping heavy loads, larger powered transport aircraft and helicopters. For a few years after the war the heavy glider could still claim to be a useful tool while these areas of military aviation matured. However, the future potential of these new technologies, linked with the budgetary restraints that were steadily reducing the size of Britain's airborne force, meant the wartime generation of gliders would never be replaced.

23 See Bill Overton, *Blackburn Beverley*, (Leicester: Midland Counties Publications, 1990).

Part Three

PERSPECTIVE

Chapter 11

Other Countries

The trio of Hamilcar, Tetrarch and Locust was the only combination of aircraft and tank to be used in action by the Western Allies, and the only combination of any country to be used to fly tanks directly into action in support of an airborne assault. However, other countries did produce gliders and aircraft capable of carrying tanks, and a comparison between these and the British effort should enable a more balanced judgment of the latter's value to be made. By far the most significant effort in this direction, and the most revealing comparison, is the tank carrying glider developed by Germany, and the powered transport aircraft developed from it.

The catalyst for the production of these aircraft was the intended German invasion of Britain, planned for 1940 after the 'Battle of Britain' had been won in the air. Researching his biography of Willy Messerschmitt, Frank Vann uncovered a letter from Messerschmitt to General Ernst Udet dated 14th April 1940, in which he proposed towing gliders capable of carrying 'heavy and very heavy tanks' across the Channel to participate in the airborne assault which would assuredly be part of any invasion.[1] His initial idea chimes in with some ideas the British were later to consider, in that he proposed bolting wings and a tail onto the chassis of the tanks rather than a fully fledged transport glider. He also proposed towing by four Ju 52 three-engined transport aircraft, using which he suggested '40 to 50 tons can easily be got into the air in a towed aircraft in one unit'. He insisted that by keeping things simple, 'a large quantity of such gliders could be produced in four months'.

Udet's reply is not recorded, but a seed had evidently been planted. In October 1940 the invasion of Britain, Operation Sealion, was officially postponed, but Hitler still hoped that, following a lightning campaign against Russia, it would be possible to return to the invasion of Britain in as little as a year. With this in mind, in the same month the German Air Ministry issued a broad specification for a *Grossraumlastensegler*, a large capacity heavyweight glider.[2] Rather than considering the lifting of only light tanks, the German specification followed Messerschmitt's lead by envisaging a glider capable of carrying the heaviest tank the Germans then deployed, the Mk IV panzer. The latest version of this tank, the Mk IVE, had entered production in September 1940 and weighed just under 21 tons. (The four earlier versions, A to D, were still operational and weighed two or three tons less). A winged tank was no longer considered sufficient, probably for the same reasons of flexibility it was ruled out in Britain, and the glider would have a hold sufficient to contain the MkIV, an 88mm anti-aircraft gun and tractor, or a

---

1 Vann, *pp. 134-135*.
2 Much of the detail that follows derives from William Green's outstanding survey of German wartime aircraft, *The Warplanes of the Third Reich*, (London: Macdonald, 1970).

self-propelled assault gun. It would also, of course, be capable of transporting men and supplies.

A very high level of urgency was attached to the programme. Messerschmitt and Junkers were both instructed to submit detailed design proposals within 14 days, and to start acquiring materials immediately for the intended production of 100 gliders. Both manufacturers established dedicated design staffs and met the deadline, and on November 6th, 1940 both were instructed to commence production of an increased total of 200 machines each. The designs were designated Me 263 and Ju 322. The Junkers design proved unsuccessful, but it did fly and so we should briefly describe its history.

Initially known in the company as the *Goliath*, the Junkers design eventually received the name *Mammut* (Mammoth). The aircraft was a quite radical solution to the problem posed, being similar to what today would be called a 'blended wing' design. The massive and thick wings had an enlarged centre section within which the hold was located, with the leading edge of the centre section forming an upward hinging door to the hold. A conventional fuselage and tail unit led from the rear of the hold, with the pilot's cockpit offset to the port side of the centre section. Wing span was a sensational 203ft 5in. Landing was on steel skids below the hold, with steel half-hoops protecting the wingtips, whilst for take off a jettisonable trolley fitted with eight pairs of wheels was used. Junkers had been told to construct their glider entirely from wood, and this produced problems from the outset. Junkers had been a pioneer of all metal aircraft and by 1940 had limited woodworking experience, and in addition the availability of suitable wood was found to be limited.

The first loading trial with a MkIV tank also produced a problem. The tank climbed the loading ramp and then tipped forward over the sill of the hold to drive into the aircraft. It would seem that the angle between ramp and hold was too sharp, and the floor too weak, as the tank crashed down abruptly on to the hold floor and smashed through it. Strengthening the floor cost nearly 882bs in weight which had to be taken off the available payload, but by early April 1941 the prototype had been repaired and was ready for its first flight. It was to be towed by a Junkers Ju 90 four engine transport, which was just powerful enough to tow the glider if the latter was loaded with minimum ballast. However, on getting airborne the Mammut proved impossible to control, and had to be cast off soon after take off to avoid causing the towplane to crash. Once released, the glider came back under control and landed safely in a field a short way from the aerodrome. Modifications, in particular a larger vertical tail, were made and more flights conducted, but handling characteristics remained bad. By May it was clear that the Messerschmitt design was working well and the Junkers project was terminated, the two completed aircraft and the 98 uncompleted airframes all being cut up. The programme had been a total failure, at a cost of 45 million Reichsmarks.

Messerschmitt had been told to use tubular steel construction for their glider, and the design they came up with was much more conventional than the Junkers, and in fact was essentially similar in form to the Hamilcar (although much larger). In constructing the glider the Messerschmitt works at Leipheim was assisted in particular by the Mannesmann-Werke at Komotau near Dusseldorf who made the steel-tube fuselage skeletons and wing spars, and the May furniture factory in

Me321 landing on its skids using the grass area of its aerodrome, following a demonstration flight (IWM)

Stuttgart which made the wooden wing ribs, tail components and fuselage fairings. By an incredible effort, the first prototype was completed 14 weeks from the receipt of instructions to go ahead. In the words of aviation historian William Green:

> Surpassed in size only by the Tupolev ANT-20bis, the construction of this immense aircraft, the second largest in the world, in so short a time was a feat without parallel. What is more, a further 11 examples were in final assembly and 62 more were in pre-assembly stage.[3]

The glider had been redesignated Me 321 and received the name *Gigant* (giant). The aircraft had a high, braced wing spanning 180ft 5in. Length was 92ft 4in. The cargo hold within the massive fuselage was 36ft 1in long, 10ft 4in wide and 10ft 10in in height. Access to the hold was by double 'clamshell' doors which formed the nose of the aircraft when closed. A single pilot occupied the cockpit which was perched atop the nose at the leading edge of the wing, and the total crew was intended to be a pilot, radio operator, loadmaster and two gunners. The latter would operate two machine guns fitted in the upper part of each nose door. If infantry were carried, provision was made for them to fire their own machine guns from stations at the fuselage windows. Four sprung skids below the forward fuselage were provided for landing, and a jetisonable trolley with four wheels was provided for take off. Maximum and minimum towing speeds were 137mph and 99mph respectively, with a normal gliding speed of 87mph. The hold was initially stressed for a load of 44,090lbs (19.7 tons). However, after development the

3 *Warplanes of the Third Reich*, p.646.

weights came out at an empty weight of 26,896lbs, a normal loaded weight of 75,840lbs , and a maximum overload of 86,860 lbs. This gave a possible load of between 48,944lbs (21.8 tons) and 59,964lbs (26.7 tons).[4] Note that a load of around twice the weight of the glider itself was achieved. An auxiliary deck could be fitted within the hold to allow up to 200 troops to be carried.

The first flight took place on 25th February 1941, and as with the *Mammut* the towplane was a Ju 90, once again just able to get the glider into the air with minimum ballast carried. The glider handled quite well, and would continue to cause few problems during its development. What was noted straight away was that the controls were very heavy, and provision was quickly made for a larger cockpit to accommodate two pilots to share the workload. This modification would be introduced after the initial 100 gliders, whose production was already underway, had been completed. The main problem to be solved was that of getting the glider into the air and towing it when fully loaded. The first part of the solution was that RATO units would be employed as standard. The initial fit was for up to four 1,102lb thrust units to be carried under each wing, and this was increased after development work to up to six 1,102lb, four 1,653lb or three 2,205lb rockets on each side. The second part of the solution was development of a specialised towplane, the Heinkel He111Z *Zwilling* (twin). This effectively took two He 111 twin-engined medium bombers, with the left wing outboard of the engine removed from one and the right wing similarly removed from the other. The two were then connected with a short constant-chord central wing, on which an additional engine was mounted, to produce a five engined towplane which it was calculated would have the power to tow the Me 321 over an acceptable distance. In the event, only 12 *Zwillings* were ever produced, two pre-production examples and ten production aircraft.

However, although work had commenced on the *Zwilling* before the first flight of the *Gigant*, a significant delay was expected before the former would become available, and an interim solution was required. Multi-aircraft towing, as originally conceived by Willy Messerschmitt in his first proposals, offered such an interim solution and the combination eventually selected was three Me 110C twin-engined fighters. This combination became known as the *Troika-Schlepp* (triple-tow) and involved the three aircraft flying in a vee formation, with the lead aircraft having a 328ft towline and the two wingmen having towlines of 262ft. The combination proved to be workable, but involved a high level of pilot skill and was always a marginal operation involving considerable risk. Preparations for take off were time consuming and made multiple launches a slow process. The fighters were close to stalling speed as they took off and there was a tendency for tow cables to tense and slacken in a series of violent jerks. Accidents during testing and training were numerous and sometimes fatal. The worst of them is described by William Green in his book, *Warplanes of the Third Reich*:

> On one occasion during operational trials with a Gigant carrying 120 troops, the take off rockets under one wing failed to ignite, the glider veered to starboard, its three Me 110 towplanes colliding, and the entire 'train' crashing to its destruction in a forest near the airfield boundary, 129 lives being lost.[5]

4 *Warplanes of the Third Reich*, p.648.
5 *Warplanes of the Third Reich*, p.647.

Panzer Mk.IVE demonstrates the technique for leaving an Me321 with jammed doors. A mock-up fuselage is in use (IWM).

Despite the accidents, the *Troika-Schlepp* was made to work and in June 1941 the first operational Me321 unit was formed, designated *Grossraumlastenseglergruppe Me 321*. By late summer 1941 the original batch of 100 Me321A gliders was complete and work was starting on production of the two-pilot Me 321B. Use in an invasion of England was now clearly not going to occur, and operational status had been achieved too late for the operation in Crete. Therefore the unit was organised in preparation for service in Russia. On achieving operational status in September, the *Gruppe* contained four *Sonderstaffeln* (*Grossraumlastensegler*), each with five Me321 and fifteen Me 110C towplanes.

In just under a year from the issue of the specification, the *Gigant* had been designed, tested and produced in significant numbers. A twenty aircraft unit was operational, with sufficient aircraft in reserve to make up losses in any operations. In contrast, from the finalisation of the Hamilcar specification in January 1941 it was 14 months before the prototype even flew. To achieve a comparable level of operational availability took roughly three years, say from January 1941 to January 1944. It is also worth noting that news of the development of these giant gliders in Germany reached Britain sometime during 1941.[6] Evidently, no real desire to emulate the achievement was stimulated.

6   See for example Wright, p.57.

In Russia the *Gruppe* was not kept together, but was split into *Staffeln* which were allocated to separate operational areas. The period of deployment was short, mainly due to the onset of the Russian winter when rain ruined unpaved airfields and weather conditions rendered flying hazardous. In addition, the gliders found themselves assigned supply and transport duties for which they were really not suited, having been designed for one-off assault operations. Only one *Staffel*, GS 1 based at Riga, seems to have been involved in assault missions, when on 14th September Me 321s landed a company of infantry on the Baltic island of Saaremaa in an unsuccessful attempt to capture the coastal fort at Kubassaare. The *Staffel* subsequently flew logistic support missions for Me 109 fighter units and ground troops active in the area. *Grossraumlastenseglergruppe ME 321* was disbanded in December 1941, but some of the aircraft stayed on in Russia for a time as (GS) Kommandos 1 and 2. These units eventually received some He111Zs around spring 1942, and the irregular use of the *Gigants* on supply missions continued on the Eastern front up to the summer of 1944, when the gliders were used on one-way trips to supply surrounded troops.[7]

Early in 1942 it seems the majority of the *Gigants* were withdrawn from frontline service in order to prepare for an operation of the type for which they were designed. This was Operation *Herkules*, the invasion of Malta, planned for July 1942. A special armoured unit was created for the operation, Panzer-Kompanie (z.b.V.) 66, later expanded to a Panzer-Abteilung of two companies.[8] The unit was equipped with Mk IV tanks, as well as special up-armoured versions of the Panzer I and Panzer II tanks, and captured Russian KV I and KV II heavy tanks.[9] The Russian vehicles were too heavy for the Me 321, but consideration was given to carrying in the lighter German types by glider. In the end, it was decided that the difficult thermal conditions which were common in the region would render operations too risky for ME 321s loaded to their maximum weight. The Gigants would be used for carrying heavy weapons and supplies. However, the operation was eventually cancelled, as were other operations in Astrakhan and the Baku oil fields which were to have involved the Me 321. In January 1943 the glider was chosen to take part in the emergency re-supply operations into Stalingrad, but the logistic problems of moving and supporting these massive aircraft meant they arrived too late. Supply missions into the Kuban bridgehead in the Crimea were carried out in early 1943, and some isolated transport missions in rear areas, but by summer 1943 most of the remaining gliders were at Istres in France. By August 1943 20 Me321s and 11 He111Zs were present here, but a major airstrike on the airfield on 17th August destroyed five of the gliders and damaged two. The problems of keeping the *Gigants* operational is demonstrated by a November 1943 report which gives 21 *Gigants* on strength in France but only four operationally ready. From July the gliders were being prepared to ferry two paratroop divisions to Sicily, using He 111Z tugs. In the event the distances involved were found to be too great, and as no intermediate landing grounds were available this operation too was cancelled. The units in France were disbanded in December 1943 and the glid-

---

7   Dabrowski, p.15.
8   z.b.V. = zur besonderen Verwendung = for special duties.
9   See Martin Tomczak, 'Further Notes On Operation Herkules', in *Miniature Wargames*, July 1998, pp.32-33.

ers scrapped.[10] As noted above, isolated operations continued on the Russian front into 1944, but it does not appear that the Me321 ever transported tanks on an operational mission. Production of the Me321 had ended in early 1942, all of the original order for 200 being completed.

Despite its very limited use as an assault glider, there is no doubt that the Me 321 would have been effective in that role. Take off distance at normal loaded weight with rocket assistance and the *Troika-Schlepp* was 1400 yds, hardly excessive, and more significantly landing distance was around 450 yards, short enough to allow landings in open country without the need for captured airfields. As a transport aircraft, however, it had serious limitations. Arrangements for moving it from place to place were complex, as it required special support for the rocket motors it used and airfields needed to be suitable for *Troika-Schlepp* operations. Once landed, it also needed a lot of effort to ground handle it. It was these considerations which led to the development of a powered Me 321 for use as a large capacity transport.

It would seem that the limitations of the ME 321, and the fact that it was unlikely to see much service in the role for which it had been designed, were appreciated quite early by the German Air Ministry. Only a few weeks after flight testing of the glider had commenced, the Messerschmitt company was asked to design two powered versions. The first was to be similar in concept to the Hamilcar X, having insufficient power (from 4 engines) to take off fully loaded without a tow, but able (unlike the Hamilcar X) to sustain level flight with the same load The other was to have 6 engines and to able to operate as a normal powered aircraft. In order to avoid using engines required for existing German aircraft, French engines were adopted. These were the Gnome-Rhone 14N, rated at 1,140hp for take off. The powered *Gigants* were produced with the minimum changes from the glider, the most significant modifications being the strengthening of the wing structure to take the engines and the adoption of a fixed, 10 wheel undercarriage. The latter was adopted to allow the heavy aircraft to operate from rough landing grounds and featured five wheels one behind the other on each side of the fuselage. The new aircraft was designated Me 323, and flight testing of one prototype of each version commenced in March-April 1942. It was soon decided that the six engined version was the preferred option, and this was put into production as the Me 323D, retaining the name *Gigant*. The powered aircraft, with the weight of the engines, fuel and reinforced structure to cope with, had a smaller available load than the glider. The maximum load was around 25,500 lbs, (11.4 tons). Two additional crew members were carried, these being flight engineers who had cabins in the wings, one on each side between the inner and mid engines. Provision for use of rocket assisted take off, as with the Me 321, was made, but the poor reliability and specialised servicing requirements of the rockets meant that that they were not often used operationally.

A total of 198 new build Me 323s, plus 15 converted from Me321s, were eventually delivered to the Luftwaffe, almost all in the two main variants, the Me 323D and the Me 323E. The latter version featured improvements to the defensive armament, structural strengthening and increased fuel load. They operated mainly in the Mediterranean theatre and on the eastern front, and were broadly considered very useful aircraft. Of course, where air superiority was not established they were

10 Dabrowski, p.15.

always vulnerable to enemy fighters, and as a result acquired quite a heavy defensive armament during their time in service. They were not cleared for flight on instruments, and so could not be flown at night to avoid enemy interference.

Operations in the Mediterranean began in November 1942 with the Gigants formed into *Kampfgeschwader* (z.b.V.) 323, with three groups of 6 aircraft plus a headquarters with three aircraft. The main task was flights from Italy to Tunis and Bizerta carrying supplies for the Afrika Korps. The *Gigants* usually flew in mixed streams with large numbers of Ju 52 three engined transports, along with a large fighter escort. The missions continued through to April 1943, but losses to fighters en-route, and on the ground in Tunisia, eventually led to the withdrawal of the aircraft. The last straw was on the 22nd of April, when 14 out of formation of 16 Me 323s were shot down by RAF fighters, with another destroyed in a strafing attack on the airfield at Tunis. During December 1942, some *Gigants* had been moved to Russia to take part in re-supply missions to Stalingrad. Operations in Russia, after withdrawal of the aircraft from the Mediterranean, continued until at least May 1944, with main bases in Warsaw, Kecskemet (Hungary) and Focsani (Rumania). The aircraft were assigned to *Transport-geschwader* 5 (Transport-wing 5), which consisted of two Gruppe, although according to William Green 'the Messerschmitt transport was never available in really substantial numbers'.[11] Production of the aircraft ceased in April 1944, and following continuous losses on the eastern front TG5 was disbanded in August 1944.

The Me 323 was used primarily as a normal transport aircraft, carrying supplies, men and fuel and evacuating casualties. There is evidence, however, that armoured vehicles were transported on at least one occasion in the Mediterranean. In Frank Vann's biography of Willy Messerschmitt he quotes the following letter to Messerschmitt regarding operations in November 1942:

> The first Me 323 flew with an assault gun and the necessary ammunition to Bizerta immediately after our landing in Tunis. It unloaded there without any trouble and returned to its home base without any damage. It was this assault gun that we have to thank for being able to break through the ring of American tanks drawn up in a circle of 12 kilometres diameter around Bizerta. On the very first day 8 tanks were destroyed by it and on the next day that total went up to 28. More assault guns were flown over with the Me 323 and these opened up for the troops the possibility of driving the Anglo-Americans even further back. [...] The transport of the assault guns was necessary because the Straits of Otranto had been completely mined by the enemy. This had the result that one of our transport ships loaded with tanks was blown up.[12]

This information might be thought to dent the unique reputation of 6th AARR as the only unit to fly tanks into action in World War Two, but it must be pointed out that the German armoured vehicles were flying as part of a transport mission rather than an assault landing. The type of assault gun is not mentioned, but they cannot have been the Wehrmacht's standard assault gun, the Sturmgeschutz III, as these vehicles would be too heavy for the Me 323. They would appear to have been one of the versions of the Marder self-propelled gun. This series of vehicles were improvised tank-hunters (*panzerjager*) using the chassis

---

11 *Warplanes of the Third Reich*, p.655.
12 *Willy Messerschmitt*, p.138.

Me323 and Marder II *Panzerjager*. This photo was probably taken during the emergency reinforcement of Tunisia, November 1942 (AXL's Plane Gallery).

of obsolete AFVs, firstly that of the French Lorraine tracked carrier (Marder I), then that of the German Panzer Mk II and the Czech Lt-38 (Marder II and III). They mounted either the German 75mm PaK40 anti-tank gun or the captured Russian 76.2mm gun. Their armament was effective but the vehicles were lightly armoured with poor crew protection and had a high profile. Their weight of about 10.5 tons was within the possible load of the Me 323, and a number of the two later versions (Marder II and III) are known to have been used in Tunisia in 1942-43. A surviving photograph shows a Marder II being unloaded at a desert airfield from an Me 323 and provides further confirmation of this supposition.[13] It seems therefore that some of these vehicles were rushed to Tunisia in Me 323s as part of the emergency reinforcement of the area which followed the Allied landings on November 8th (Operation Torch). It would also seem that they played a worthwhile role in what became known as the 'Race for Tunis', an unsuccessful attack eastwards by the Allies towards the Tunis area in late November and December which was defeated by hastily assembled German forces.

An interesting endpiece to the Me321/323 story is provided by a War Office note from August 1944, which considers the potential usefulness of the Me323 to the Allies in the Far East. Noting the aircraft's unique capabilities, the note concludes 'even a few of these aircraft would be of immense value to us in the war against Japan'.[14] It suggested that existing aircraft could be procured and more pro-

13 The photo may be found (in colour) on the Axl's Planes Gallery website – www.studenten.net/customasp/axl/index.asp. See also Dabrowski, p.22.
14 PRO file WO233/44 Long term Glider Sub-Committee.

duced, (presumably when the factories in Germany had been captured), and shipped to the Far East. It was an idea unlikely to be realised, and evidently not pursued, but it was a tribute to Messerschmitt's design achievement.

The second country to consider in our comparison is Russia. Three developments are of interest here: the carriage of light tanks as underslung loads in pre-war trials, a project for a winged light tank, and a military glider comparable with the Hamilcar. It should be noted that information on these projects is scanty in this country, and sometimes contradictory. Wherever possible, the latest information from recent websites has been used to update the material in those published sources which do exist.

During the 1930s, Russia was a pioneer of massed airborne forces. The reader may recall that early in this book the experience of General Wavell as an observer to the 1936 Russian Army manoeuvres was mentioned. He was treated to a demonstration during which 1200 paratroops and 18 light field guns were dropped. Other, even larger drops, were taking place in Russia on a regular basis during the mid-late 1930s. With this in mind, it is no surprise that the first carriage of tanks by air in any country took place in the Soviet Union. The development of the twin engined Tupolev TB-1 and four engined Tupolev TB-3 bombers had, from the 1920s, given the Soviet Union aircraft with sufficient load carrying capacity to enable experiments with the carriage of light tanks and tankettes to take place. The TB-1 (also known as the ANT-4) was the world's first all metal heavy bomber, and first flew in November 1925. The aircraft had a wingspan of 97 feet 1 inch, and a length of 56 feet 9 inches (about Halifax size). The TB-3 (or ANT-6) was to be a larger and more capable successor to the TB-1 and first flew in December 1930. This aircraft had a span of 132 feet 10 inches and a length of 79 feet 4 inches, which made it significantly bigger than the Halifax. Both Russian aircraft were very advanced for their time, though obsolete by the time the Second World War started. For example, the maximum speed of the TB-1 was about 125mph, and of the TB-3 only 140mph.[15]

With both aircraft, the vehicles were carried rigidly secured directly under the fuselage between the undercarriage legs and were normally unloaded after landing (but see below). The earliest date so far given for flight with armoured vehicles is 1930, when some imported Vickers Carden Loyd (VCL) tankettes (either Mk.IVs or Mk.VIs, sources disagree) were attached to cradles beneath TB-1 bombers.[16] The concept was persevered with, as by 1935 T-27 tankettes (a Soviet development of the VCL tankette) were apparently being flown secured under TB-3 bombers during military manoeuvres. Since 1933, one company of T-27s had been included in each of four 'motorised airborne battalions' which had initially formed in 1930. The T-27 appears to have participated in the airborne role in the 1936 and 1937 manoeuvres as well.

As has been stated, the T-27 was not a tank, but a 'tankette', a two man machine gun carrier which represented about the smallest practicable armoured fight-

---

15 See Gunston, *Tupolev Aircraft Since 1922*, (London: Putnam, 1995) and Paul Duffy and Andrei Kandalov, *Tupolev: The Man And His Aircraft* (Shrewsbury: Airlife, 1996) for details of these aircraft.
16 See Zaloga and Grandsen, p.51.

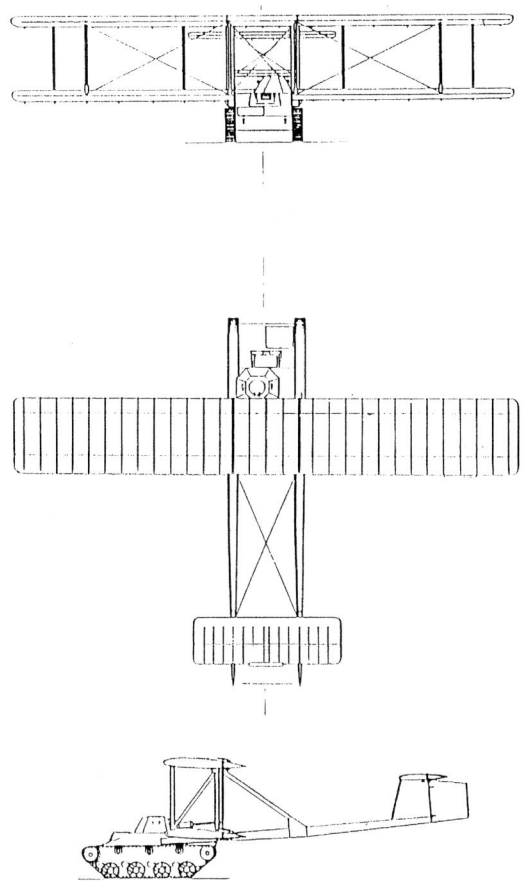

The Russian KT tank glider (Museum of Army Flying).

ing vehicle available. In Britain, development of this type of vehicle eventually led to the Universal Carrier which has featured so extensively in this book. The T-27 was armed with a 7.62mm machine gun, had a maximum armour thickness of 10mm, and weighed 2700kg (2.66 tons). The VCL tankettes used in earlier trials would have weighed the same or slightly less.[17]

The other armoured vehicle generally agreed to have been flown by the Russians was the T-37 light amphibious tank. As the limitations of tankettes were recognised, this vehicle replaced the T-27 from 1933, both within the Red Army as a whole and within the armoured companies of airborne units. The T-37 was only slightly heavier than the T-27 at 2900kg, and retained a two man crew, but was slightly larger all round and mounted its machine gun in a turret rather than the hull front. From 1937 the T-37 was itself replaced by the T-38, which was an improved version of the earlier light tank.

17 Additional detail on the T-27 from the page 'The T-27 Tankette', from the website The Russian Battlefield, August 2002.

Both the T-37 and T-38 were flown in trials and exercises secured beneath TB-3 bombers. From the published sources available, it is not clear whether these tanks replaced the T-27 or supplemented it during the manoeuvres carried out around 1935-38. Besides the main concept of transporting and landing with the tanks, it seems experiments were also carried out investigating the dropping of tanks or tankettes (without parachutes) at very low level and as slow as possible, both into water and onto land. 'Very low level' meant as low as one metre. The TB-3 had a landing speed around 65-75mph, depending on version, and so presumably could fly a little slower than this if required. There is no published information as to how successful these trials were. More conventional paradropping trials may also have taken place from as early as 1930, but again information is scarce. One operational deployment of airlanded light tanks is reported during the seizure by the Soviet Union of Bessarabia from Rumania in 1940. Presumably, T-37s or T-38s were used. One source indicates the tanks were dropped onto captured airfields by low and slow flying TB-3s, without crews, though simply landing and unloading would seem the more logical and safer choice.[18]

Whilst many details, including the number of tanks used, are unknown regarding all the trials, manoeuvres and operations described above, it should be emphasised that during the 1930s such activities meant that the Soviet Union was the world pioneer both in the carriage of armoured vehicles by air and in the development of airborne forces in general. However, the development of the airborne tank concept seems to have ceased at the end of the 1930s, and during the war itself, Russia made only a limited use of airborne forces, on a much lower scale than the Western Allies. Exactly why this was so remains to be fully explained, but at least part of the reason may be that the kind of independent minded and forward thinking officers that were required for the development of airborne forces were exactly the kind of officers who would have been the target of Stalin's purges of the 1930s. Zaloga and Grandsen give the lack of sufficient transport aircraft as the main reason.[19] Certainly, the largest glider deployed operationally during World War Two appears to have been the Antonov A-7, which carried only eight troops.

There was to be only one further experiment in airborne tanks before the war ended, and this was initiated during the autumn of 1941 by the aviation engineer O.K. Antonov. His idea was for a T-60 light tank to be attached to a set of biplane wings and a twin boom tail, to be towed into action as a glider. The tank would land on its tracks and the wings and tail would be removed to ready the tank for combat. Antonov was authorised to go ahead with his idea. The T-60 was the latest Soviet light scout tank at this time and was eventually produced in substantial numbers, commencing in July 1941. The tank weighed 5800 kg (5.7 tons), had a crew of two, armour up to 20mm thick and was armed with a 20mm cannon. The wings for the tank had a span of 18 metres (59 feet) and the length of the glider was 12.06 metres (39 feet 7 inches). For the first (and apparently sole) test flight, the tank was lightened by removing armament, ammunition, headlights and most of its normal fuel load.[20] Various designations have been given for this flying tank, in-

18 Zaloga and Grandsen, p.192.
19 Zaloga and Grandsen, p.193.
20 Detail taken from the page 'Modifications of the T-60', from the website The Russian Battlefield, August 2002.

cluding AT-1 or A40-T, but the correct one seems to have been simply KT, for *Kryl'ya Tanka* , meaning 'tank's wings'. Total weight of the KT contraption was 7804kg (7.68 tons). The towing aircraft was to be the TB-3 or the more modern twin engined DB-3F bomber, though for the test flight a TB-3 was used. This flight took place in the autumn of 1942. The TB-3 experienced considerable difficulty in building up flying speed due to the rolling resistance of the tank's tracks (which as we have seen were used instead of undercarriage), and once airborne the high drag of the biplane glider with its tank fuselage also proved to be a considerable strain for the towplane. The TB-3's engines overheated and the glider was released early, but is reported to have flown well after release and made a safe landing. The tank's engine was apparently started in the air so that the tracks were turning prior to landing in order to reduce the strain on the running gear. The wings and tail were removed successfully and the tank driven back to its base. However, the problems experienced by the tug aircraft were sufficient to prompt a decision to abandon the project.[21]

Although a number of gliders were developed in Russia during the war, only two types seem to have seen service in any numbers. Besides the A-7 already mentioned there was the Gribouskii G-11 which was comparable in capacity to the Horsa. Only post war was a glider comparable to the Hamilcar built. This was the Ilyushin IL-32, completed in 1948. The IL-32 was a high wing, all metal glider with a very box-like fuselage. Both the nose (including the cockpit) and the tail aft of the wings swung to one side to allow full access to the cargo compartment. The potential load is given as 7000kg (6.9 tons) or 60 troops, with two crew seated side by side. Wing span was about 117 feet, length 81 feet, and maximum weight 16600 kg (16.3 tons), so the glider was very comparable to the Hamilcar in size and performance if not in construction. I have discovered no details of any vehicle loads, though the design was clearly intended to be able to carry light trucks or possibly light armoured vehicles. Only a few, perhaps only one, were built.[22] As far as the period of the Second World War is concerned, the Soviets had clearly given up their early lead in air transportable armoured vehicles.

The main American project for the carriage of airborne tanks has already been described. This was the plan to carry the Locust underneath the C-54 Skymaster cargo plane. Whether this form of carriage was influenced by Russian pre-war activities is not known, but for the long distances of the Pacific war this form of transport would have had advantages over a glider combination, particularly in range and reliability (there was no tow rope to break).

Nevertheless, despite the fact the relatively small Waco CG-4A (or Hadrian as the British called it) was the only American glider deployed operationally by the US during the war, and that for some operations the US actually used Horsas when they felt they needed some larger capacity gliders, the American glider programme was the largest of any nation during this period. According to James Mrazek, al-

21 Zaloga and Grandsen, pp.192-193. See also *History of the World's Glider Forces*, p.292, and *Fighting Gliders of World War Two*, pp170-172.
22 *History of the World's Glider Forces*, p.293, and *Fighting Glidersof World War Two*, pp.167-168. A three view drawing is available on the 'Ilyushin IL-32' page of the Russian Power website.

most 16,000 training and transport gliders were produced for the military, nearly 14,000 being CG-4As.[23] A few types of heavy capacity glider were developed, most notably the Waco CG-13A and the Laister-Kauffman CG-10. Both of these could carry loads up to about 10,000 lbs (around 4.5 tons), and were designed to carry artillery pieces with their towing vehicles as well as cargo and troops. A contract for 1000 CG-10s was placed in 1945, but the end of the war meant only seven were completed. Of the CG-13A, 132 were completed. It seems likely both of these types would have been used in the invasion of Japan had this gone ahead, and in this event the British were interested in operating the CG-13 themselves to supplement their glider capacity in this theatre.[24]

Only two prototype gliders comparable with the Hamilcar were flown, and details regarding them are scarce. These were the XCG-20 and the XLRN-1, the latter being developed by the US Navy. The XCG-20 was developed from December 1946 by Chase Aircraft, and was an all metal high wing glider reminiscent in overall shape of the present day C-130 Hercules transport. It had a wingspan of 110 feet and a length of 77 feet, and a cargo capacity of 16,000 lbs (7.1 tons) which was loaded via a combined door and loading ramp in the rear fuselage. It was equipped with a fully retractable tricycle landing gear. Details of what armoured vehicle loads the glider may have carried have not been discovered. Even less has been published on the XLRN-1, and I have found only one photograph and no drawings of this aircraft. It had a wingspan of 110 feet and a length of 67.5 feet, with a cargo capacity of at least 18,000 lbs (8 tons), and possibly nearly 20,000lbs. The layout was similar to the Hamilcar, with a high wing and boxy fuselage, but tricycle landing gear was fitted. One detail that is known is that the towplane was a Navy Douglas R5D, which was simply the Navy designation of the C-54.[25] About all that can be said regarding both gliders is that they were successfully flown, but were too late for the war. Only one example of each seems to have been produced. The XCG-20 airframe was the basis for the well known C-123 Provider twin engined transport aircraft. Apparently, it seemed more logical to the Air Force to provide the airframe with engines and make it a transport aircraft than persist with towing it around, and in fact the powered version flew five months ahead of the glider, in October 1949. The glider itself received two twin J-47 jet engine pods, one under each wing, in 1951 and became America's first jet transport, although once again this was only a trials aircraft and was not produced.

On the subject of towplanes, it is worth noting that in the powerful and modern C-54 the Americans had the advantage of deploying what was probably the most advanced transport aircraft in the world, and an aircraft that could be used to tow heavy gliders without taking bombers away from their primary role. The American four engined bomber fleet was nevertheless also a potential source of capable tugs, such as the B-17 Flying Fortress, B-24 Liberator and, if a really powerful tug were needed, the B-29 Superfortress.

23 *Fighting Gliders of World War Two*, p.99.
24 See PRO file WO233/44, Long Term Glider Sub-Committee.
25 Once again, the sources here are *History of the World's Glider Forces*, pp.280-284, and *Fighting Gliders of World War Two*, pp.99-152.

The final country to develop a glider capable of carrying a tank was Japan. As with Britain and the United States, it was the use of assault gliders by Germany in 1940 which seems to have inspired Japan to develop its own glider force. However, Japanese airborne operations in general were quite limited, and only one glider was produced in significant numbers and used operationally. This was the Kokusai KU-8, which had a wingspan of 76 feet and could carry 18 equipped troops or 4000 lbs of cargo. The usual towplane was the Mitsubishi Ki-21 'Sally' twin engined bomber. The KU-8, developed and produced through 1942 and 1943, does not appear to have been employed in the assault role, but saw some service for transport purposes. Of a number of experimental gliders, two are of interest to this study, the Maeda Ku-6 and the Kokusai Ku-7. The Ku-6 (named *Sora-sha*, or later *Kuro-sha*) was another attempt, comparable to the British Baynes-Muntz carrier wing concept and the Russian KT design, to make a winged tank. Work on the concept started before the Pacific War began, in 1939, but the single prototype did not appear until January 1945, a very long development period indeed.[26] I have found only one drawing of this aircraft, showing a monoplane pair of wings, with a high T-tail set on a simple tail boom. Landing may have been on skids or the tank's tracks. The airframe was attached to a special light tank developed by Mitsubishi. Wingspan was 72 feet, and the available cargo weight is given as 6174 lbs (2.76 tons), so we can see that that the tank itself must have been a very small one, barely more than a tankette. The original idea was to provide a means of moving tanks quickly over long distances between the Japanese home islands to resist a seaborne attack, though by the time the Pacific war started the small tank to be used can hardly have been considered of worthwhile combat value. Details of towplanes and the success or otherwise of test flights are once again not available in any easily accessible sources.

A more capable aircraft, once again comparable to the Hamilcar, was the Ku-7 Manazuru or 'Crane'. Development of the aircraft commenced in late 1942, and resulted in a large glider of twin-boom design, that is having a pod-like fuselage with the tailplane carried on two booms which were attached to the wings, similar to the German Gotha Go 242 design but significantly bigger. Wingspan was 114 feet, length 64 feet, and the cargo compartment measured 17 feet long, 10 feet wide and 7 feet high. Total weight with cargo was 26,455 lbs, with a cargo capacity of 16,455 lbs (7.35 tons). A tricycle undercarriage was fitted, with a single nose wheel and two mainwheels in tandem on each side of the fuselage. Cargo was loaded via the back of the fuselage, which opened to one side in a manner similar to the nose of the Hamilcar. The first Ku-7 was tested in August 1944, and it seems the glider flew well. Normal tugs were the Nakajima Ki-49 'Helen' and the Mitsubishi Ki-67 'Peggy' twin engined heavy bombers. Nine Ku-7s were built, but testing was still taking place when the war ended. What type of tank it was intended to carry is not given in the available sources, but the cargo load makes it obvious it must have been a light tank of the Tetrarch class. A powered version of the Ku-7 was developed, eventually known as the Ki-105. This involved the fitting of two 940hp Mitsubishi engines to produce an aircraft weighing 1100 lbs more than the glider but with a much reduced payload of 7275 lbs. The aircraft was appar-

---

26 The only significant published source on this glider is Mrazek's *Fighting Gliders of World War Two*, p.87.

ently specifically intended to carry oil from wells in Sumatra to the Japanese mainland.[27] Testing began in April 1945, and a production programme was planned, but once again the end of the war intervened.

The period from, say, five years before World War Two to five years after was the only period during which military gliders were considered seriously as weapons of war. During this time, a surprising variety of nations entered the field, even if only with prototype gliders. The list includes (for example) Argentina, France, China, Turkey, Australia, India, Italy and Czechoslovakia. Taking into account the state of development of transport aircraft at this time, the glider offered the best chance of lifting large and heavy loads like tanks. This chapter has covered, I believe, all the countries which built gliders capable of carrying tanks. It is clear that, with the exception of Germany, Britain had the lead in this field with the Hamilcar, all the other nations developing their heavy gliders in very small numbers and usually too late to take part in the war. The German case is, however, vital in putting the Hamilcar into perspective. The German glider was much more capable, developed in much less time, and produced in significant numbers. The two main reasons seem to be that the Me 321 was given top priority and was developed with the involvement of one of the world's leading design teams, indeed with the personal involvement of Willi Messerschmitt himself. With all due respect to GAL, they simply could not equal the vision and capabilities of such a world class aircraft company. It also seems fairly obvious that nothing approaching the extreme urgency attached to the Me321 was ever given to the Hamilcar.

The Me321 proves that early 1940s technology was perfectly capable of producing a glider which could take into action a worthwhile tank, and that the Air Ministry, the War Office and GAL were wrong to limit themselves to tanks of around 8 tons. We do not need hindsight to tell us that the Tetrarch and Locust were incapable of supplying worthwhile armoured support to airborne forces: this fact was known at the time these vehicles were selected, as has been demonstrated in this book. If the effort was to be made to develop an airborne tank force, the British, like the Germans, should have taken their best tanks as the starting point. A good and obvious choice would have been the Valentine, which was available when the Hamilcar was being designed. It was a compact tank and weighed slightly less than the Mk IV which the Germans used as their yardstick. Although obsolescent by 1944, it had been developed to the extent that it had by that time the same gun, and armour only slightly thinner, than contemporary main battle tanks such as the Sherman and Cromwell. It was a little slow and suffered from a three man crew, but was a very reliable tank. It is suggested here not as the ideal vehicle with which to support the airborne divisions, but as a tank around which a glider could realistically have been designed in 1941 and which would still have been worth having during 1944-45. An alternative might have been the development of a specialised airborne tank, but anyone with even a basic knowledge of British problems in developing new tanks during the Second World War would not want to bet on such a project coming up with anything worthwhile in an acceptable timescale.

27 *History of the World's Glider Forces*, p.297.

Chapter 12

Conclusion

> The purpose of the Hamilcar is to transport massive military weapons and ancillaries straight to the scene of action. In the case of a continental invasion, such a type has proved its value without question, and more may be heard in the future of the flying tank which will have the advantage of overcoming in simple fashion all those obstacles to advances now such a feature of military operations – minefields, tank traps, road blocks and the like.[1]
>
> *The Aeroplane*, 15th December 1944

> The General Aircraft Hamilcar has a rather unorthodox history in that the original concept was such stuff as dreams are made of. During 1940 the authorities responsible for our prosecution of the war were looking clearly into the future with such uninhibited perception as appears farcical when applied to the stolid Englishman of fable.[2]
>
> *Flight*, 14th December 1944

The conclusions of these two respected magazines were typical of accounts of the Hamilcar published in the late war and immediate post-war period, following the press debut of the aircraft and its 'flying tanks' in July 1944. In the understandable euphoria consequent upon the successful invasion of Europe and the defeat of Hitler's armies, the Hamilcar, Tetrarch and Locust were promoted in the public arena as one of the many advanced and powerful weapons which had given the Allies victory. The Hamilcar was genuinely admired during the war (as some of the quotes in this book have shown), not just in propaganda but by those who flew it and went into action in it. Indeed, it would seem most who encountered it were impressed by its size and capabilities. It is my conclusion that the perspective of history allows us to take a more critical view, though we should balance hindsight with a proper appreciation of the problems and uncertainties which faced those working at the time.

If we regard the combination of Hamilcar, Tetrarch and Locust as a weapon *system*, the individual components of the system are an interesting combination of success and failure. The Hamilcar was a genuine leap in the dark for the British aircraft industry in 1941 when it began to be designed and built, and an even greater leap in the dark for a relatively small company like GAL. Yet it was ready in sufficient numbers for D-Day, and performed all the functions required of it with very few problems. The Tetrarch was a fine light tank in the late 1930s when it was first produced, and up to perhaps 1940 could claim to be one of the best light tanks in the world, with excellent mobility and a powerful gun for its class. The Locust was also a successful design within the limitations set for it. It had some early teething

---

1 'The General Aircraft Hamilcar', *The Aeroplane*, December 15th, 1944.
2 'Hamilcar Glider', *Flight*, December 14th 1944.

problems, but was a neat and compact vehicle which, in the end, did what was required of it.

Viewed from another perspective, however, things can be put differently. Due to inefficiencies and errors during its development and production, the Hamilcar was slow to be produced and was not available for the first massed airborne operation in Sicily. Although a fundamental reason for its design had been the transport of armoured support for airborne forces, it was incapable of carrying a tank large enough to fulfill that role in a worthwhile way. The Tetrarch and Locust were, by 1944, virtually powerless on the battlefield as fighting tanks, due to their thin armour and weak armament. Furthermore, the German Me321 was proof that an assault glider capable of carrying a worthwhile tank *could* be produced (and produced quickly) with the technology of the early 1940s. One is left, therefore, with the paradox of acknowledging a unique achievement whilst bemoaning the fact that what was achieved was fundamentally inadequate.

The two quotes at the head of this chapter are therefore seriously distorted by propaganda and wishful thinking. The *Aeroplane* talked of the future, but after D-Day the airborne tanks had a very limited future, being ignored for Arnhem and then deployed in much reduced numbers during Varsity. This reflected serious doubts about the value of taking up precious Hamilcar space with these vehicles, so they had clearly not proved their value 'without question'. As for *Flight's* idea of the 'authorities' with 'unlimited perception', a bit of true perception would have put the crews of 6th AARR in tanks which had a chance of tackling the enemy on more equal terms.

Whatever our respect for designers doing their best in difficult circumstances, and our admiration for the courage and skill of those who took these weapons into action, the conclusion is straightforward. Considered as a method of providing airborne forces with armoured support, the Hamilcar/Tetrarch/Locust weapon system was a failure. What was possibly worse, it was known by those in charge of its development in the War Office and the Air Ministry to be such from almost the moment of its creation. There was a fundamental lack of vision, and this resulted in the failure to take a worthwhile load as the starting point of the design process. In this, government departments lacked the guidance of a truly world class aircraft company. With all due respect to GAL, they did not possess the potential to see what was genuinely possible, in the way that Messerschmitt did in Germany. Consequently, the official role of the tanks had to be changed to one of reconnaissance, and other uses found for the glider that carried them.

It is on the credit side that the Hamilcar had been designed from the outset to be flexible enough to carry other loads apart from tanks. With the paradropping of really heavy loads in its infancy, and with the absence of large capacity transport aircraft within the RAF during World War Two, the Hamilcar was a useful aircraft for airborne forces to have around. The most valuable load it carried was not the Locust or Tetrarch, but the 17pdr anti-tank gun and tractor, one of the most powerful anti-tank guns of the war and vital if the airborne troops were to fight off the powerful tanks deployed by the Germans in the late war period. The Universal Carrier also represented a very useful source of armoured transport for the hard-pressed airborne soldiers, and the ability to carry in earth-moving equipment to rapidly create advanced landing grounds was also worthwhile, even if not actually used. The large capacity of the Hamilcar also made it a cost effective method of bringing in stores, provided it was flying in to landing zones already properly secured.

However, even if we take the limitations of the Hamilcar glider/tank combination as read, it is still possible to question the way in which it was used. Before D-Day, knowing the weakness of the Tetrarch and Locust, it would surely have been worth exploring the possibility of converting either chassis to a self-propelled mounting for a 6pdr anti-tank gun (or even a 17pdr) or 95mm howitzer. Such weapons could have given valuable support during the early stages of an airborne landing. On D-Day itself, the most obvious question mark lies over the whole concept of Parkerforce. With the expectations of immediate armoured counter-attack from the Germans, the sending out of a highly vulnerable force of light tanks, jeep borne infantry and a handful of anti-tank guns and howitzers, and expecting them to form a firm base *outside* the airborne perimeter, seems a highly unrealistic concept. However, Major-General Gale was by all accounts a highly capable officer. He led 6th Airborne Division in Normandy with considerable distinction, and went on to become one of Britain's most distinguished soldiers.[3] With this in mind it is possible to give the plan the benefit of the doubt, as a scheme designed to take advantage of conditions significantly more open than those actually encountered and which was sensibly cancelled in good time. It is worth recalling that in his post war account, Gale stood by the idea of Parkerforce.

It is nevertheless also possible to question why the Tetrarchs were sent in at all, and if they were to be sent, why they didn't go in earlier. With 34 Hamilcars to play with, only four flew in 17pdr anti-tank guns. Gale himself was fully aware that counter attacks with tanks by the Germans could be expected from the word go, so why didn't he leave behind his light tanks and take more 17pdrs? We have already seen that a case for Parkerforce can be made, and Gale may have been under orders to have plans ready for the insertion of recce forces if the opportunity presented itself. It may also be that the creation and training of such a unique unit as 6th AARR created its own momentum, and that Gale felt obliged to find a role for the unit on D-Day. As to timing, if the light tanks were to provide what support they could to the paras, it would perhaps have been a good idea to fly them in at dawn on D-Day during the most critical phase of the operation, rather than waiting until the evening.

Of course, a good deal of the above is speculation. However, what seems plain is that 6th AARR arrived in Normandy ill-equipped for their prospective missions. For reconnaissance, the best combination of vehicles had been established soon after the war started, using the small, quiet and manoeuvrable Daimler scout cars backed up by armoured cars. 6th AARR's jeeps were too vulnerable, their carriers and Tetrarchs too noisy, and in the case of the tank, also too big, for the recce task. For support of troops, the unit's vehicles were again too vulnerable, and in addition too lightly armed. Perhaps one positive thing that can be said is that once the tanks arrived, their relatively low casualties during the succeeding weeks indicate that

---

3 He was C-in-C of the British Army of the Rhine 1952-56 and went on to take over from Montgomery as Deputy Supreme Allied Commander Europe 1958-60. See General Sir Richard Gale, *Call To Arms: An Autobiography*, (London: Hutchinson, 1968).

they were used sensibly, providing useful fire support where possible but not being misused as battle tanks in formal attacks. For the latter purpose, tank units from outside 6th Airborne Division were used.

Of the three major actions fought by airborne forces in northwest Europe (D-Day, Arnhem and Varsity), Arnhem would appear to be the one where some light tanks had the chance to make a difference, but was of course the only one of the three where they were absent. Indeed, Arnhem would seem to be exactly the kind of operation envisaged when the role of the original Light Tank Squadron was being developed. It would be foolish to argue that a few light tanks would have changed the outcome of Market Garden, but if the planners were willing to entrust the initial rush to the bridges to the jeeps of the 1st Airborne Reconnaissance Squadron, it was surely worth increasing their chances of success by allocating perhaps six or twelve light tanks to help them. The airlift was certainly available, but the idea was evidently not viewed as sufficiently important to make it a priority.

Of course, if more effective tanks had been available for airlanding, they could have been an extremely useful tool in *any* airborne operation. The point that a more worthwhile glider/tank combination could have been developed in Britain has already been made. It was surely not beyond the aircraft industry that created the Mosquito, Spitfire and Lancaster to produce a glider capable of lifting a twenty ton tank. I have already offered the Valentine, which in fact weighed 16 to 17 tons, as a ready made solution to the problem of an airborne tank. It was compact and reliable, and though available from 1940 it was still viable, in the Mk.IX version, in 1944-45. The most likely towing solution would have been a twin tow using Lancasters or Halifaxes.

The main mitigating factor of the above criticisms regarding Britain's flying tanks is the high level of uncertainty that prevailed when airborne forces were first being developed. These forces had to be created from scratch in the UK, and just about everything concerning them was initially a matter for debate, including the argument as to whether they were worth having at all. There was also the constant struggle for resources for a force which would make heavy and specialist demands at a time when even basic weapons were in short supply. With this in mind, the failure to make the right choices in the field of airborne tanks may be thought more understandable. Nevertheless, that failure occurred.

Turning to the operational record of 6th AARR, we are on much simpler and more positive ground. It should not be forgotten what a singular unit the regiment was. Quite apart from its unique role in delivering tanks to the battlefield by air, 6th AARR fielded an extraordinary range of vehicles and weapons during its short life, including main battle tanks, light tanks, scout cars, universal carriers, jeeps, motorcycles, medium and heavy mortars, medium machine guns and the full range of infantry weapons. The men of the unit also had to master a wide range of skills, from tank tactics to reconnaissance methods, infantry tactics, indirect fire support up to divisional level, and parachuting. Both the Royal Armoured Corps and the Reconnaissance Corps had cause to regard themselves as something of an elite, and the spirit of both corps had to be upheld in 6th AARR. Furthermore, those of the regiment from cavalry units had their own unique traditions to maintain. All these were further encompassed by the inclusion of the unit as part of a new elite, the airborne forces. By dint of hard training and with the leadership of a well respected CO, the regiment lived up to all expectations.

As this book has shown, the unit had an excellent record as a recce regiment in the Normandy breakout, the Ardennes and the advance across Germany after Varsity. The tankmen of the unit also won respect for being willing to expose themselves to danger to provide support for the troops of the parachute and airlanding battalions. The crews of the Tetrarchs and Locusts were well aware of the limitations of their vehicles, but were determined to make their contribution by supporting the efforts of their regimental colleagues, and providing what support they could for the rest of the division.

Despite the variety of experiences which this book describes, the abiding image in this author's mind is of men manning tanks shackled inside gliders, being towed perhaps 2000 feet above the Channel or the European countryside, not knowing exactly what awaited them at their destination, or even if they would achieve a safe landing. What an extraordinary way to go into battle, and what an extraordinary experience it must have been. The matter-of-fact professionalism (and even humour) with which this truly unique task was approached, which I hope has been evident in the surviving accounts printed in this book, is an enduring tribute to the abilities, character and courage of the men concerned.

Bibliography

Primary Sources

The main sources of primary material for this book have been mentioned in the Acknowledgments section. Details of individual sources are in the footnotes.

Secondary Sources

Books

Arthur, Max, *Men of the Red Beret: Airborne Forces 1940-1990* (London: Hutchinson, 1990)
Ashworth, Chris, *Action Stations: 5, Military Airfields of the South-West* (Wellingborough: Patrick Stephens, 1982)
Barnes, C.H., *Shorts Aircraft Since 1900* (London: Putnam, 1967)
Beale, Peter, *Death By Design: British Tank Development in the Second World War* (Stroud: Sutton Publishing, 1998)
Bernage, Georges, *The Red Berets in Normandy* (Bayeux: Heimdal, 2002)
Bolitho, Hector, *The Galloping Third: The Story of The 3rd The King's Own Hussars* (London: John Murray, 1963)
Bowyer, Michael J.F., *Aircraft for the Many: A Detailed Survey of the RAF's Aircraft in June 1944* (Sparkford: Patrick Stephens, 1995)
Bright, Joan, *History of the Queen's Royal Hussars*, (Np, nd)
Buckley, Christopher, *Five Ventures*, (London: HMSO, 1954)
Chatterton, Brigadier George, *The Wings of Pegasus: The Story of the Glider Pilot Regiment* (Nashville: Battery Press, 1982)
Crookenden, Napier, *Drop Zone Normandy* (London: Ian Allan, 1976)
Crow, Duncan, (ed.) *American AFVs of World War 2* (Windsor: Profile Publications, 1972)
Crow, Duncan, (ed.) *British AFVs 1919-1940* (Windsor: Profile Publications, 1970)
Dabrowski, H.P., *Messerschmitt Me321/323: Giants of the Luftwaffe* (Atglen, PA: Schiffer Publishing, 1994)
Dank, Milton, *The Glider Gang* (London: Cassell, 1977)
Dawson, Leslie, *Wings Over Dorset* (Wincanton: Dorset Publishing Company, 1989)
Doherty, Richard, *Only the Enemy in Front (Every Other Bugger Behind): The Recce Corps at War 1940-46* (London: Tom Donovan, 1994)
Duffy, Paul & Kandalov, Andrei, *Tupolev: The Man and His Aircraft* (Shrewsbury: Airlife Publishing, 1996)
Ellis, Major L.F., *Victory in the West: Vol I – The Battle of Normandy, Vol II – The Defeat of Germany* (London: HMSO, 1962 & 1968)
Facer, John, *Flying at Sherburn: The Story of a Yorkshire Airfield* (Ouseburn, Yorkshire: Silver Quill, 1998)
Fairley, John, *Remember Arnhem* (Aldershot: Pegasus Journal, 1978)
Fletcher, David, *Mechanised Force: British Tanks Between the Wars* (London: HMSO, 1991)

Fletcher, David, *The Great Tank Scandal: British Armour in the Second World War, Part 1* (London: HMSO, 1989)
Fletcher, David, *The Universal Tank: British Armour in the Second World War, Part 2* (london: HMSO, 1993)
Foss, Christopher & McKenzie, Peter, *The Vickers Tanks: From Landships to Challenger* (Wellingborough: Patrick Stephens, 1988)
Gale, General Sir Richard, *Call to Arms: An Autobiography* (London: Hutchinson, 1968)
Gale, Lt. General Richard, *With 6th Airborne in Normandy* (London: Sampson Low, 1948)
Green, William, *Warplanes of the Third Reich* (London: Macdonald, 1970)
Gunston, Bill, *Tupolev Aircraft Since 1922* (London: Putnam, 1995)
Hamilton, Nigel, *Monty: The Battles of Field Marshall Bernard Montgomery* (London: Hodder & Stoughton, 1994)
Harclerode, Peter, *"Go To It!": The Illustrated History of the 6th Airborne Division* (London: Bloomsbury, 1990)
Harris, J.P., *Men, Ideas and Tanks: British Military Thought and Armoured Forces, 1903-1939* (Manchester: Manchester University Press, 1995)
Hunnicut, R.P., *Stuart: A History of the American Light Tank* (Novato Ca.: Presidio Press, 1992)
Jarrett, Philip, (ed.), *Aircraft of the Second World War: The Development of the Warplane 1939-1945* (London: Putnam, 1997)
Kershaw, Robert, *D-Day: Piercing the Atlantic Wall* (Shepperton: Ian Allan, 1993)
Ladd, James, *Commandos and Rangers of World War 2* (London: Macdonald & Jane's, 1978)
Lake, Jon, *Halifax Squadrons of World War 2* (Oxford: Osprey Publishing, 1999)
Macksey, Kenneth, *Tank Versus Tank: The Illustrated Story of Armoured Battlefield Conflict in the Twentieth Century* (Leicester: Magna Books, 1991)
Middlebrook, Martin, *Arnhem 1944: The Airborne Battle* (London: Viking, 1994)
Milsom, John, *Russian Tanks 1900-1970* (London: Arms & Armour Press, 1970)
Ministry of Information, *By Air To Battle: The Official Account of the British Airborne Divisions* (London: HMSO, 1945)
Mrazek, James, *The Glider War* (London: Robert Hale, 1975)
Mrazek, James, *Fighting Gliders of World War 2* (London: Robert Hale, 1977)
Neillands, Robin & De Normann, Roderick, *D-Day 1944: Voices From Normandy* (London: Orion, 1994)
Otway, Lt. Col. T.B.H., *Airborne Forces* (London: IWM Reprint, 1990)
Overton, Bill, *Blackburn Beverley* (Leicester: Midland Counties Publications, 1990)
Polmar, Norman & Mersky, Peter, *Amphibious Warfare: An Illustrated History* (London: Blandford Press, 1988)
Roskill, Captain S.W., *The War At Sea 1939-45, Vol. II: The Period of Balance* (London: HMSO, 1956)

Shannon, Kevin & Wright, Stephen, *One Night in June* (Shrewsbury: Airlife, 1994)
Smith, Claude, *The History of the Glider Pilot Regiment* (London: Leo Cooper, 1992)
Smith, J.R., *German Aircraft of the Second World War* (London: Putnam, 1972)
Tapper, Oliver, *Armstrong Whitworth Aircraft Since 1913* (London: Putnam, 1973)
Taylor, Jeremy, *This Band of Brothers: A History of the Recce Corps of the British Army* (Bristol: White Swan Press, 1947)
Van Hees, Arie-Jan, *Tugs and Gliders to Arnhem* (Eijsden, Netherlands: pub. by the author, 2000)
Vann, Frank, *Willy Messerschmitt: First Full Biography of an Aeronautical Genius* (Yeovil: Patrick Stephens, 1993)
Walklett, Bob, *Ginetta: The Inside Story* (Oxford: Bookmarque Publishing, 1994)
Warner, Philip, *The D-Day Landings* (London: Kimber, 1980)
Weeks, John, *Men Against Tanks: A History of Anti-Tank Warfare* (London: David & Charles, 1975)
Wilmot, Chester, *The Struggle for Europe* (London: Collins, 1952)
Wood, Alan, *History of the World's Glider Forces* (London: Patrick Stephens, 1990)
Wood, Alan, *The Glider Soldiers* (Tunbridge Wells: Spellmount, 1992)
Wright, Lawrence, *The Wooden Sword* (London: Elek Books, 1967)
Zaloga, Steven & Grandsen, James, *Soviet Tanks & Combat Vehicles of World War 2* (London: Arms & Armour Press, 1984)

Journals and Magazines

Anon., 'Hamilcar Glider', *Flight*, December 14th 1944
Anon., 'The General Aircraft Hamilcar', *The Aeroplane*, December 15th 1944
Anon., 'Madagascar and the Special Service Squadrons', *Royal Hussars Journal*, vol.20, summer 1990
Anon., 'The Airborne Light Tank Squadron – 6th Airborne Armoured Reconnaissance Regiment', *Royal Hussars Journal*, vol.20, summer 1990
Bowyer, Michael, 'Enter the Horsa', *Airfix Magazine*, September 1976
Bowyer, Michael, 'Hamilcar Tank Transports', *Airfix Magazine*, March and April 1977
Bowyer, Michael, 'Hamilcars in Action', *Airfix Magazine*, May 1977
Collins, C.L., 'Flying Tanks', *Pegasus Journal*, 1949
Cox, Steve & Middleton, Paul, 'The Airborne Armoured Reconnaissance Regiment', *Tankette – Magazine of the Miniature Armoured Fighting Vehicle Association*, vol.30, no.6, 1995
Fletcher, David, 'The Flying Tank', *Military Illustrated*, no.100, September 1996
Gunston, Bill, 'Hamilcar Tank Carrying Glider', *Aeroplane Monthly*, December 1977
Jarrett, Philip, 'Nothing Ventured...', *Aeroplane Monthly*, February 1982

Knowles, Eric, 'With Armoured Cars to France', *The Journal of the Society of Twentieth Century Wargamers*, no.34
Lowman, Brigadier F.H., 'The 6th Airborne Divisional Engineers on D-Day' *The Royal Engineers Journal*, June 1982
Prower, Charles W., 'Gliding Tanks', *Aeroplane Monthly*, July 1993
Prower, Charles W., 'Gliding into Battle', *Aeroplane Monthly*, August 1993
Shiner, J.S., 'The Grangues Memorial', *Pegasus Journal*, December 1997
Stockman, Jim, 'Madagascar 1942', *British Army Review*, no.83, August 1986
Tomczak, Martin, 'Further Notes on Operation Herkules', *Miniature Wargames*, July 1998
White, B.T., 'The Special Service Squadrons', *Tankette – Magazine of the Miniature Armoured Fighting Vehicle Association*, date unknown

Web Sites

Many websites were visited during research for this book. Basic and sometimes inaccurate information on 6th AARR and the Tetrarch, Locust and Hamilcar can be found on a number of sites. The following four sites provided particular information on specific subjects which was additional to that available in printed sources.
'6th Airborne Division in Palestine': www.britains-smallwars.com/Palestine/6TH.htm
'AXL's Plane Gallery': www.studenten.net/customasp/axl/index.asp
'The Russian Battlefield, Tank Development': www.battlefield.ru/map.html
'Russian Power, IL-32 Glider': legion.wplus.net/guide/air/t/il32.shtml